COMPUTER
PROGRAMMING
FOR TEENS

MARY FARRELL

Course Technology PTR

A part of Cengage Learning

COURSE TECHNOLOGY
CENGAGE Learning™

Australia • Brazil • Japan • Korea • Mexico • Singapore • Spain • United Kingdom • United States

COURSE TECHNOLOGY
CENGAGE Learning

Computer Programming for Teens
Mary Farrell

Publisher and General Manager, Course Technology PTR: Stacy L. Hiquet

Associate Director of Marketing: Sarah Panella

Manager of Editorial Services: Heather Talbot

Marketing Manager: Mark Hughes

Acquisitions Editor: Mitzi Koontz

Project Editor and Copy Editor: Kim Benbow

Technical Reviewer: Keith Davenport

Teen Reviewer: JT Hiquet

PTR Editorial Services Coordinator: Erin Johnson

Interior Layout Tech: ICC Macmillan Inc.

Cover Designer: Mike Tanamachi

CD-ROM Producer: Brandon Penticuff

Indexer: Sharon Hilgenberg

Proofreader: Kate Shoup

For product information and technology assistance, contact us at
Cengage Learning Customer & Sales Support, 1-800-354-9706

For permission to use material from this text or product, submit all requests online at **cengage.com/permissions**
Further permissions questions can be emailed to
permissionrequest@cengage.com

Computer Programming for Teens are trademarks of Microsoft Corporation. Java is a trademark of Sun Microsystems, Inc. in the United States and other countries. Python is a trademark of the Python Software Foundation. All other trademarks are the property of their respective owners.

Library of Congress Catalog Card Number: 2007938243

ISBN-10: 1-59863-446-1

ISBN-13: 978-1-59863-446-4

Course Technology
25 Thomson Place
Boston, MA 02210
USA

Cengage Learning is a leading provider of customized learning solutions with office locations around the globe, including Singapore, the United Kingdom, Australia, Mexico, Brazil, and Japan. Locate your local office at: **international.cengage.com/region**

Cengage Learning products are represented in Canada by Nelson Education, Ltd.

For your lifelong learning solutions, visit **courseptr.com**

Visit our corporate Web site at **cengage.com**

Printed in the U.S.A.
3 4 5 6 7 11

ELIZABETH IMOLEOLUWA

ATANSUYI

For my parents

ACKNOWLEDGMENTS

I would like to thank my editors, Kim Benbow and Keith Davenport, for their helpful suggestions. I would also like to thank my co-workers, Charlie Drane and Morgan Soutter, who have always been helpful when I had questions. I would also like to thank Gerald Bilodeau, who first gave me the opportunity to teach computer science.

Lastly, I would like to thank all of my students, past and present. Their questions have made me a better teacher and a better learner.

ABOUT THE AUTHOR

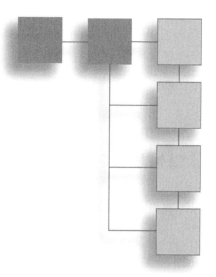

Mary Farrell teaches computer science, mathematics, and Japanese at Boston College High School, where she has been teaching for the past 17 years. She is an avid learner of spoken languages as well as computer languages and travels frequently to practice. She lives south of Boston, Massachusetts.

CONTENTS

INTRODUCTION

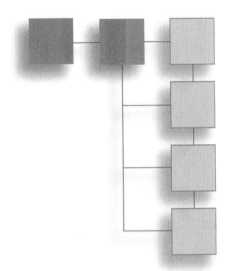

Computer Programming for Teens is an introduction to the topic of computer programming. The focus of the book is on the common elements of programming in any language. The book begins with understanding the computer as a machine, and then proceeds to help you develop an understanding of the data structures and control statements that allow you to program.

What You'll Find in This Book

There is an exhaustive list of programming topics common to all languages. This book will introduce you to algorithms, loops, decisions, and data structures, like arrays, records, and matrices. It will also cover strings, objects, and pointer variables, as well as more advanced topics like searching, sorting, and recursion.

Who This Book Is For

This book is for teenagers and anyone interested in understanding the subject of programming from a general point of view. While other books focus on the minutiae of computer programming language grammar, this book attempts to focus on the bigger concepts in programming. So if you want to understand the fundamentals of programming, such as how to write loops and make decisions, you will find this book useful.

How This Book Is Organized

Computer Programming for Teens is organized into chapters, beginning with the most fundamental topics, like data storage, and progressing through decisions, loops, design, and complex data structures. Each chapter deals with one topic as a point of focus, and material is developed sequentially.

- **Chapter 1, "First Things First,"** explains the basics of algorithms and how computers are able to process instructions.

- **Chapter 2, "Variables: The Holders of Information,"** covers variables, the necessary holders of data. It examines the different kinds of data, how variables are classified according to the data they hold, and how data is assigned to a variable.

- **Chapter 3, "Everything You Ever Wanted to Know About Operators,"** explains how mathematical operators can be used to process data.

- **Chapter 4, "Programming: It's Now or Never,"** introduces some short programs and covers how a program acquires data and displays data.

- **Chapter 5, "Design: It's Best to Start Here,"** covers the basic top-down design used in most programs.

- **Chapter 6, "True or False: The Basis for All Decisions,"** examines how decisions are made by a computer and covers the `if` statement, which implements decisions.

- **Chapter 7, "Loops, or How to Spin Effectively!,"** introduces the three main kinds of loops: `for` loops, `while` loops, and `do` loops.

- **Chapter 8, "Function Calls: That's What It's All About—Get Somebody Else to Do the Work,"** explains what functions are and how they are called by the program to execute some particular task.

- **Chapter 9, "Using Functions in Graphics,"** covers the basics of graphics and how functions are used in graphics.

- **Chapter 10, "Running Out of Holders? It's Time for the Array,"** introduces the array as a holder for groups of data that are similar in type.

- **Chapter 11, "All About Strings,"** explains different functions used to manipulate strings.

- **Chapter 12, "The Matrix—Before the Movie,"** explains what matrices are and how to assign data to them.

- **Chapter 13, "Debugging: More Important Than You Think,"** explains what a bug is and then makes helpful suggestions for debugging a program.

- **Chapter 14, "But What If Things Are Different? Structures, Records, and Fields,"** covers different data holders, like structures and records. These holders are used for groups of data that are not of the same type.

- **Chapter 15, "Objects and Classes: Being Organized Is Better Than Not,"** introduces the object and the topic of object-oriented programming. Objects are also covered in the online appendixes.

- **Chapter 16, "Dealing with the Outside World: Files,"** explains how files can communicate with programs. Files are read and written by programs. Files are useful for storing large amounts of data needed by a program.

- **Chapter 17, "Pointers: Who Is Looking at Whom?"** introduces pointer variables, which shed light on the connection between memory and data storage.

- **Chapter 18, "Searching: Did You Find It Yet?"** explains how to search for specific values. There are two main algorithms that accomplish this work.

- **Chapter 19, "Let's Put Things in Order: Sorting,"** introduces the topic of sorting, specifically the selection sort and merge sort.

- **Chapter 20, "Recursion: Calling Yourself Over and Over Again,"** covers recursion, the process of designing a solution for a smaller case of the same problem and building on that solution to find the answer to the original problem.

Appendixes A, B, and C are dedicated to specific programming languages: HTML, C++, and Java. In Appendix D, you will find an ASCII chart, and Appendix E includes exercises for the chapters, where appropriate. You can find all the appendixes online at **www.courseptr.com/downloads**.

On the CD-ROM you'll find examples of programs, as mentioned in specific chapters. While most chapters give accurate examples of code, the chapters dealing with strings and files are more general to avoid hardware-dependent considerations and more advanced topics that go beyond the scope of this book.

If you wish to learn more about computer programming, java.sun.com is very useful for information on Java, while www.w3.org is a good reference point for HTML. There are several web sites devoted to C++, including www.cplusplus .com and others, which you can find easily through an Internet search.

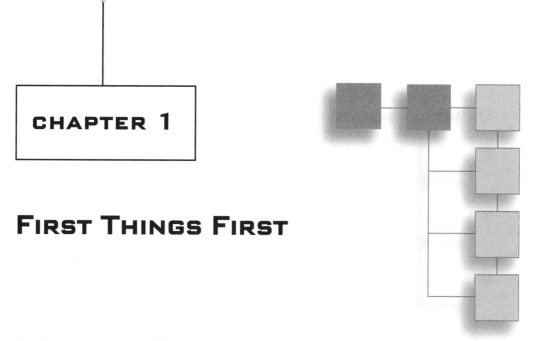

CHAPTER 1

FIRST THINGS FIRST

In this chapter, we will look at the differences between hardware and software and define the principal parts of a computer. Since the computer is an electronic machine, all information it uses must be reduced to electronic states. These states are represented by binary digits (or *bits*) Changing sounds or images to pieces of data represented by bits is the process of digitization of information. Once information has been digitized, it can be fed into a computer and manipulated. Machine language operates with bits, while other languages need to be translated into machine language so the computer can execute their commands. You'll learn about the algorithm, which is necessary in the design of solutions to problems and which programmers can code in any number of languages.

In This Chapter

- Important hardware components and software

- The concept of digitization

- Binary digits, bits, bytes

- The computer, an electronic machine

- Languages: high-level vs. low-level

- A first look at the algorithm and its relationship to programming

Introduction

Computer technology is all around us—not only on our personal computers, but also on ATM machines, fuel injection in cars, digital cameras, and telephone communications. None of this technology would be possible without computer programming. Programming provides instructions that tell the machine how to operate. In your personal computer, everything it does—from playing video games and music to typing simple documents in Microsoft Word—requires a set of instructions.

This book will provide you with a basic knowledge of computer programming. It will tell you how to control the computer so that it can do something over and over again, make a decision, and store information in the right kind of holder, contingent on what that information looks like. These are just a few of the things you will learn.

It is important to cover certain fundamentals before learning to program. The more you understand the machine and how it works, the easier it will be for you to grasp the concepts of programming.

Hardware and Software

A computer is usually hooked up to a printer, an external drive, and various other peripheral devices, such as scanners, modems, and so on. All the physical components of a computer make up its *hardware*. Think of the word "hardware" as describing those parts of a computer that are hard or can be touched. You can touch a printer, but you cannot touch programs that are running on a computer. Programs represent *software*. Any programs, whether they are commercial programs, games, word processing applications, or programs that make the computer itself operate, are all examples of software.

Programs are sets of steps that tell a computer what to do. There are directions for everything that happens in the computer. For example, saving a file on the hard drive occurs because inside the computer a program is "telling" the computer to save a file rather than delete it. Saving a file, printing a file, or deleting it are just a few of the programs called *system programs*. They are also referred to as the *operating system*. These programs allow the computer to handle its basic operations: opening and closing files and saving or deleting files. Likewise, getting an application, such as Microsoft Word, to open up and start running is the task of the operating system.

Application programs are programs sold on the market, for example, WinZip, iTunes, Microsoft Office, Adobe Acrobat, Skype, and so on. The word "application" refers to a set of programs "applied" to some real-life task to make it easier to do. Some of the earliest application programs—such as Microsoft Word, Word-Perfect, and ClarisWorks—were created to facilitate typing long documents.

Tip

System software is the set of programs that enables the computer to store data, retrieve data, save files, delete files, and, generally, allow the computer to operate application programs.

Let's look at a list of the main parts of a computer:

- Keyboard
- Mouse
- Printer
- Hard drive
- External drive
- RAM (random access memory)
- CPU (computer processing unit)

The Keyboard, Mouse, and Printer

The *keyboard* is used to communicate with the computer; so is the *mouse.* The keyboard is used for typed commands, while the mouse is used for "clicking" and interacting with the graphical user interface (GUI). The printer delivers on paper what's on the screen.

Hard Drive vs. External Drive

The *hard drive* is the internal memory of a computer. Application programs are saved here, as are system files. Think of the hard drive as the permanent storage space a computer has. A house with a basement and an attic has much more storage area than an apartment with only closets for storage. Computers with a large hard drive, for example, 500 gigabytes (GB), are in demand because of their capacity to save very large applications. Metrowerks CodeWarrior, for example, needs at least 300 megabytes (MB) of storage space. Devices known as *solid state drives* can provide more portable hard memory using flash technology.

An *external drive* is used to expand storage capacity outside of the computer itself. As recently as the early 1990s, many personal computers had little memory in the hard drive, necessitating storage outside of the computer. Memory needed for application programs at that time was not what it is today. Although internal hard drive capacities are much greater today than in the past, there are still many uses for external drives, such as flash drives for storing pictures, video clips, and so on.

RAM: Random Access Memory

The *RAM* is really the workspace for the computer. Think of the RAM as a large table onto which you place many different things. If you have only a small workspace, you can't open too many things at once because they won't fit on the table. For example, if your operating system uses 128 MB, while Microsoft Office uses 256 MB and Adobe Acrobat uses 128 MB, you could have both applications open at the same time as the operating system (a total of 512 MB) if your computer has 1 GB of RAM. Now if you run a game, such as *Master of Defense*, you'll need another 128 MB just for that application. (Compare that with *Battleground*, which requires 512 MB!) Again, running the operating system alone with that game brings your total to 642 MB; and that's why you want a computer with a good size RAM, like 1 GB, if you usually play such games. Opening several applications at once and not running out of memory is desirable.

RAM is temporary memory and is lost once the computer is turned off. The term *volatile* is used to describe this memory, since anything not saved will be lost in a sudden, abrupt fashion. For example, when a plug is suddenly pulled on a machine or if you have to reset your computer for some reason, everything in the RAM will be lost.

Fortunately, there is always a "backup plan" for storage on a computer and this is called a *swap file*. The swap file is memory taken from the hard disk space as well as from the RAM in case of an emergency. It is used only in the event that the RAM becomes exhausted and some emergency storage is needed.

ROM: Read-Only Memory

ROM, or read-only memory, is memory that's not lost when the machine is turned off. Certain instructions for the computer are permanently etched onto a chip at the time the computer is manufactured. Thus ROM is permanent memory and is never lost.

CPU: Central Processing Unit

The main part of the computer is the *central processing unit*, or CPU. This is where the computer stores, processes, and retrieves data. The CPU manages all the functions of the computer, including processing data—manipulating data by sending it from one place to another or by performing some math on the data. The CPU contains the *arithmetic/logic unit*, or ALU, and the *control unit* of a computer. The CPU is found within the system unit and should not be confused with it. The system unit houses the internal pieces of the computer like the motherboard, the internal memory, and so on.

The ALU: Arithmetic/Logic Unit

The *ALU* affects programmers the most. When you write a program for a computer, its ALU will be called into use to perform some math (the arithmetic part) or to evaluate a decision (the logic part) by the programmer. That's why we need the arithmetic/logic unit. The logic portion is the part of the unit that can handle decisions. Most interesting programs need the ability to make a decision.

The Control Unit

The control unit of the CPU is used to regulate program flow. This unit executes statements in sequence and will only repeat steps or skip steps if programmed to do so.

If you write a program putting a number like 5 into a holder called x and decide to increase the value of x from 5 to 7, the ALU will be used to do this task. If you want to print the message "I have had enough!" 250 times on a computer screen, then the control unit will have to do work because the programmer is asking the computer to do something over and over. Thus the programmer controls how long or how many times the computer does something; in this case, printing a message 250 times.

I mentioned earlier that the computer can store, process, and retrieve data, and the CPU will handle that work.

Digitization: Using Numbers to Represent Information

To understand how the computer does what it does, you can examine a situation in the real world to see how numbers can be used to give information about that situation. Imagine four towns, roughly equidistant, as shown in Figure 1.1. A bad snowstorm has closed some of the roads between these towns while others are still open.

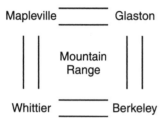

Figure 1.1

Between Mapleville and Glaston the roads are closed, as are the roads between Whittier and Mapleville. The roads between Glaston and Berkeley are open, and the roads between Berkeley and Whittier are open. If the number one (1) represents the roads being open, and the number zero (0) represents the roads being closed, then the picture can be redrawn to look like Figure 1.2.

Mapleville ___0___ Glaston

| 0 | Mountain Range | 1 |

Whittier ___1___ Berkeley

Figure 1.2

Now you can describe the road situation using numbers:

From	To	Road Situation	Number Description
Mapleville	Glaston	closed	0
Glaston	Berkeley	open	1
Berkeley	Whittier	open	1
Whittier	Mapleville	closed	0

The use of zeros and ones to describe a situation is a way of *digitizing* it. What was described with English words, like *open* and *closed*, has now been described by the numbers *zero* and *one*. These two digits are called *binary digits*—the word "binary" implying there are only two of them, specifically zero and one. The term *bits* is formed from the boldfaced letters of the two words "**bi**nary dig**its**."

Now let's expand on the situation of the roads. What if someone from a nearby town inquires, "Can I get from Mapleville to Glaston and from Glaston to Berkeley?" (The towns surround a mountain range, which prevents driving directly from one town to the other.) The answer would be, "No, but you could go from Glaston to Berkeley."

> MAPLEVILLE → GLASTON → BERKELEY
> closed   open

If we digitized the answer, it would look like this:

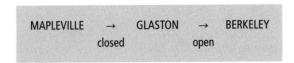

If we dropped all English words, the answer would be the two bits:

> 0   1

For the next question, someone asks, "Can I go from Whittier to Glaston via Berkeley?" The answer would be yes, since the road from Whittier to Berkeley is open, as is the road from Berkeley to Glaston."

Now we digitize the answer:

> 1   1

The first 1 represents that the road is open from Whittier to Berkeley, and the second 1 represents the road being open from Berkeley to Glaston.

Now look at an expanded map of the area, shown in Figure 1.3, this time adding the names of smaller towns between the larger towns.

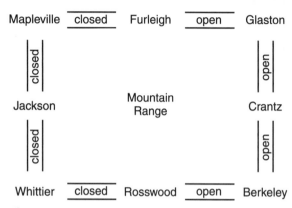

Figure 1.3

From	To	Road Situation	Digit Description
Mapleville	Furleigh	closed	0
Furleigh	Glaston	open	1
Glaston	Crantz	open	1
Crantz	Berkeley	open	1
Berkeley	Rosswood	open	1
Rosswood	Whittier	closed	0
Whittier	Jackson	closed	0
Jackson	Mapleville	closed	0

A description of the road situation from Mapleville to Berkeley via Glaston would look like the following:

MAPLEVILLE	→	FURLEIGH	→	GLASTON	→	CRANTZ	→	BERKELEY
	closed		open		open		open	
	0		1		1		1	

or just the four bits:

0	1	1	1

If you wanted to describe the road situations starting at Mapleville and going through Furleigh, Glaston, Crantz, Berkeley, Rosswood, Whittier, Jackson and back to Mapleville, you would be looking at these bits:

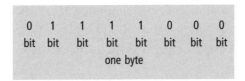

Any sequence of 8 bits is called a *byte*. So the sequence we just used is a byte of information.

Binary digits, or bits, can be used to describe many situations in the real world aside from the road conditions mentioned. When these numbers or digits are used to represent a particular situation or bit of information, we have *digitized* information. What other examples are there of digitization? We digitize photos when we scan them—all the colors used to create images that we recognize are represented digitally. The music you hear on a CD has been digitized because musical notes can be associated with numbers as well. A password for a person using a bankcard at an ATM can be digitized. In Chapter 2, I will discuss how letters and words are digitized.

Note

Digitizing information means using numbers to represent something other than a number. We digitize sound, color, and even images. Once digitized, they can be handled by a machine that can recognize these two integers: 1 and 0.

The Computer: An Electronic Machine

In order to be a good programmer, it is important to start with some of the fundamentals of how the computer operates. You must understand what kind of machine you're using and why it can do what it does.

The computer is an electronic machine. Thus it needs electricity to operate. The electricity comes from batteries or a plug in a wall and travels through elaborate circuitry etched onto highly sensitive material (like silicon) on a chip.

Electricity: On or Off

By manipulating electricity through the circuitry on a chip, we can go back and forth between two states: electricity flowing and electricity stopped.

If we assign the zero bit (0) to the stopped state and the one bit (1) to the flowing state, these bits can be connected to the internal workings of the machine.

The machine's capacity for manipulating electronic states is used to create a language of zeros and ones called *machine language*. It is called machine language because it is the elementary language of the machine. Without getting bogged down in the details, the computer expresses all information with these bits and bytes of machine language.

Computer Languages

Languages are used in everyday life for communication. All of us speak a native language and, depending on how much we read or write, we can develop a deep understanding of that language. The important thing about language is that you use it effectively to communicate your intentions, needs, wishes, or feelings.

Computer languages are similar to spoken languages in that you must use them very precisely so that you are not misunderstood by the computer. Each language has its own grammar, or *syntax*, which must be followed for the computer to understand that language.

Consider these examples from spoken languages:

English: Hello, how are you?

French: Bonjour! Ça va bien?

German: Guten tag. Wie geht's?

Japanese: Konnichi wa. O genki desu ka?

All of these examples mean the same thing: each sentence has a greeting followed by a question asking how you are. But each example is a completely different group of words. Unless you know these languages, you would not know that each means the same thing.

Computer languages are similar in that there are basic tasks that any computer language must do for a programmer. The programmer just has to learn to "speak" the language. One advantage of a computer language over a spoken language is that is does not take that long to become fluent in a computer language! Many programmers learn several languages during their careers.

Now read these examples from some computer languages:

*Python

```
BASIC    if (x > 5) print "greater."
Pascal   if x > 5 then writeln (greater.);
C++      if (x > 5) cout << "greater.";
Java     if (x > 5) System.out.println ("greater.");
```

All of these statements accomplish the same task: if the contents in the variable called x is greater than the number 5, then we will print a message on the computer screen—the word "greater."

Levels of Language: High and Low

All programming languages need to be translated into machine language, the native language of the computer. Machine language is comprised of binary code and therefore is extremely tedious to read and understand. Since the computer can only execute commands that have been written in its native machine language, other languages must be translated into machine language before being understood by the computer. There are two levels of language among programming languages: *high-level languages* and *low-level languages*.

High-Level Languages

High-level languages are languages that are "high" above the language of the computer—its machine language—the language it "understands" most naturally. High-level languages are removed from the reality of how computers process data—that is, in terms of bits. They are as removed from machine language as a king or queen is removed from the everyday worries of life—like making money, paying bills, and so on. Machine language is made of all binary digits, but high-level languages use English words to give directions to the computer. In order to understand the phrase *high-level*, consider first the following analogies.

Let's say you want to have a party for over 100 people. A "high-level" party giver would simply pick a date for the party, invite friends via e-mail or the telephone, and then the party would take place. A "low-level" party giver would have to handle all the details, that is renting a place, hiring a caterer, a band, and so forth. The party would not just "happen." You would have to deal with all the details, which the well-heeled "high-level" party giver can ignore.

Suppose you need to get your car fixed. A "high-level" approach to repair would be to bring the car to the repair shop and pick it up when the work is done. A "low-level" approach would be to lift the hood yourself and examine the parts, looking for the problem. Once the problem part was found, you would have to repair it yourself and then close the hood.

These analogies apply to programmers as well. The high-level language programmer doesn't need to know anything about how the computer itself goes about its work. He states a problem at a higher level without being involved in the nitty-gritty of how the computer performs its tasks. For this reason, high-level languages use commands that relate directly to the problem being programmed as opposed to the internal workings of the machine.

Programs written in high-level languages run more slowly on the computer because these languages need to be translated into machine language. Languages are defined in terms of their proximity to machine language: the higher the level, the more translation required before the program can be executed by the machine. Programs written in a high-level language require fewer lines of code than those written in a low-level language. It's much easier to say "let's give a party" or "fix the car" than say "call the caterer, order the food, rent the hall, and so on." Pascal, Cobol, Fortran, BASIC, C, C++, Perl, and Java are some examples of high-level languages.

Note

Computers "understand" machine language, which is generated from the electronic states determined by the current and circuitry of the machine.

Low-Level Languages

Low-level languages are just above machine language level. As such, they do not undergo as much translation as the high-level languages. They are, however, more difficult to understand because they rely on a greater understanding of the internal workings of the machine. Assembly languages are low-level languages. To a BASIC programmer, C might be considered a low-level language, since it allows the programmer to have more control at a lower level than the BASIC programmer.

Language Helpers: Translators

Translators break down high-level and low-level language code into machine language understood by the particular processor in the CPU. There are two kinds of translators: interpreters and compilers.

Interpreters and Compilers

Translators can work in two different ways: as interpreters or compilers. *Interpreters* will translate one line of code at a time and generate error messages immediately. *Compilers* translate an entire file of code all at once, rather than line by line. The compiler will not generate error messages until all code has been translated. The original file or program that the programmer writes is called *source code*. *Object code* is the result of translation and is the machine language version of the original file. C++ is an example of a compiled language, while BASIC is an interpreted one.

Note

Translators change high-level language or low-level language into machine language that is readily understood by the computer's processor.

The Algorithm: The Basis for All Designs to Solutions of Programming Problems

We are almost ready to begin the subject of programming—taking problems in the real world and writing them in a language that the computer can "understand" or execute. Before you get to the stage of programming your problems, you must design a suitable way of solving problems. An *algorithm* is a set of steps for solving a problem. These steps may repeat and may involve some decisions, such as a choice of two or more things.

Consider the following example of an algorithm for buying a ticket to a movie.

1. Go to the theatre.

2. Walk to the ticket counter.

3. Select a movie.

4. Pay the price.

5. Receive the ticket.

What about an algorithm for finding the smallest number among three numbers?

1. Compare the first number with the second number.

2. Discard the bigger number from step 1.

3. Compare the third number with the number that's left.

4. Discard the bigger number from step 3.

5. Whatever number is left is the smallest of all three.

The Three Parts of Any Algorithm

An algorithm has three parts:

1. The steps are finite (i.e., they do not go on forever).

2. Steps may be repeated.

3. Steps may involve decision making.

Tip

Each step of an algorithm should follow the step before. If necessary, repeat some of the steps and skip others if a decision calls for that action.

Examples of Algorithms in the Real World

Some examples of other algorithms follow.

Buying Fries at Burger King

1. Select the size of fries that you want.

2. Take out enough money to pay for them.

3. Hand over the money.

4. Receive change if necessary.

5. Take fries with you.

Dialing a Friend Who Lives Locally

1. Pick up receiver.

2. Dial seven digits.

3. Wait for friend's voice.

Programming a VCR's Timer to Tape a Show

1. Select menu button on remote control.

2. Select program menu from the given menu.

3. Complete table information about program's start time, finish time, channel, and speed of programming.

4. Press menu button on remote control.

5. Press power button of VCR.

6. Check for red light on VCR.

Programming

Now we are ready to discuss the subject of *programming*—taking a problem or task and designing an algorithm to handle this task, then using a programming language to express that algorithm so the computer will be able to execute that code.

Most people think of programming as being just about code—the lines of symbols and words that all of us have seen if we have ever opened a book on programming. It is more than code, however; it is a way of thinking about a problem and designing a solution that can then be written in a programming language.

Look at this short C++ program that prints the message "Could you please say that again?" 250 times on the machine.

```
# include <iostream.h>
# include <string.h>

int main ()
{ int x;
  string first_phrase;
  first_phrase = "Could you please say that again?";

    for (x = 0; x < 250; x++)
       {
          cout << first_phrase << endl;
       }
  return 0;
}
```

Here is another version of the same program in Pascal.

```
program printmessage ()
  var
     x : integer; first_phrase :string;
   begin
first_phrase := "Could you please say that again?";

  for x := 0 to 250 do
   begin
   writeln (first_phrase);
   x := x + 1;
   end
 end
```

Each of these examples could have been written in any language. The main point of these programs is that they both contain a loop, which is another way of saying that a particular task is being executed over and over again.

The point of showing both of these programs is to focus on how they are similar rather than their language differences. As you move through the chapters that follow, keep in mind that languages will always change to suit the development of technology. Certain concepts remain the same regardless of language. If you learn these concepts well, you will have no problem becoming a serious programmer.

Summary

We looked at the basics of the computer, including its hardware and software. We examined the computer as an electronic machine that can recognize changes in states of "on" and "off"; these states represent the basis of the digitization of information for the computer. Programming relies on the ability to write clear, step-by-step solutions called algorithms in a language. Some languages are high-level and easy to use, while other languages are more difficult to learn because they are low-level and closer to the machine's "understanding." In Chapter 2, we will look at the first major concept of programming: understanding variables.

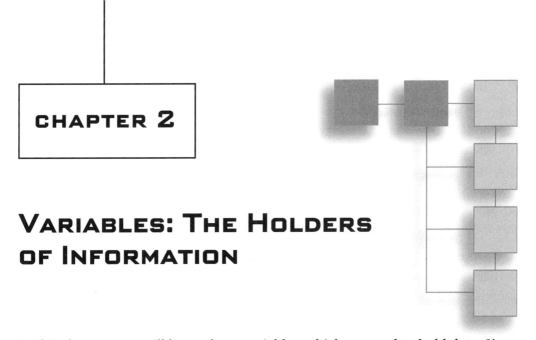

CHAPTER 2

VARIABLES: THE HOLDERS OF INFORMATION

In this chapter, you will learn about variables, which are used to hold data. Since we use computers primarily to manipulate data, we need to begin the study of programming with learning about variables. We will examine the different kinds of data and how variables are classified according to the data they hold. Once you understand variables, you can begin to learn about programming statements, which are the fundamental building blocks of programs. The first statement we will examine is the assignment statement, which allows you to store data into a variable. I'll cover the topic of variables as necessary holders for data. You'll examine variables by their types—that is, what kind of data they are intended to hold. I'll define programming statements, the necessary building blocks of programs. Next I'll cover how to introduce a variable into a program: variable declaration. Finally the topic of loading variables with data will be covered—how the variable is assigned its data.

In This Chapter
- Variables as holders of data
- Types of variables: integer, real, character and string
- Variable declaration
- Programming statements
- Assignment (by the programmer or by the user)

17

A Place to Put Data

One of the computer's most treasured assets is its capacity to store and manipulate information. *Data* (plural for *datum*) is another term for this information. Most programs that programmers write will need to put this data or information into some type of holder in order to manipulate it in some manner. We see the need to manipulate data everywhere in our society. Changes of address, phone numbers, new passwords for accounts, and editing manuscripts illustrate the need to manipulate information. Programs are constantly updated.

A programmer might want to edit some information, change it, print it, or perhaps send the data over the Internet through some file. Data has to be put somewhere and programmers use holders for it. Three examples of data are

- The number 365 to represent the days in the year

- The number −20 F to represent the Fahrenheit temperature in Alaska on a winter day

- The name of a favorite actor, Tommy Lee Jones

These three pieces of data, 365, −20 F, and Tommy Lee Jones are all pieces of information that a programmer would have to store in holders. When we use holders, we try to give them descriptive names so that readers of the programs can understand what we are trying to do in our program.

Let's devise some appropriately named holders for our data. We could put the number 365 into a holder called days, the number −20 F into a holder called temperature and the name Tommy Lee Jones into a holder called actor. Now instead of referring to 365, −20 F, or Tommy Lee Jones directly, we refer to the holders—days, temperature, or actor—which a programmer uses to manipulate data that often changes, or *varies*, over time.

Suppose you want to change 365 to 366 because you are dealing with a leap year. A programmer would manipulate the holder days rather than the number directly. Should you want to change the name of your favorite actor to Will Smith, you need to put the new name inside the holder actor. Likewise, to reflect temperature changes in Alaska, we use the holder temperature to alter the degrees.

One can never be certain whether data in a program will change right away or later on; you also don't know how often a piece of data will change during the running of a program. Having a holder that contains data facilitates managing

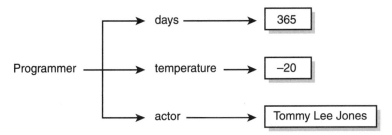

Figure 2.1
The programmer accesses data through the holder names used in his program.

that data. Here are some examples. A programmer would write instructions to do the following:

1. Increase the number in days by one.

2. Get another name of an actor and put that name into the holder actor.

3. Change the value in the temperature holder to the current reading.

These examples illustrate the need for a programmer to manipulate the values through their holders, since the instructions can be written for the holders rather than the numbers themselves. The programmer thus controls the data via the holder name. See Figure 2.1.

Now to the real name of these holders—variables. *Variables* are holders of data, in particular, data we expect to change, or *vary*, over time. In computer languages, the word variable differs slightly from its meaning in algebra. Variable names are not simply the letters of the alphabet, like x and y, which many of you might remember from your study of algebra. Variables can be any *descriptive* names that help us understand *what the data means*. That's why we used variables named days, temperature, and actor to label or identify the raw data 365, −20, and Tommy Lee Jones.

Note

Variables in algebra are letters of the alphabet, like x and y, but in computer languages, they can also be any *descriptive* names like sum, answer, or first_value.

Tip

If you want to link two words together to make an interesting variable name, use the *underscore* character, (_) for example, first_sum and my_last_answer.

Examples Using Variables

This example shows why it is easier to write a program using a variable rather than a number/value directly. The temperature variable from the previous section could be used as a holder for a given daily temperature in Anchorage, Alaska during the last week of February. As the temperature changes each day, a new value is put inside of the temperature holder or variable.

	Sun.	Mon.	Tues.	Wed.	Thurs.	Fri.	Sat.
Temperature	15	18	6	21	19	−4	2

One way to view what a variable might look like as its values are changing is to show the variable and its values as they are being replaced. Each new value replaces the previous one until the final value is left there (at least for now!).

Temperature
   15
   18
    6
   21
   19
   −4
    2

If a programmer wanted to write a program to print the average daily temperatures during the first four days of the week, he could devise two algorithms to do this—one using the variable temperature and one without that variable.

Algorithm with temperature as the Variable	Algorithm without Variable
1. Enter a value in temperature.	Print 15
2. Print actual temperature for second day.	Print 18
3. Print actual temperature for third day.	Print 6
4. Print actual temperature for fourth day.	Print 21

The algorithm *without* the variable is very inefficient and it is dependent on exact values being known at all times. The algorithm using the variable `temperature` is *not* dependent on knowing what value is within `temperature`. It is enough to know that whatever the temperature is, it will be printed.

Comparison of Two Variables

In another example, we will use two variables and continually compare one value against a second value in terms of whether the first value is less than, greater than, or equal to the second value. Think of a flight of stairs with one variable representing the number of steps you have climbed and the other variable representing the top step. The first variable will be called `count_steps`, and the second variable will be called `top_step`. See Figure 2.2.

We will continually increase the value of `count_steps`, and each time check its value against `top_step`'s value. If `count_steps` is still less than `top_step`, it means we have not yet reached the top of the stairs, and so we should continue to increase `count_steps` by 1. When `count_steps` and `top_step` are equal, we know that `count_steps` has "reached" the top of the flight of stairs and the program should end.

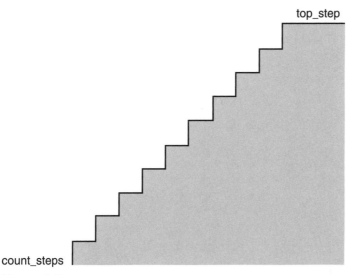

Figure 2.2
`count_steps` is shown on the landing at the bottom of a flight of stairs, and `top_step` is shown at the top of the steps.

In this example, the number 10 is placed in the variable top_step. The value 0 is placed into count_steps to represent the fact that we are at the bottom of the flight of stairs.

Look at the values of count_steps at the beginning of the program.

count_steps

0   This statement reports that count_steps starts off as zero.

1   count_steps changes to 1.

Now count_steps is compared with top_step in terms of being less than, greater than, or equal to top_step's value.

count_steps   <   top_step

1   <   10

"is less than"

Since count_steps' value is less than top_step's value, the execution of the program continues; count_steps increases to 2.

count_steps   <   top_step

2   <   10

"is less than"

This pattern continues:

count_steps   <   top_step

3   <   10

"is less than"

count_steps   <   top_step

4   <   10

"is less than"

This pattern continues until we view the program near the end of execution.

count_steps   <   top_step

9   <   10

"is less than"

Until now, the variable count_steps has been less than the top_step of 10. But now

count_steps = top_step

    10   =   10

         "equals"

The last value for count_steps is 10, and it is compared with the value in top_step. Since count_steps' value is not less than top_step but equal to it, *the program stops.*

This example illustrates the ability of the computer to alter one variable repeatedly. The decision to alter this variable depends on its value in comparison to another fixed value, top_step. As the program executes, the focus shifts back and forth between count_steps and top_step, with count_steps steadily increasing as the program runs. In one programming statement, count_steps is increased, and in the next statement it is compared to top_step. The programmer uses this algorithm to do all the work.

Here is an algorithm to count the number of steps, and then ring a bell when you get to the top.

1. Set count_steps to 0.

2. Set top_step to 10.

3. Increase count_steps' own value by 1.

4. Check count_steps' value against top_step's.

5. If count_steps is less than top_step go back to step 3; otherwise, go to step 6.

6. Ring a bell.

On the CD

A program that increases count_steps and compares it with top_step is written in C++.

Different Types of Variables

Now that we have both introduced the term *variables* and looked at some examples involving them, it is important to classify variables according to their type. The *type* of a variable is the kind of holder needed for the kind of data being

DATA TYPES

General Subdivision

- -

Specific Types

Figure 2.3
In the first diagram, the four main groups of data types are listed under their appropriate headings. Then another diagram gives the specific names of these four main groups.

stored *inside* the variable. In our previous examples, days and temperature were holders for the same kind of data: a *number*. The actor variable is a different type because it contains three words (Tommy Lee Jones).

So what types of variables are there in most computer languages? The main division in data types is between numbers and letters. Data is then further subdivided into groups under those headings. See Figure 2.3.

The Integer Type

Integers, in computer languages, are defined as numbers that have no fractional parts. Some examples of integers:

-20 42   13   1, 475 -234 0

The Real Type

Numbers that are *not* integers can be called *real*. In the computer language C++, real numbers are stored in a type called *double*, which refers to the fact that two bytes of memory are needed for its storage.

14.62 $58\frac{1}{3}$ -5.76 0.213   17.36   8.0

Each of the numbers in this list has a fractional or leftover part, so to speak. This puts them in our second category: the *real* type. The term *real* refers to all other numbers that are not integers:

14.62 $58\frac{1}{3}$ −5.76   0.213   17.36   8.0

The Character Type

Now consider the *character* type. The character type is a variable that will hold a letter of the alphabet or a symbol found on your keyboard, like '#', '*', '!', and so on. We use single quotes to set off characters to distinguish them from variables, which sometimes can be taken for characters—compare the character 'A' with the variable called A. Which symbols or letters are considered characters? There is a standard list of characters in the American Standard Code for Information Interchange, also known as the ASCII (pronounced *askey*) chart. It includes the alphabet in both upper- and lower-case, as well as all the symbols on a keyboard. If you use any of these letters or symbols, you will need a character type variable to hold it. For a copy of the ASCII chart, please see Appendix D. Examples of non-ASCII characters would be special letters from foreign languages, such as ç, for example, or special mathematics symbols like pi (π).

More Examples

'G'

'%'

'+'

'k'

Tip

Characters are generally displayed with single quotations to avoid confusion with variables that have the same name as a character. In the previous example, the letter G could be the variable named G or it could be the letter 'G'. By putting single quotes around it, we emphasize that we are talking about the letter 'G'.

The String Type

The *string* type is a variable holder that can only contain strings or groups of letters or symbols. The string type allows words to be stored by the computer. The ability of a user to enter a word is via the string type. Strings are used for a sequence of characters because the character type can only hold one character at a

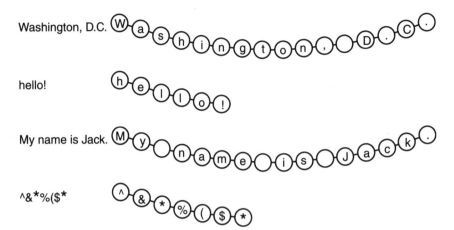

Washington, D.C.

hello!

My name is Jack.

^&*%($*

Figure 2.4
Each example is shown as a string of beads in a necklace to emphasize that each letter is separate but also connected to the next letter, as far as the computer is concerned.

time. Later we will see that there are other ways to handle a sequence of letters. Here are some examples:

```
"Washington, D.C."
"hello!"
"My name is Jack."
"^&*%($*".
```

Think of a string as a string of beads in a necklace. Except here, we mean a string of characters strung together. See Figure 2.4.

Note

The word *type* in computer programming languages refers to the kind of holder needed for data.

TYPE	EXAMPLES
Integers	1, 2, −38, 327, 10, etc.
Reals	3.82, −14.6, 0.005, π
Characters	'G', '%', '+', 'k'
String	"robot", "Stars and Stripes", "Wow!!"

Introducing a Variable for the First Time in a Program

Now for an explanation of the most interesting and basic part of programming—the ability to store data/information in a variable. The initial step in writing a computer program is to tell the computer how much memory to *allocate*, or set aside, for the variables used in the program.

The computer must know whether the variable being used requires a lot of *memory*, or space, for instance. Once the computer knows what type of variable is being used, all the rules that govern that particular type must be followed. These rules will be explored later as you learn more about programming.

In order to tell the computer what type of variable will be used and how much memory is required, we must declare a variable. *Declaring* a variable is the same as *introducing* a variable. It is the first time you tell the computer what the variable's part will be in the program. The relationship or type of a variable must be identified so the computer can respond appropriately. The different types of variables previously mentioned—integer, real, character, and string— all make different demands on the computer. For example, different types require more memory than others. A character requires less space for storage than a string. Likewise, an integer requires less memory than a real type on most computers. By stating the type of variable used in the program, a programmer is instructing the computer to allocate a certain amount of memory for that variable.

An Analogy: Telling the Audience Who Is Who

The analogy of a playbill is useful, since we are likening the computer to an audience. An audience wants to know who is playing what part as well as the kinds of roles in the play. The computer is the same way: it needs to know what part each variable is playing so it can respond accordingly. Variables have different memory requirements for storage, and the manner in which they are stored depends on their type. A computer has to "know" this before the variable appears later in the program.

Think of the play *Hamlet* by William Shakespeare. When you open the playbill to the first page, the list of characters and their parts in relation to the whole are listed (see Figure 2.5).

Hamlet is a prince, while Rosencrantz and Gildenstern are courtiers. Lesser-known Francisco is a soldier. Gertrude is a queen, and Hamlet's father a ghost. A playbill lets the audience know who's involved in the play and what part each character plays by the description of the character. From reading the cast of *Hamlet*, we know that Gertrude is a member of royalty, while Rosencrantz and Guildenstern are not.

Cast of Hamlet

Claudius, the new king of Denmark.
Hamlet, son to the late, and nephew to the present king.
Fortinbras, prince of Norway.
Polonius, a lord and high official (probably Lord Chamberlain).
Laertes, his son.
Horatio, the friend of Hamlet.
Voltimand
Cornelius
Rosencrantz   } Courtiers
Guildenstern
Osric
Marcellus, a Danish officer.
Francisco
Bernardo   } soldiers on sentry duty.
Reynaldo, servant to Polonius.
A Norwegian Captain.
Players on Tour.
Two clowns, gravediggers.
English ambassador, a priest, a gentleman, soldiers, sailor, messenger,
    and various attendants.
Gertrude, Queen of Denmark and mother of Hamlet.
Ophelia, daughter of Polonius.
Ghost of Hamlet's father.

Figure 2.5
This shows the entire cast of *Hamlet*.

Imagine a playbill with the following heading:

"My First Computer Program!!"

Starring

the integer	my_first_sum
the integer	my_last_sum
the real	answer
the character	middle_initial
the string	last_name

The type of each variable is written on the left, while the name of the variable is written on the right. This playbill is useful because we can find out that there are two integers in this program—one called my_first_sum and another called my_last_sum. There is one real called answer, a character called middle_initial and a string called last_name.

Each of these "players" has a proper name, a name that the audience would recognize. my_first_sum, my_last_sum, answer, middle_initial, and last_name are the names of the players in this program. They take part in the program and appear at different points in the program in order to perform different tasks. The fact that one of the variables is an integer, while another is a real, is comparable to saying that one of the characters in *Hamlet* is a queen, while another character is a maid.

This play, "My First Computer Program!!" also has two integers in it: my_first_sum and my_last_sum. These names are useful since they allow you to distinguish one integer from another. Most programs have several variables and often a few from each type category. Using the proper name to refer to the variable is a way of distinguishing among variables of the same type. This proper name is called the *identifier* of the variable to distinguish it from its *type*.

Look at the following chart that mixes some of the types from both the program and the play. Each character in the play has a type, just as each variable does. Is the character in the play a friend of Hamlet's, a relative, a member of the ruling class? Is a variable an integer, a character, a string, or a real?

CHARACTERS IN PLAY	VARIABLES IN PROGRAM
King: *Claudius*	integer: my_first_sum
Queen: *Gertrude*	integer: my_last_sum
Courtier: *Rosencrantz*	real: answer

TYPE	IDENTIFIER
queen	Gertrude
prince	Hamlet
king	Claudius
integer	my_first_sum
integer	my_last_sum
courtier	Rosencrantz
courtier	Guildenstern
real	answer

All programs require that variables be *declared*: that is, their type and name are stated before they are used in the program to do something really useful. Imagine what would happen if you were watching a play and an unidentified character appeared in Scene III, for example, and spoke with other characters before leaving the stage. Your first instinct would be to check the playbill and make sure you had not overlooked this character. However, what would you think if the character wasn't listed there? You would have to spend the rest of the play trying to figure out what connection that character had to the other characters in the play and the play as a whole.

The computer is the same way. It cannot encounter a variable halfway through a program unless it has been declared prior to use. This is one of the most important concepts that must be understood. It's not that all languages require that all variables be listed at the top of a program (though many do!), but they must at least be declared prior to being used in the program.

Note

Names for variables, as essential as the names of characters in a play, should be *descriptive* to enable any reader to follow what the variable will be used for in the program (e.g., check_sum, last_name, initial_balance, etc.).

Caution

Don't underestimate the importance of declaring a variable because the computer *must know* how much memory to set aside for it. This must be done *before* the variable is used in the program.

A Word about Statements

Computer languages like spoken languages have a certain grammar that must be followed. The first point about writing in a programming language is to write in sentences or statements. Computer *statements* are the building blocks of programs, just as sentences are the building blocks of paragraphs and essays. A program is comprised of statements. There are different kinds of programming statements: loop statements, if...then statements, assignment statements, and print statements—just to name a few.

A statement in a computer language has rigorous grammar. As you learn each of these statements, you will take a moment to learn the *grammar*, often called *syntax*, of each statement type. This will save you a lot of time when you start to run programs. There is little or no room for variation because the "reader" of your programs is a machine, which will not understand what you mean to say if you do not expressly say it according to the grammar it understands.

Termination of Statements

The first point about programming is to understand how your computer language ends its statements. Do the statements end in a period (.) or a semicolon (;)? Most languages use the semicolon to indicate the end of a statement.

Let's look at these statements from various languages. It is not important that you understand the statements—only that you recognize that each one ends in a semicolon.

Example 1	`c := 14;`
Example 2	`answer = 58;`
Example 3	`while (x < 14)`
	`    cout << "hello! \ n";`

In each of these examples, the semicolon is the last mark of punctuation after the group of words and symbols in the statements. In Example 3, we have a statement that wraps to the next line, indicating that programming statements do not need to fit entirely on one line.

Note

Programming statements terminate with some sort of punctuation; usually it is the semicolon.

Must Statements Fit on One Line?

A programming statement need not fit on one line. Sometimes one statement, because of its complexity, will last several lines, and the semicolon will appear finally to indicate that the statement is complete.

Another point about programming statements is that programmers like to indent. Indentation makes the programs easier to read and understand. In Example 3, the line

```
while (x < 14)
   cout << "hello\n.";
```

could have fit on one line, but writing it on two lines makes it easier to understand as you will see later after studying this kind of statement.

Note

A programming statement is not defined by its length. It may be longer than one line or it may wrap to the next line. Lines that wrap to the next line are easier to read and understand.

Putting a Value into a Variable

Once variables have been declared, you are now ready to put a value into the variable: this is called *assigning the variable*. By assigning the variable, you are giving it a value for later use. If we try to print the contents of a variable on the screen, and that variable is unassigned (or empty), then we have a problem.

Caution

Sometimes programmers forget to assign a variable and then later try to use a variable's value, which produces erroneous and unpredictable results. Remember to assign the variable before using it.

There are different ways of assigning a variable, depending on who does the assigning of values. So now I will formally introduce two important people in programming: the programmer and the user.

The Programmer

The *programmer* is the person who writes the program. When a programmer puts values into variables, he is the only person controlling what data is assigned to those variables. The programmer might use his own data to load the variables, or he might use an external source for that data, such as a file. But the bottom line still holds; he is responsible for acquiring the data and assigning it to the variables.

The User

The *user* is the person who interacts with the program. He will use the program much like the person who purchases an application (like Microsoft Word) at the store and uses it after installation on the computer. The user runs the program and responds to what the program asks. If the programmer has written statements to cause the program to pause and wait for a response from the user, then the user will be the one to assign variables. The user is *prompted*, or asked, by the programmer with some message that appears on the screen. See Figure 2.6.

Please type a number
|

Figure 2.6
A message followed by a blinking cursor appears on the screen. Whatever the user types in response will go into the variable associated with this prompting statement.

How the Programmer Assigns Variables

In an *assignment* statement a programmer writes a variable followed by some symbol to denote that a value is being assigned (sent into) a variable. To the right of the symbol is the value itself or another variable.

The syntax is as follows:

VARIABLE	ASSIGNMENT SYMBOL	VALUE;
left-hand side	=	right-hand side

Look at each of the following assignment statements written in their respective languages:

VARIABLE	IS ASSIGNED	VALUE	LANGUAGE
A	:=	35 ;	Pascal
A	=	35 ;	C++; JAVA
Let A	=	35	BASIC

Everything on the left-hand side is the variable A, while everything on the right hand side is the value 35. The value 35 is being placed into a variable called A. The emphasis in assignment is that some value from the right-hand side is being shifted into the left-hand side of the assignment symbol. In the examples that follow, different values are assigned to different types of variables.

Another important rule about assignment is that you must be careful about what values you put into which types of variables. In general, you must put a value into a variable of the same type. Integers go into integer type variables, reals go into real type variables, and so on. Here are some examples:

```
answer = −14              Integers are being assigned to integer variables
sum = 27;
first_initial = 'M';      Characters are being assigned to character variables
last_initial = 'W';
name = "Janet";           Strings are being assigned to string variables
cousin = "Mike";
balance = 1234.56;        Reals are being assigned to real variables
amount = 78.00;
```

The one exception is that *integers can fit into real types* because integers are easily converted to real numbers, and the memory required for storing a real is generally larger than that required for storing an integer.

Before the assignment statement is executed, a variable is empty and has no contents. Once the assignment statement is executed, the value is put into the variable. See Figure 2.7.

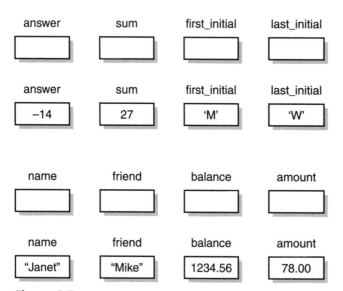

Figure 2.7
Each variable is shown initially empty, or *unassigned*, and then is shown with its value inside it.

Assigning One Variable to Another Variable

It is also possible to assign to a variable the contents of another variable. Let's say you want an extra copy of a value that already exists in a variable, called first_val. All you have to do is declare another variable called copy_val and assign to copy_val first_val's value. The syntax is as follows:

The variable on the right-hand side of the assignment symbol will have the value *inside it* copied into the variable on the left-hand side of the assignment symbol. If the variable is not empty, whatever is in it will be *replaced* with the new value. This is called assigning one variable to another. See Figure 2.8.

In another example, a variable is empty before being assigned the contents of a second variable. See Figure 2.9.

Caution

The left-hand side must *always* be a variable, while the right-hand side can either be a value or another variable. When one variable is assigned to another, the right-hand variable *does not* change. Only the contents of the left-hand variable do.

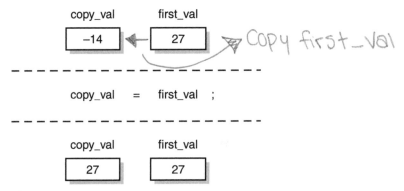

copy_val   =   first_val   ;

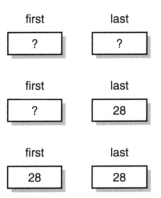

Figure 2.8
Variables first_val and copy_val are shown with their respective values. Then the assignment statement is executed. Now the variables are shown again—this time copy_val's value (−14) has changed to show the same value that is in first_val (27).

first   last

?   ?

first   last

?   28

first   last

28   28

Figure 2.9
The variable first, initially empty, is assigned the contents of the variable, last. Then, first is shown as an empty variable and last with its value, 28. Then the assignment statement is executed after which first has the same value as last: 28.

How the User Assigns Variables

It is important to let the user think of values for variables. The programmer should not be the only one thinking of values that will be assigned to variables. Think of the word "input" in English. Sometimes a friend will ask you, "What is your input?" She is really asking, "What do you think about something?" When we look for the user's input, we are interested in what the user wants for values.

There are two steps involved in understanding how you can get a response from the user stored into a variable. The first step is understanding how programming languages use the keyboard as a source of input.

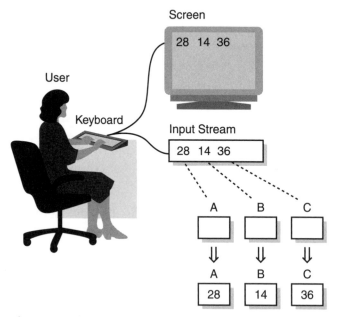

Figure 2.10
A drawing shows the connection among the user, the keyboard, the screen, the input stream, and three variables being assigned.

Input Streams

Programming languages use an *input stream* as a source of values. Think of a stream in a computer language in the same way as you would a stream or rivulet (a small river). Streams flow into larger bodies of water. In programming languages, an input stream is like a small channel that feeds from the keyboard. Anything that is typed at the keyboard will be sent to this stream. (It is also visible on the screen.) The stream is then a source of values (data) for the variables that will be assigned. See Figure 2.10.

Variables Are Assigned Their Values from This Stream

Programming languages will differ in the way that they handle the stream. One thing is common, however: every programming language uses some word to indicate that an input stream is the source of values for variables that will be assigned. The programmer must also *list* the variables that are to be assigned values from this stream. Let's concentrate on the C++ programming language, which uses its input stream name cin directly.

A Stream Used for Input: cin

cin (pronounced "see-in") is the name of the input stream in the C++ programming language. When you use a cin statement with a list of one or more variables, you are assigning data from the cin channel to the variables that follow. Anything that was sent to this stream will eventually end up in the variables connected to the stream.

The syntax for using the cin stream goes as follows. You name the stream **cin**. Then you follow with an *extraction operator* that indicates something is being *pulled out* of the stream and sent into a variable. (The word extraction means "pull out"; that's why when you get a tooth pulled by the dentist, it is called an extraction!) The extraction operator is this double arrow symbol: >>. Next, you list the variable that you wish to load (assign) with the value that came from the stream. Let's look at some examples.

```
int second_val;
cin >> second_val;

string my_name;
cin >> my_name;
```

In the first example, we are taking a number (an integer) from the cin stream and assigning it to the variable, second_val. In the second example, we are taking a word (typed at the keyboard by the user) from the stream cin and assigning that word to the variable my_name. Notice how the variables always appear to the right of the extraction operator (>>).

On the CD

C++ has one of the simplest approaches to getting the user's input for assigning variables. Compare the previous example with these ones written in BASIC and JAVA, respectively.

Assigning Two Variables at Once

When you wish to assign more than one variable at a time with input from the user, you need to use the extraction operator *before* each variable in a list. We use the cin stream followed by the extraction operator, the first variable we are assigning, the extraction operator (again), and the second variable. (Remember we are assigning two variables with two numbers "extracted from" the stream.)

In both examples that follow, more than one item is pulled from the stream so the extraction operator is placed in front of each variable assigned.

```
cin >>first_val >> second_val;//two vars. are assigned

int a ; int b; int c;
cin >> a >> b >> c ;//three vars. are assigned
```

Note

Any input from the user will first travel to the `cin` stream. You need the extraction operator, `>>`. If there is more than one number or word of input, put the extraction operator *before* each variable. You need a variable for each value and the variable should have the same type as the expected value.

Tip

As the user types at the keyboard, she may make a mistake and need to backspace or delete. Her data will only become finalized after she presses the Enter or Return key—then the data goes to the input stream.

Summary

In this chapter, you learned that variables are the holders of data. Different types of variables were introduced: integer, real, character, and string. Next the topic of declaration, or how a variable is first introduced in a program, was covered. If a variable is not introduced, the computer will not know what the variable's role in the program is. Furthermore, the computer will not know how much memory to set aside for that variable. Programs consist of statements, which proceed in sequence like the algorithms mentioned earlier. Statements are like sentences, which have punctuation to show that they have terminated. Most computer statements end in a semicolon. Each computer statement has its own grammar, or syntax, which must be followed rigorously.

Finally, the topic of assigning variables and who does that assignment, the programmer or the user, was discussed. If the programmer assigns the variables, we expect to see an assignment symbol surrounded by variables on one side and variables or values on the other side. If the user assigns the variables, the user will type values at the keyboard. These values will be sent to an input stream. Variables are assigned values that come from this stream. This is how the user can assign values to variables.

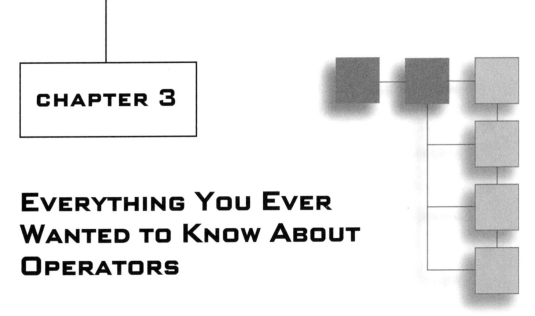

CHAPTER 3

EVERYTHING YOU EVER WANTED TO KNOW ABOUT OPERATORS

Now that you have learned to store values in variables, what can you do with those variables? Most programs involve some form of computation: computing the balance in a checking account, comparing an identification number with an existing one to see if it is the same, updating the information on an individual's age stored in a data file. In order to perform any kind of computation, we must first understand something about manipulating values within a computer language environment. Chapter 2 was all about how to put values into variables. Now that you have those values inside of variables, you'll want to start performing computations on those values. *Operators* allow you to do that.

In This Chapter

- Operators defined

- PEMDAS (Please Excuse My Dear Aunt Sally)

- Binary and unary operators

- Arithmetic operators

- Relational operators

- Logic operators

- Mod operator

What Are Operators Anyway?

Operators are the names for the actions that we perform on numbers. What usually come to mind are the actions of addition (+), subtraction (−), multiplication (*), and division (/). Each of these symbols are examples of operators because they act on the numbers around them to generate an answer. Following are some examples:

5 + 6	Produces the answer 11
13 * 5	Produces the answer 65
12/2	Produces the answer 6

Not all operators are like the +, −, *, and / operators. Some operators are more subtle—they produce answers that are not numbers but *true* or *false* answers. The examples that follow use the less than (<) and greater than (>) operators:

15 < 37	15 is less than 37
Produces the answer *true*	
14 > 100	14 is greater than 100
Produces the answer *false*	

We get an answer, but it is not a number. It is a true or false answer.

The reason to use operators, namely +, −, * (multiplication), and / (division), is to enhance the ability of the machine to carry out simple tasks that involve some computation (e.g., computing the interest in a savings account, finding the average of a set of test scores, calculating the cost of an item that has been discounted, or determining whether someone's checking account balance is greater than the amount written on a check).

If you want to control this machine, it will be necessary to understand how computations, which involve operators, are performed. The easiest thing to do will be to understand the order of operations that already exists in the real world, namely those used in arithmetic and algebra.

The Order of Operations

Not all operators are the same. Some are more important than others in the sense that they are given priority over another operator. Here we use the term *precedence*. The *precedence* of one operator over another means that one operator ranks higher than another: it has *greater precedence*. If you use more than one operator in a programming statement, you will need to understand the precedence of your operators so that you get the desired result from any computations you wish the computer to perform.

The operator with the highest rank/priority will be executed *first* by the computer. Then any other operators in the statement will be executed in the appropriate ranking order. If we write an addition or subtraction operator and a multiplication or division operator in the same expression, the multiplication/division operator will be given precedence: that means that it will be executed first before the addition/subtraction operator.

Let's look at the following examples where each operator has a number beneath it to indicate the order in which its operation is performed.

Examples

3 + 2 * 5

In the preceding example, the multiplication is the ranking operation so 2 * 5 will be executed first—it is given precedence. Once performed (2 * 5 = 10), then the addition operator is activated (3 + 10), and the answer is 13. Here is another example:

Ranking operators		1st		2nd	
		⇓		⇓	
	4	*	6	–	3
		⇓			
Becomes	24	–	3		
		⇓			
Which then becomes	21				

In this example, 4 * 6 is computed first. Next, 3 is subtracted from 24 to give 21.

Ranking operators		1st		2nd	
		⇓		⇓	
	8	/	2	–	5
		⇓			
Becomes	4	–	5		
		⇓			
Which then becomes	−1				

In this example, 8/2 is computed first. Next, 5 is subtracted from 4 to give −1.

PEMDAS (Please Excuse My Dear Aunt Sally)

Although the above phrase is perhaps a little outdated, it continues to serve its purpose well—namely to give instruction regarding the precedence of the operators. The acronym, PEMDAS, refers to the following: parentheses, exponents, multiplication, division, addition, and subtraction. These operators should be executed in the order they appear in the acronym. So parentheses are first, followed by exponents, then multiplication and division follow—with addition and subtraction last.

In the previous examples, the multiplication and division operators always precede the addition and subtraction operators. Division and multiplication have equal precedence, and they both rank higher than addition and subtraction. Likewise, addition and subtraction have equal precedence, and they both rank lower than multiplication and division.

Parentheses Still Rule

Parentheses are perhaps the most interesting operator because they tell the computer that what appears *inside* of them should be given precedence over all other operators—that is, they should be executed *first*.

Examples

	$8 (5 + 2) - 7$
	2nd 1st 3rd
Becomes	$8 (7) - 7$
	$56 - 7$
	49

Because the parentheses are present, $(5 + 2)$ is executed first. Next, 8 is multiplied by 7 to give 56. Then 7 is subtracted from 56 to give 49.

	$15 + 3 (2 - 5) * 6$
	4th 2nd 1st 3rd
Becomes	$15 + 3 (-3) * 6$
	$15 + -9 * 6$
	$15 + -54$
	-39

Note

Remember that when the same operator appears more than once in a programming statement, each of those operators will be executed in order from left to right.

Operators: Are They Binary or Unary?

Operators can be classified according to the number of operands required by the operator. An *operand* is a number on which an action is being performed. In the example $2 + 2$, the 2s are the operands because the operation of addition is being performed on them. As you will see in the examples that follow, almost all operators require two operands. Any of our arithmetic operations, like addition, subtraction, multiplication, and division, are *binary* operations because they require two numbers to add, subtract, multiply, or divide. (Recall that binary means *two*.)

Binary Operators

Binary operators are operators that require two operands, one on either side of the operator. The two operands are needed for the operator to function properly. Most of the operators you will encounter will be binary operators.

Examples

$6 + 7$
The + sign needs two operands, the 6 and 7, to work on.

$3 * 8$
The * sign works on both the 3 and 8 on either side of it.

$6 - 18$
The − sign allows the 18 to be subtracted from the 6.

sum $= 24$
The = sign allows the value 24 to be stored into sum. It needs a variable on the left-hand side and either a number or a variable (containing a number) on the right-hand side.

Unary Operators

Unary operators are operators that require only one operand to function properly. The *negative* sign (–) can be an example of a unary operator. For example, if we put a negative sign in front of a number (5), it makes it negative (–5). If we put a negative sign in front of an already negative number, it will make it positive: $-(-6)$ becomes 6.

We can also put a negative sign in front of a variable to change whatever is inside the variable. Consider this example:

X = 15

Y = –X

Now Y contains -15 because X's contents were *negated* before Y was assigned the value inside X.

Examples of Unary and Binary Operators

Unary
-4
The only operand is the 4. The result is the number -4.

Binary
$3 + 2$
There are two operands: 3 and 2.

Unary and Binary
$-(8 + 7)$
The + is a *binary* operator. Its operands are 8 and 7. The *unary* operator is the negative sign. Its operand is the 15 that results from executing $8 + 7$ first.

Remember the assignment symbol (=) from the last chapter? The assignment symbol is a binary operator because it always takes two operands: the variable to be assigned as the left operand and the value it is given as a right operand. Some examples:

```
a  = 15;
b  = -34;
m = b;
```

Tip

Most calculators will distinguish between the subtraction operator (a binary operator) and the negative sign (a unary operator).

Arithmetic Operators

Every computer language will use the arithmetic operators to perform simple calculations. These operators are readily recognized as the same as those on a calculator, except perhaps, for the multiplication symbol (*).

+   The addition sign

−   The negative sign or the subtraction sign, depending on how it is used .

*   The multiplication sign

/   The division sign

Division: a Special Case

Except for the division sign, the other operators perform as they do in arithmetic. The division operator performs according to the type of the operands, those numbers used on either side of its operator. See Figure 3.1.

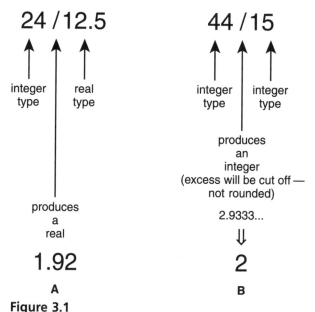

Figure 3.1
Two division problems, A and B, and their results are shown. If integers are used exclusively, as in problem B, an integer will be produced.

Division works just as you would expect, *except* when integers alone are used with the division sign. If the division symbol is used with two integers, only an integer will be produced and any fractional part *will be dropped.*

Examples

6/4 produces 1 instead of 1.5
(0.5 is thrown away)

8/4 produces 2

−143/7 produces −20
(0.429 is thrown away)

Examples with Variables

```
a = 14;
b = 12;
c = a/b;
(c is 1)

answer = 67;
sum = -23;
new_answer = answer/sum;
(new_answer is -2)
```

Caution

Always notice which types you are using around a division symbol. The division symbol "recognizes" its operands and performs accordingly. Either the fractional part is dropped (with integers) or it is retained (with all others).

The Relational Operators

Another group of operators is very useful because operators allow values to be compared to other values. When you *compare* one value to another, you are interested in knowing whether one value is greater than, less than, or equal to another value. The result of using a relational operator with its operands is a *true/ false* answer rather than an *arithmetic* answer.

The first relational operators that we will use are as follows: <, <=, >, >=, ==. The last operator deserves some mention. The double equal symbol is used to emphasize that this is not the assignment operator from Chapter 2 (=) but the relational operator, meaning equivalent to.

Examples

Operation	Result
15 < 16	True
15 is less than 16	
−13 > 100	False
−13 is greater than 100	
25 == 25	True
25 is equal to 25	
35 == 4	False
35 is equal to 4	

In addition to the < (less than), > (greater than), and == (equal to) operators, there are the additional <= (less than or equal to) and >= (greater than or equal to) operators.

Operation	Result
57 <= 69	True
57 is less than or equal to 69	
12.5 >= 12.5	True
12.5 is greater than or equal to 12.5	
−26 <= −27	False
−26 is less than or equal to −27	

Finally computer languages provide an operator that means *not equal to*: ≠.

In the computer language called C++, it looks like an exclamation point followed by an equal sign: !=.

Operation	Result
28 != 28	False
28 is not equal to 28	
0 != 7	True
0 is not equal to 7	

Logic Operators

The logic operators are a group of operators that allow the computer to make a complex decision. Let's start with examining the logic involved in some statements that you encounter in everyday life. Then we will take what we have learned and apply it to our context of programming in a language.

Logic Operators in the Real World

Imagine a situation where you are only allowed to go to a party if exactly one of the following numbered choices is fulfilled:

You can go to the party if

1. You take out the garbage *and* you clean your room.

2. You take out the garbage *or* you clean your room.

3. You rake the leaves *or* you wash the floor.

4. You rake the leaves *and* you wash the floor.

Which of these numbered conditions seems the most appealing? If you think of each of these situations *logically*, #2 and #3 are the easiest to fulfill. This is not because of the simplicity of the tasks involved. (Let's ignore the fact that you would do anything to avoid washing the floor.)

Choices #2 and #3 are easiest because of what is meant by the word "or" linking the two tasks. By using this word, the underlying assumption is that you have a *choice* in what to do in order to gain permission to go to the party. Choices #1 and #4 give you no choice: you must do *both* tasks before getting permission. Look at the following table and examine all the possibilities of doing either, both, or neither of the tasks and the resulting permission. (A check means that a task is completed and an X means that a task is not done.)

Tasks		Permission
You take out the garbage *and* you clean your room		
✓	X	NO
You take out the garbage *and* you clean your room		
X	✓	NO
You take out the garbage *and* you clean your room		
✓	✓	YES

You take out the garbage *and* you clean your room		
X	X	NO
You rake the leaves *or* you wash the floor		
✓	X	YES
You rake the leaves *or* you wash the floor		
X	✓	YES
You rake the leaves *or* you wash the floor		
X	X	NO
You rake the leaves *or* you wash the floor		
✓	✓	YES

Look at each situation to see why permission was given or denied. What can we say about the *and* conjunction? It requires *both* conditions to be executed. In contrast, the *or* conjunction needs only one condition to be checked to get permission. Each of these conjunctions is called a *logic operator*. The *and* conjunction has been used with one task on either side of it; therefore, it behaves like a binary operator. Likewise, the *or* conjunction has been used with one task on either side of it, and so is also a binary operator. Both words are called logic operators because they evaluate a statement just as you would in everyday circumstances.

Logic Operators in the Computer Language Environment

In the context of computer programming, we do not deal with tasks but true/false results that are generated by *relational expressions*. (Recall that a relational expression uses a relational operator for comparison—like greater than, less than, not equal to, etc.) Each task in the real world is a relational expression in the computer language environment. Let's compare one of our previous examples with an example appropriate in a programming environment.

Real-world example: You take out the garbage *and* you clean your room

Programming example: x must be greater than 24 *and* x must be less than 30

$$x > 24 \quad and \quad x < 30$$

Real-world example: You rake the leaves *or* you wash the floor

Programming example: y is less than 0 *or* y is greater than 100

$$y < 0 \quad or \quad y > 100$$

Recall that if both tasks are done (in the case of the *and* operator), then permission is granted or access given, and so forth. In the programming example, a *relational expression* will appear on both sides of the operator. Depending on whether one or both of these expressions are true, the result will be true or false.

The logic operators are these words: *and* and *or*. Like any binary operators, they must have an operand on either side. The operand on each side must be an expression that has a true or false value: so far, only the relational expression gives such a value. *Arithmetic expressions* yield numbers and are not acceptable as operands for the logic operators. Consider this example: $5 + 9$ *and* $6 - 3$ does not make sense in a computer language. However, $5 + 9 == 14$ and $6 - 3 != 4$ are true statements and can be written in any programming language.

When you evaluate a logic expression, keep in mind two things: once there is a false expression on one side of an *and* operator, the *whole statement is false*. Once there is a true expression on one side of the *or* operator, the *whole statement is true*.

Examples with Variables

sum > 12 *or* sum < 0

What will be the result if sum contains 14?

What will be the result if sum contains −25?

What will be the result if sum contains 12?

In the first example, $14 > 12$, so we have one true result in an *or* statement. Therefore the entire statement is true regardless of the second relational expression's result.

In the second example, −25 is not > 12 but $-25 < 0$ so a false or true result is overall true.

In the last example, 12 is not > 12 and 12 is not < 0 so false or false produces false.

Example

answer > -5 *and* answer < 20

What will be the result if answer contains 10?

What will be the result if answer contains −65?

What will be the result if answer contains 28?

In the first example, $10 > -5$ *and* $10 < 20$, so we have a true result on either side of the *and*. Therefore the entire statement is true. In the second example, −65 is not

> −5 although −65 is < 20, but the entire statement is false because we have a false on one side of the *and*. In the last example, 28 is > 12 but 28 is not < 20, so true and false produces false.

Tip

The logic operator *and* has to have all relational expressions around it to be true for it to generate an overall true answer. The logic operator *or* needs only one of its operands to be true to generate an overall true answer.

Note

The *and* operator is usually the word *and* or double ampersands: &&. The *or* operator is the word or, or it is represented symbolically as two vertical bars: ||.

Examples

x > 3 *and* x < 10	is the same as	x < 3 && x < 10
y > 100 *or* y < 0	is the same as	y > 100 || y < 0

A Special Logic Operator: The Not Operator

Our last logic operator is the word *not*. What does a *not* operator do? In order to understand the *not* operator, let's look at an example from the real world. Imagine that you have a very contrary friend (lucky you!). Everything you say, she changes. Let's look at some of your conversations.

You: That movie was great!

Her: No, it was horrible!

You: I liked the opening scene.

Her: No, you didn't. You said it was lame.

You: I didn't like the ending, however.

Her: Yes, you did. You were laughing all during it.

After a series of conversations like these, you might want to avoid your friend for a while. Your friend behaves like the *not* operator. Everything that you have said gets changed, *logically*. If you said you liked something, the *not* operator (your friend) will say you didn't like it. If you say you didn't like something, the *not* operator (your friend) will say you liked it by altering what you said to its *logical opposite*. Let's take a few sentences and apply the *not* operator to them, and then see what that does to the meaning of those statements. Notice that the *not* operator *precedes* the statement that will be altered.

Operator	Statement	Resulting Statement
not	(It's raining outside.)	It's *not raining* outside.
not	(I have no homework.)	I *have* homework!
not	(I disliked the movie *Gladiator*)	I *liked* the movie *Gladiator.*

The *not* in front of each of these statements changes the logic of whatever it is applied to. It changes every statement or expression it operates on. It is a unary operator because it only needs one operand on which to work.

In the next set of examples, we will look at a resulting statement and determine how a *not* statement was used to create it.

Resulting Statement	not	Original Statement
I love the summer.	*not*	(I don't like summer.)
He reads a lot.	*not*	(He doesn't read much.)
She did not write a letter.	*not*	(She did write a letter.)

Tip

The *not* operator could be the word *not* or the exclamation point (!).

Examples

not (x < 3)	is the same as	! (x < 3)
not (y > 100)	is the same as	! (y > 100)

Caution

The *not* operator does not always produce a negative statement; it produces the *opposite* of its operand.

Consider these examples with variables. In each example, a variable is first assigned a value and then a *not* expression is used. Follow each example to see what the result is for each.

Expression	Result
sum = 14;	
! (sum > 12)	
14 > 12	
⇓	
true	
not true	false

Because 14 *is* greater than 12, the original statement (sum > 12) is true. However, the use of the *not* operator on the result, true, has the effect of changing the overall expression to the value, false. To be not true is to be false.

```
answer = -60;
! (answer >= 78)
    -60 >= 78
       ⇓
     false
  not false        true
```

In this example, the original statement, "negative 60 is greater than or equal to 78," is false. By using the *not* operator, however, the value of the entire expression becomes true. To be not false is to be true.

```
first_ans = 0;
! (first_ans == 0)
     0 == 0
        ⇓
      true
   not true        false
```

In this example, the relational expression inside the parentheses is done first. Since 0 is equal to 0, the relational expression is true. After that, the *not* operator changes the value true to false.

The *not* operator is always used with parentheses, as you have seen in the previous examples. Why is this so? It is important to group together what is being altered. By using parentheses around the expression, the computer is being instructed to find the value of the expression in parentheses (PEMDAS) first, before altering the value by applying the *not* operator. In the following examples, we will use two relational expressions with a logic operator outside the parentheses. See how these work.

Expression	Result
$y = 36;$	
$! (14.5 < y \mid\mid y > 39)$	
$14.5 < 36 \mid\mid 36 > 39$	
(true *or* false)	
⇓	
true	
not true	false

Since parentheses are to be done first, we evaluate the relational expressions within. The first relational expression (14.5 < 36) is true and the second (36 > 39) is false. Because the operator *or* is used between them, true *or* false gives us the value true. (Notice that we wait to use the *not* operator because we are still inside of the parentheses.) In the last step, the *not* operator changes the value from true to false.

$val = 35;$	
$! (val > 23 \&\& val < 30)$	
$35 > 23 \&\& 35 < 30$	
(true *and* false)	
⇓	
false	
not false	true

Again, we evaluate what is inside the parentheses first. The first relational expression (35 > 23) is true and the second relational expression (35 < 30) is false. However, since the operator *and* is used between them, true *and* false yields false. The last step with the *not* operator produces true because not false is true.

A Powerful Operator for Any Computer Language: Mod

In addition to each of the arithmetic operators already mentioned, most languages provide an additional operator in division. It is called the *mod* operator, short for *modulus* in Latin, or *remainder*. In order to understand what it does, let us revisit

division between two integers. The *mod* operator, when used between two operands, produces the remainder of a long division problem between the two integer
operands. The *mod* operator is usually represented by the percent (%) symbol or
the word *mod.* In the next section, I will show you how it is used in programming.

28	*mod*	14	is	0	because there is no remainder.
172	*mod*	35	is	32	because 172 ÷ 35 = 4 with a remainder of 32.
1943	*mod*	7	is	4	because 1943 ÷ 7 = 277 with a remainder of 4.
18	*mod*	17	is	1	because 18 ÷ 17 = 1 with a remainder of 1.

In each case, the number to be divided is of greater value than the one it is being
divided by (the *divisor*)—for example, 1943 is being divided by 7. In all of these
cases, there *has* to be a remainder (even when it is 0). See Figure 3.2.

Now consider some interesting examples where the divisor, the number by which
you divide, is greater than the *dividend,* the number under the long division
symbol. Also notice what happens when you use negatives with the mod operator.

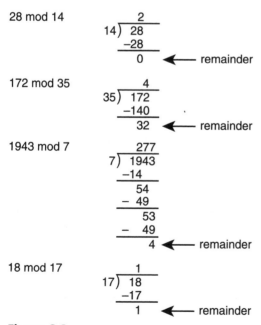

Figure 3.2
Each equation is a long division problem where the remainder is what you get after you complete the
last subtraction in long division.

38 *mod* 47 is 38

Remember that the *mod* operator produces the remainder, so $38 \div 47 = 0$ with a remainder of 38.

−14 *mod* 5 is −4
When we divide −14 by 5 we get −2 with a remainder of −4.

−32 *mod* −6 is −2
We see that −32 divided by −6 is 5 with a remainder that is negative (−2).

Caution

It is very easy to make mistakes with the *mod* using negatives. The answers you get always come from the arithmetic of a long division problem—not the rules from algebra regarding negatives and positives.

If you ever have an example using the *mod* operator, and you do not understand why the answer is negative, revisit a long division problem to see how the negative answer is generated. See Figure 3.3.

Caution

The *mod* operator is used *only between two integers.* It is not designed for use with real numbers (numbers with decimals, and so forth). An error results from trying to use the *mod* operator with anything other than integers.

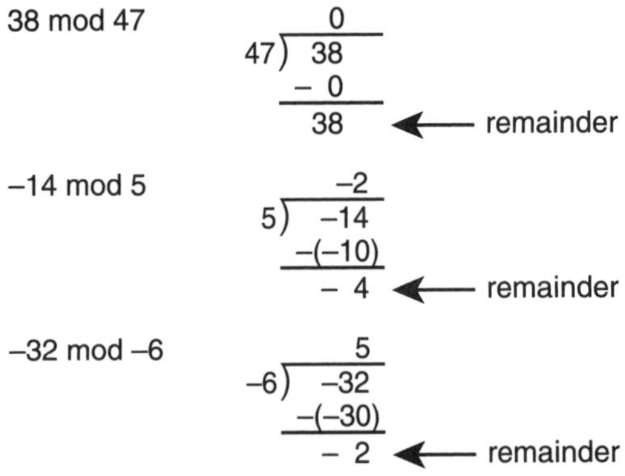

Figure 3.3
In each example, the long division shows the remainder that is produced. When using the *mod* operator and a negative integer, note whether the remainder is positive or negative.

How Is the Mod Operator Used in Programming?

This operator can be used in very interesting ways. By being able to tell whether there is a remainder from doing a division problem between two numbers, you can tell whether one number fits *exactly* into another number. Why would this be useful? Look at these questions, which the *mod* operator can answer if used appropriately.

1. Do we have a divisor of another number?

   Is 35 a divisor of 70? Yes, since 70 % 35 is 0. If the result of using the *mod* operator between two integers is zero, then the right-hand operand (35) is a divisor of the left-hand operand (70). So 35 is a divisor of 70 because it fits perfectly into it with no remainder (i.e., zero remainder).

2. Do we have an even number?

   An *even* number is a number divisible by 2. Let's say that you have an unknown number contained in the variable *x*. If *x* % 2 is 0, then *x* is an even number. Some examples: 46 % 2 is 0, 8 % 2 is 0.

3. Do we have an odd number?

   Similarly, if an unknown number contained in *y* is used in a *mod* statement, you can determine whether *y* is an odd number. If *y* % 2 is 1, then you have an odd number. Some examples: 13 % 2 is 1, 25 % 2 is 1.

Summary

We defined *operators* as the actions taken on numbers or variables. The *precedence* of an operator or its *priority* in terms of when it should be executed was introduced. The terms *binary* and *unary* operators were defined in terms of the number of operands required for an operator to function properly.

Next, different kinds of operators were defined: *arithmetic, relational,* and *logic* operators. The arithmetic operators are the most familiar because they involve the operations of addition, subtraction, multiplication, and division. There is a special case in division—division between two integers—where any fractional part in the answer will be dropped. The relational operators ($<$, $<=$, $>$, $>=$, $==$, $!=$) produce true or false answers as do the logic operators ($\&\&$, $||$, $!$).

Finally, the *mod* operator (%) was defined and some instances of its use in programming were given. In the next chapter, you will begin to look at some short programs using what you have learned from Chapters 2 and 3.

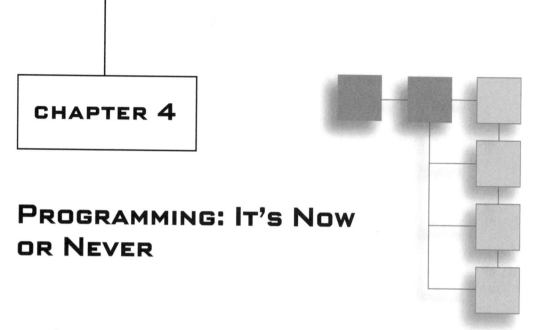

CHAPTER 4

PROGRAMMING: IT'S NOW OR NEVER

Now that you have been introduced to variables and how to assign data to them, you can begin to program. Through output and input statements, your program will allow a user to interact with a program. You'll learn the basic elements of any C++ program: namely the `main` section, the `return` statement, and the input and output statements, `cout` and `cin`. Statements like `cout` and `cin` allow you to display and retrieve data within a program.

In This Chapter

- Review of declaration and assignment

- Writing an output statement

- Understanding the `cout` stream

- The `endl` command

- How to insert comments into a program

- Introduction of compiler directives

- The `main` section of a program

- The `return` statement

- Three short programs

Putting a Program Together

We are almost ready to write some short programs. In the past two chapters, we have looked at some of the initial aspects of programming—namely, declaring and assigning variables, and manipulating those variables through operators. Throughout this chapter and the following ones, we will use the C++ programming language commands.

Declare, Assign, and Manipulate

If you recall, when *declaring* a variable, we tell the computer that a variable is of a certain *type* so that the computer can set aside the appropriate amount of memory. In C++, the word for integer is shortened to int. Let's declare two integer variables as follows:

```
int first_val, second_val;
```

Now we have told the computer that two variables called first_val and second_val will be used in our program. We have just declared the variables (that is, introduced them) to the computer. The next step is to *assign* the variables. We will let the programmer assign the first_val variable. (Let's leave the second variable, second_val, alone for a moment.) The following statement will accomplish first_val's assignment.

```
first_val = 25;
```

The third part of this process involves using one of our operators from Chapter 3. We will use an arithmetic operator, the multiplication sign (*). Here we will also use the second variable to hold twice the contents of first_val's value.

```
second_val = 2 * first_val;
```

This means that second_val has the value of 50 because 2 * first_val (25) is 50.

Time for an Output Statement

In our next stage of writing a program, we should show the contents of second_val on the screen so that our user will know we doubled the value of first_val and produced second_val as a result. We want the user to be able to see his *output*, the data that the computer has generated through the manipulations we performed. An *output statement* is a programming *language statement* that generates output—data contained within variables or messages to the user to be directed to the screen.

An output statement in C++ will have three key parts: a stream name, an insertion operator, and a variable or message. The *stream name* is the name of a channel where data is sent before it goes onto the screen. An *insertion operator* is an operator that inserts data into that stream. After the insertion operator, either a variable or a message can be placed. The variable's *value* will be inserted into the stream and then shown on the screen.

Because C++ is a high-level language, you do not have to worry about how the stream sends its data to the screen. That does not concern us. We just need to ensure that we are sending all data and messages properly to the stream.

Cout

cout (pronounced "see-out") is the name of the stream where data gets sent before it is channeled to the screen. (This stream is the opposite of the cin stream introduced in Chapter 3.) When you use a cout statement, you are really sending data to the screen through the cout channel. Anything that is sent to this stream will eventually end up on the screen where it can be viewed.

The syntax for using the cout stream goes as follows. You name the stream cout, then you follow with the insertion operator symbol (<<) that indicates something is going out into the stream. Next, you put the variable name or message that you wish sent to the screen (via the stream). Messages must be in quotation marks. Let's look at some examples.

Examples
```
cout << first_val;
cout << "hello.";
```

In the first example, we are sending a variable to the stream, which "feeds into" the screen—that really means that the contents of the variable will appear on the screen. In the second example, a message is sent to the stream and will be displayed on the screen next to the number in first_val. It will look like this:

```
25  hello.
```

When you wish to put more than one item into the stream, you need to use the insertion operator *before* each item. Let's look at some other examples where we use the cout stream. In both examples that follow, more than one item is sent to the stream so the insertion operator is placed in front of each variable or message.

```
cout << "Here is the first value:" << first_val;
```

Produces

```
Here is the first value: 25
```

and

```
cout << first_value << second_val;
```

Produces

```
25    50
```

In our third set of examples, let's say you wish to use a period (.) to finish a sentence that included a variable. You would need to use the insertion operator *between* the variable and the period because the period is a string following a variable.

```
cout << "The content's of second_val is"<< second_val << ".";
```

Caution

Any output should follow the cout command and the insertion operator (<<); if there is more than one item of output (i.e. multiple variables or messages), put the insertion operator *before* each item.

Now let's say that you were using the string type mentioned in Chapter 2. Recall that a string can hold *several* characters or words. The string type could hold a message if you assign the message to the string. Let's declare and assign a message to a string type.

```
string    my_message;
my_message = " Have a nice day." ;
```

Now we can send the message to the stream without using any quotation marks because we will use the variable, my_message, to hold the sentence.

```
cout << my_message;
```

Tip

Remember that variables do not need quotation marks; it is assumed that when a variable is sent to the cout stream, its value will be sent to the stream, and ultimately, to the screen.

How to Execute a Line Feed: endl

The endl (pronounced "end line") command (in C++) causes a line feed on the screen. In order to have data and messages appear on separate lines, you need to direct a line feed to the screen. The way to do this in C++ is to put the endl command *into* the cout stream. When the data "flows" from the stream onto the screen, the endl command will cause a line feed so that anything that follows this command will be on a new line. It is very important to notice that if endl is used at the end of a cout statement, the *next* cout statement will show data on the next line.

Let's look at some examples with and without the endl command.

```
cout << first_val;
cout << "Goodbye.";
```

Screen output:

```
25    Goodbye.
```

```
cout << first_val << endl;
cout << "Goodbye.";
```

Screen output:

```
25
Goodbye.
```

```
cout << "Hello" << endl << endl << "Goodbye.";
```

Screen output:

```
Hello

Goodbye
```

Notice that there were two line feeds—so that Goodbye is on the line *after* the next line.

Comments

Another useful tool in programming languages is the ability to *comment* in a program, or put descriptive remarks next to a programming statement or statements. The reason for putting comments into a program is to make the code clearer for any reader of the program. As programs become more complex, it's useful to clarify what a section of a program does so that you or another programmer can go back to the program to make changes.

Look at this example in everyday life.

Sentence	Comment
Jack will be late today.	Jack is the man who used to work with Marie.

Programming Statement	Comment
`first_val = 25;`	`//first_val is the original number` `of people who wanted tickets.`

Notice the symbol (//) used to the left of the comment. When you write a comment for a program, you do not want the compiler to think that your comment is part of the code that is being executed. Before every comment you write, the symbol (//) tells the compiler to ignore what follows on that line. Recall that the compiler is the translator of your code. It tries to make sense of every command you give it, so the symbol (//) is a way of telling the compiler not to translate what follows.

If your comment is longer than one line, you need to use two different symbols— one to indicate the beginning of the block to be ignored (/*) and then another to indicate the end of the block (*/). These symbols function like parentheses. After the second symbol is read, the compiler "knows" it can start executing code again.

```
/* Everything to the right of these symbols is ignored.
Write whatever you want in here
since this code will be ignored.
The end of the block is to the right. -> */
```

Compiler Directives

Now that we have seen four parts of early program writing—declaring variables, assigning them, manipulating their values, and displaying output—what else does a program need?

Compiler directives sounds like a complicated term, but it is not. The first thing is to recall what the compiler does. The *compiler* translates high-level language code into low-level code, and ultimately machine language code, that the computer understands.

A *directive* is just a fancy word for *direction*. So compiler directives are special directions for the compiler. Although there might be several compiler directives, we are only interested in a specific directive, the *include* directive.

The Include Directive

The *include* directive is a special instruction (in C++) for the compiler to get a specific file that we ask for and insert it at the top of our program. That way, our program can benefit from any of the capabilities that the included file offers. When the compiler starts to translate our program into low-level code, it first gets the file that was mentioned at the top of the program and starts to translate that code. Whatever that file can do, our program can now benefit from it.

There are several files that we might like to use in any program that we write in C++. These files have names that all end in the extension .h, which stands for the classification of a *header* file. An *extension* is an appendage used to indicate what type of file you have. (You may have seen other extensions that are attached to file names, like .jpg and .gif, which refer to files that made up of pictures.) A *header* file is a file that can be placed at the top of a program and accomplishes certain tasks that the file including it needs. (Later, in Chapter 16, I will discuss header files in more depth.) Here are some examples of header files we might like to use at some point in our programming:

Header File Name	Description
iostream.h	Manages the streams used for input and output of data
string.h	Manages the string type variable
math.h	Allows many math functions to be performed on data—similar to those on a calculator, such as sin(x), abs(x), and so on.

If you recall, *input* is necessary when someone other than the programmer wishes to load data into variables. That is, the user wishes to send values into variables. *Output,* or sending data to the screen, is a basic aspect of most programs. There are very few programs that would not send some results to the screen to be viewed. For these reasons, practically all programs need access to the streams that channel data to and from the keyboard and screen. The iostream.h (pronounced "eye-oh-stream dot h") file allows us to use both the cout stream for displaying output on the screen and the cin stream (from Chapter 2), which allows the user to assign variables through keyboard input. These two streams are part of this file.

At the top of our program (written in C++), we must give the compiler directive to get iostream.h. The directive looks like this:

```
# include < iostream.h>
```

The number symbol (#) indicates that this is a directive to the compiler. `iostream.h` is the name of the file that manages input and output. In the appendix on C++ (Appendix B), you will learn more about these header files.

Tip

> We will put `# include < iostream.h>` at the top of *every* program we write in C++ because we always expect to have input and output in our programs.

The Main Section of a Program

Programs are broken into sections. At the top of a program are any files that might help our program accomplish its task. After that, a program can be broken into sections where each section accomplishes a specific task. The reason for the subsections is really one of *organization*. By blocking code into separate sections, you are organizing the code so that any reader can understand it or fix it, if necessary. (This is especially important if there are *errors* in the language code.)

The Main Section

The `main` section contains the body of a program. With the first programs we write, it is not necessary for us to move away from the `main` to other subsections. All the code that we write to execute some task will be contained in this `main` section. Later we will learn how to compartmentalize a large program—that is, break it into sections that each do some task rather than having all the code in the `main`.

The `main` section has a *heading* (like a title) and is followed by two *braces*: an opening brace { and a closing brace } to indicate where the `main` section both begins and ends. Inside the braces go the programming statements that you write.

```
int main ( ) // the heading of the main section
{            // the opening brace

//***Your programming statements go between these braces.***

return 0;    //the return statement
}            //the closing brace
```

In the heading, you see the word for an integer, `int`, followed by the word `main` and then some empty parentheses followed by the braces that begin and end the `main` section. In Chapter 8, I will explain the syntax of this heading. Just use it for now.

The Return Statement

The `return` statement is the last statement of the `main` section, and you might consider the return statement in the following way. Imagine that the compiler has been given a key to the main room—the control room of the program. This room is usually locked because it is the control center, and we don't want just anyone going in there. When the compiler is done with the `main` section, it "returns" the key to the room—for security reasons. This "key" is an integer according to the first word in the heading of the `main`. The compiler is being directed to return an integer before it leaves the `main` section.

Since many programs don't necessarily produce an integer, we come up with the idea of returning the integer 0 as a matter of simplicity. By using the `return 0` ("return zero") command at the bottom of the main section, the programmer is satisfying the compiler's requirements to generate an integer before leaving the `main` section and closing the program for good. Once it does that, the program is over and the compiler's work is finished. In Chapter 8 we will learn more about how this statement works, but for now, this explanation should suffice.

```
int main ( )
{

//Your programming statements go between these braces.

return 0;
}
```

The heading gives some information about how the `main` must function. An integer must be produced before we can "close" the `main`. The last command, `return 0`, allows the compiler to *leave* the `main` section carrying the integer 0 and "know" that it has finished its work there.

Building a Program Outline

We are now ready to build an *outline* of a program. The first part of the program should include any directives to the compiler. The next part will be the `main` section blocked off by the opening and closing braces: { }. So now our outline looks like this:

```
#include <iostream.h>     // the compiler directive

int main ( )       // the heading
{

// Your programming statements go between these braces.

return 0;    //returning an integer so that we can satisfy
//the heading's requirement of an integer being produced.
}
```

Now let's look at some of the code (programming statements) talked about previously. I mentioned that it was necessary to include the declaration of a variable. The program outline can be completed in this way:

```
#include <iostream.h>
int main ( )
{
   int first_val, second_val; // the declaration section


return 0;
}
```

Next we can insert the code that causes assignment of values to variables.

```
#include <iostream.h>
int main ( )
{
   int first_val, second_val;

first_val = 25;      // the variable is assigned
second_val = 2 * first_val; // second_val assigned with
                            // twice first_val's value

return 0;
}
```

In the next example, we include the output statement.

```
#include <iostream.h>
int main ( )
```

```
{
   int first_val, second_val; // the declaration section

first_val = 25;      // the variable is assigned
second_val = 2 * first_val; // second_val assigned with
                             // twice first_val's value.
cout << second_val << endl; // second_val's value is printed.
return 0; //Execution of the main section will now end.
}
```

Some Short Programs

Now that we have examined the outline of a program, we are ready to see some sample programs. In each program we write, look at the basic structure of the program and keep in mind that it will probably contain three to four elements:

1. Declaration of variables

2. Assignment of variables

3. Manipulation of those variables

4. Variables' values printed on the screen.

Example 1

A program that computes the average of three numbers.

Description

We will declare three variables to hold three distinct real numbers (assigned by the programmer), and then we will compute the average of those numbers and display it on the screen. In addition to declaring three doubles to hold three real (non-integer) numbers, we need to declare a variable to hold the average; we'll call that variable average.

Notice the use of the two arithmetic operators + and / to compute the average. Since we are using doubles (non-integers) with the division symbol, it will perform division just as a calculator would by displaying the remainder in decimal form.

After examining the code in the following program, look at the output produced if the program is run on a computer. Recall that output is anything displayed on the screen—the data values that the variables contain after those variables have been manipulated.

The Program

```
#include <iostream.h>
int main ( )
{
double first_val, second_val, third_val, average;
                            //declaration section

first_val = 25;        //programmer has assigned all
second_val = 38.9;     // three variables.
third_val = 42.7
average = ( first_val + second_val + third_val) /3;
cout << "The average of the three numbers is "<< average
<< "." << endl;
// Note how this line wrapped to the next line.
return 0;
}
```

The Output

```
The average of the three numbers is 35.53.
```

Example 2

A program that computes the average of three numbers from the user.

Description

Let's take that same program and let *the user* assign the variables. Remember that we should ask the user first for the values so that he will understand what to do.

The Program

```
#include <iostream.h>
int main ( )
{
double first_val, second_val, third_val, average;
                            //declaration section
cout << "Please type three numbers." << endl;

cin >> first_val >> second_val >> third_val;//the user is
```

```
//assigning variables by typing numbers at the keyboard.

average = ( first_val + second_val + third_val) /3;
cout << "The average of the three numbers is " << average

<<"."<< endl;
// Note how this line wrapped to the next line.
return 0;
}
```

The Output

```
Please type three numbers.
25 38.9 42.7
The average of the three numbers is 35.53.
```

Of course, the value shown will depend on what the user types.

Example 3

A program that prints the user's name on the screen.

Description

In this third example, we will ask the user for his name and store that value in a string. Then we will display the string's value on the screen.

The Program

```
#include <iostream.h>
#include <string.h> // Here is the second directive to the compiler.

int main ( )
{ using namespace::std;
string name;    // declaration section
cout << "What is your name?" << endl;
cin >> name;//User assigns value by typing it at the keyboard.
cout << "Your name is "<< name << ".";
return 0;
}
```

The Output

```
What is your name?
Jack
Your name is Jack.
```

Example 4

A program that updates a checking account balance by recording an amount as a debit—something to be deducted from an account balance.

Description

In the fourth example, let's ask the user for the amount he wishes to subtract from his checking account balance. Then we will subtract that amount and display the new balance.

The Program

```
#include <iostream.h>
int main ( )
{ double balance, amount; //declaration section
cout << "What is your balance?" << endl;
cin >> balance;
cout << "What is the amount of your check?" << endl;
cin >> amount;
balance = balance - amount;
cout << "Your balance is now " << balance << "." << endl;
return 0;
}
```

The Output

```
What is your balance?
345.67
What is the amount of your check?
26.75
Your balance is now 318.92.
```

Although these programs are limited in what they do, they give you an idea of how a program is structured. You need to remember that all variables should be declared *prior* to use, then assigned by the programmer or by the user. After that, you can manipulate the variables and display output.

In Chapter 6, you will learn to make decisions on the computer—this will allow you to write a lot more interesting programs. Some examples of programs that involve decisions would be choosing the largest of a group of numbers or giving the user a choice in responding to a menu of choices. None of these possibilities could be accomplished without some sort of decision-making ability in a programming language.

On the CD

The four programs in this chapter are written in Java so you can see the difference between Java and C++.

Summary

In this chapter, we looked at the essential elements of a program: declaration, assignment, and manipulation. To be really effective, most programs will display their results on the screen: what is displayed on the screen is known as *output*. The use of the `cout` stream and the insertion operator (`<<`) allows us to produce output. The `endl` command allows us to execute line feeds on the screen.

Another good feature of clear programming is the careful use of comments. Comments can be used to explain the purpose of programming statements to any reader of a program. When you comment a program, you need to use some symbol so that the compiler "knows" it is not executing a command. In C++, this symbol is the one-line comment symbol (`//`) or, for multiple-line comments, the symbols `/*` and `*/` to begin and end the section.

Before writing a program in C++, we need to learn a few useful parts that comprise all C++ programs. The first is to include a directive to the compiler regarding input and output. In order to be able to display messages on the screen or get data from the user, you need to include the `iostream.h` header file. This file allows you to display messages and take in data.

Another part of all C++ programs is the `main` section. The `main` is the body of the program. The *heading* of the `main` requires that an integer be generated before the `main` section is completed. Opening and closing braces, `{ }`, show us where the `main` begins and ends. Once the `main` has been completely executed, the statement `return 0` causes the compiler to exit the `main` properly—thereby ending the program.

In the last part of the chapter, there are some examples tying all these elements together into four programs. In the next chapter, we will learn how to design a program so that it is well organized and easy to follow what tasks are being done.

CHAPTER 5

DESIGN: IT'S BEST TO START HERE

Design sounds like a trivial consideration when there are so many more pressing concerns, such as writing a loop, controlling decision flow, and so on; but none of these concerns are as important as deciding how you attack a program. You need to think about the design of your solution and how to go about getting it ready for programming.

Writing a program can be like having a huge problem to solve and trying to figure out the best way to solve it. Let's start by considering some problems in the real world and figuring out how we might solve them from a design point of view. Then we'll consider designs for problems for a computer.

In This Chapter

- Top-down design
- Stepwise refinement

What Is Top-Down Design?

Imagine a satellite view of the Earth. Google Earth will come to mind! Let's say you want to find your house. Initially you only see the outline of your state, and then as you zoom in, everything becomes clearer. You can make out the rivers, lakes, and maybe even the contours. Zooming in closer allows you to see more detail.

Google Earth provides a great analogy of how top-down design works. The outline of the land mass is the most generic picture. As you zoom in, you recognize more and more things. Top-down design works the same way. At first we have one big problem, but we try to break it into separate manageable tasks— just as an amorphous land mass, upon closer inspection, becomes separate countries and states.

Programming tasks can often be too general at first, but after you consider them, you decide how to subdivide them to make them more manageable. Always start by making an outline of your problem. Try to break your problem into separate tasks. Then work on refining those tasks so that you can write simple code to execute them.

Real-World Problems and Design

If you recall, we talked about algorithms in Chapter 1, and they are an important consideration in designing a solution to any problem. An *algorithm* is a finite set of instructions to solve a problem. As mentioned before, those steps can repeat as well as be skipped, according to what happens in a given step.

As your programming tasks become more complicated, it's imperative that you have an organizational plan in place before you write your first line of code. This plan is what we call the *design* of the solution.

In computer programming terms, there is one kind of design that is very important: *top-down design*. With top-down design you consider the outline— the rough sketch of what you want your program to do without worrying about the details. The opposite of that is called *bottom-up design* and involves focusing on the smaller tasks first before looking at the big picture.

Top-down design gives the programmer the organizational structure to attack a big program. With top-down design, you subdivide a big problem into little tasks. Each of these tasks can then be worked on and tested for effectiveness.

There are several reasons for designing a program before starting to write code. The design will allow you to consider realistically what you need to write to make the program work. A little planning on your part now can prevent you from running into serious problems later.

Imagine if you were to undertake some huge project, like building a house, without considering all the different aspects first. You might run out of money in the middle of construction!

So first let's consider some simple examples.

Example 1

Let's say I want to go on a hike during summer break. I am in the White Mountains of New Hampshire. I need to consider a few things before I go. If I have never hiked before, I might think that there isn't much to do other than follow a trail. However, many times ignorant hikers run into problems if the weather turns bad, they didn't pack enough water or food, or they get lost. These are the general tasks I would consider first.

1. Pick a trail.

2. Pack a knapsack.

3. Wear the right clothing.

4. Find someone to hike with.

5. Tell someone else where we are going.

6. Go.

Each of these tasks could be elaborated on, since I am not really sure of the details for any of these steps. Now look at a more elaborate list of tasks.

1. Pick a trail. Decide whether you want to do an overnight trip or a day trip. Decide the length of the trail you want to take. This decision will affect how much clothing and food you bring.

2. Pack a knapsack. Get food ready. Get water ready. Get all necessary maps and a compass. Include first aid items. Include miscellaneous items.

3. Wear the right clothing. Find both short-sleeve and long-sleeve shirts. Include warmer fleece. Decide whether you will wear pants or shorts. Include rain gear.

4. Find someone to hike with. Call various friends who like to walk in the woods all day. If friends are not available, call a relative.

5. Tell someone else where we are going. Call and leave a voicemail. E-mail name of the trail we are taking.

6. Go. Purchase a parking permit. Drive car to base of trail. Lock car and keep keys.

This is just a simple example to show the difference between a list of tasks that show little detail and another list, which is more explicit. It can seem trivial, but if you don't outline each of the big tasks first, you may run into problems later. I have, for example, driven to the base of a trail and then realized I had to drive another 10 miles to get a parking permit first. If you are planning on hiking a long trail during daylight hours, the extra time spent getting the permit can affect your plans. You may not be able to get in and out from your destination before dark.

Outlining the major tasks before the minor tasks serves two purposes. The first is one of organization. Considering the big problems as separate tasks allows you to focus on them and develop them more thoroughly. The second purpose is that you can delegate work to someone else if you have already outlined what needs to be accomplished.

In the hiking example, you can delegate the decision of where to go. That person then completes all the subtasks of choosing a trail, acquiring maps, getting tent gear, and so on.

Let's look at another example and list the tasks involved.

Example 2

Let's say I have been collecting VHS videos for years and recently switched to collecting DVDs. I've purchased several movies on DVD that I already had on VHS, and I now have two copies—one in each format. I decide to take inventory and get rid of the old duplicate VHS movies. How should I approach this problem?

The top-down design approach is where you delineate the big tasks and then break those tasks into smaller tasks. The video collection problem involves these tasks:

1. Make a list of all movies.

2. Next to each movie classify it as DVD, VHS, or Both.

3. Separate the movies with the tag Both from those without that tag.

4. Throw out the videos of the Both collection.

5. Alphabetize the entire collection.

If I want to refine the tasks in this problem, I would take a task and add more steps. Look at what I would do here:

1. Make a list of all movies. Get the title of each movie and then alphabetize those movies.

2. Next to each movie write DVD, VHS, or Both.

3. Separate the movies with the tag Both from those without that tag.

4. Throw out the videos of the Both collection. Put them into boxes and deliver to a Goodwill location. Change all words Both to DVD.

5. Alphabetize the entire collection.

Notice how steps 1 and 4 became more detailed in the second list. We refined those steps by giving them more detail. This process is known as *stepwise refinement*. Stepwise refinement is useful because it helps the programmer outline the code he must write. In step 1, I could write a separate function called getTitle and another called alphabetizeList. When I set out to write this code, I will have a clear idea of what I need to accomplish. If I don't refine the steps, I have less of an idea of what I need to do, since step 1 initially only says, "Make a list of all movies."

Stepwise refinement is important because it trains the programmer to move step by step, the way a computer works. Every time you refine a task by making it more specific, you are getting closer to being able to write these instructions in a programming language. As a beginning programmer, you need to learn how to organize solutions in a systematic way so that they can be processed. If your tasks are too vague, then chances are you will have a tough time writing them in a language.

Here is a third example where we write the big tasks first and then refine them in the second list.

Example 3

Suppose I have a list of customers and I want to get a list of those who have more than three DVDs overdue from my rental shop. Here are the tasks I need to think of first.

1. Separate customers who are renting a DVD from those who are not renting any.

2. Find out how many rentals each person has.

3. Look at each person who has more than three DVDs rented out and check the dates they were due.

4. Make a list of these people.

Let's look at each of these steps to see which ones can be refined with more explicit tasks.

1. Separate customers who are renting a DVD from those who are not renting any.

2. Find out how many rentals each person has. Count the number of rentals currently out with a person. Separate those with more than three from those with fewer than three.

3. Look at each person who has more than three DVDs rented out and check the dates they were due. Put a flag next to each person with more than three late DVDs.

4. Make a list of those who were flagged from the previous step.

What we have done in both examples is to try to give more detail for some of the steps involved. If I focus on small tasks first, I might lose sight of the big picture. This approach of looking at small tasks first is called a *bottom-up approach.*

Example 4

Here is another example of taking a large task and breaking it into smaller tasks using a top-down approach. Consider what you would do if you were buying a car. Most of us would not just go to the store and buy it without doing a few separate tasks. Each major task must be broken into subtasks that give more detail. See Table 5.1.

Buying a car is really a set of other smaller tasks, like finding out how much money you can spend and making choices about the car. You would need to choose a car's make, its type, and its color before deciding whether the car was the one you wanted to buy. You also have to get the money together for the car. Are you going to need a bank check written instead of a personal check? Most likely!

Table 5.1 Buying a Car

Task	Steps to Complete Task (Subtask)
How much money do I have?	Check first bank account. Check second bank account. Add all accounts
Choose a car.	Select make. Select type (sedan, coup, SUV, etc.) Select color.
Pay $$.	Get bank check ready. Bring check to dealer.

As you can see, the tasks on the left have been broken down on the right to make each task more clearly defined.

Computer Problems and Design

Now we will examine some practical examples that you can program. Each example involves a main task that requires some refinement. As you read each example, try to identify which task will be refined and how it will be refined.

Many of the problems that we solve on a computer involve some kind of numeric tasks. The numeric work you do will generally be in the most refined section of the program.

Example 1

In this example, we will consider a math problem involving prime numbers. We need to make a list of all the primes less than or equal to the number 500. This sounds like a big task, since there are 500 numbers to check, and we have to keep a list of all those that are prime.

Let's start by looking at the primes less than 10. There are four primes less than the number 10 (1 is not considered prime)—2, 3, 5, and 7. Now we have to find out which numbers in the number set 1, 2, ... , 499, 500 are prime. Let's look at this algorithm:

1. Start a number counter called myNum at 2, since 2 is the first number we will check.

2. Check to see whether myNum is prime.

3. If myNum is prime, write it down.

4. Increase myNum by 1 so that you can check the next number.

5. Go back to step 2 until you hit 501.

Most of these steps are clear, but we need to elaborate on how we would determine whether a number is prime. So step 2 needs to be refined. In this step we would have to articulate how a prime number is recognized. We would have to think about what we could write in programming terms that would allow the computer to recognize a prime number. In fact, it is not that difficult a task, but it is good that we have drawn attention to it by separating that work from the other steps in the algorithm.

Example 2

In this example, we will find the youngest person in a group of 50 people. At first, this problem can seem difficult to program. However, I have developed a list of steps that you can follow to complete this task. Again, as with the previous example, consider what step needs to be clarified.

1. Find the first person's birth date.

2. Find the next person's birth date. Retain the more recent birth date.

3. Go back to step 2 if there are more people.

4. Stop when there are no more people to check.

The step that needs the most refinement is step 2, where we have to retain the more recent birth date. That would involve some subtasks of comparing years of birth, and if those were the same, we would compare months and then days, if necessary.

1. Find the first person's birth date. Get the year, the month, and the day.

2. Find the next person's birth date. Get the year, the month, and the day. Retain the more recent birth date. Compare years, then months, if necessary, and days, if necessary.

3. Go back to step 2 if there are more people. Check the list of people.

4. Stop when there are no more people to check.

Both of these are examples of top-down design. As you continue to learn about programming and encounter more elaborate programs, you will find this perspective useful. The process of developing separate blocks of codes, to accomplish separate tasks called *modules* or *functions*, will be developed in Chapter 8.

Summary

Each time you break a big problem into other smaller problems, you are using a process of top-down design, which we also call stepwise refinement. Each set of tasks is refined by adding more steps to indicate how the big task is accomplished. By trying to break your tasks into other smaller tasks, you are starting to develop a modular approach to a program. This approach will be ideal for learning about functions in Chapter 8.

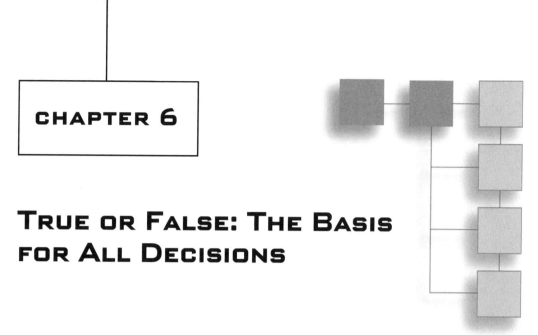

CHAPTER 6

TRUE OR FALSE: THE BASIS FOR ALL DECISIONS

In Chapter 3, we examined different kinds of operators, namely the arithmetic and relational operators, as well as the logic operators. The arithmetic operators produce a number. The relational and logic operators produce a true/false result. They require a different type variable for holding this result—it is called the *boolean* type. We will use the boolean type in the decisions that we learn to program on the computer. We will also examine the basic control statement, the `if` statement, which allows us to *program* decisions on a computer.

In This Chapter

- The boolean type

- Developing a model of a decision

- Program flow

- Control statements

- The `if` statement

- The `if...else` statement

- The `switch/case` statement

The Boolean Type

In addition to the types we have already studied—the integer, double, character, and string types—there is another type, the *boolean*, named after the mathematician George Boole, who did extensive work in the subject of logic. It is a variable type that holds the result true or false. These values are not the strings `true` or `false`. They are the *values* true or false. The only way to get these values is to use the relational operators (<, >, etc.) and/or the logic operators (*and, or, not*) from Chapter 3. When you compare two numbers with a relational operator, you get a value of true or false.

Example	Result
16 > 15	True
8.5 <= 8.2	False
–12 < 4	True

Now let's declare some boolean variables and use them in assignment statements with these examples. Because we want to declare *more than one* boolean variable at once, we will make *a* list of variables after the type boolean. Just separate the variables by commas before ending the declaration statement with the semicolon. Let's use the name `flag` for one of the boolean variables, since flag reminds us of the expression "to raise a flag" and catches our attention. You will later see why this is useful.

variable type variable, variable,	etc.;
boolean flag, x, answer;	//flag, x and answer are all //boolean type variables

Example	Result
flag = 16 > 15;	flag holds true
x = 8.5 <= 8.2;	x holds false
answer = –12 < 4;	answer holds true

Now let's consider some examples where the boolean type is used with some *variables* in relational expressions. In the previous examples, the values were used directly in the relational expressions.

```
int a, b, c ; //declaring three integers in a list
boolean answer, flag, result; //declaring three booleans

a = 14;
b = 0;
c = 7;
```

Example	Result
answer = a < c ;	answer holds false because 14 is *not* less than 7 14 < 7
flag = b > c;	flag holds false because 0 is *not* greater than 7 0 > 7
result = a > b;	result holds true because 14 *is* greater than 0 14 > 0

Tip

When you want to declare more than one variable of the same type, declare the type and then follow with the list of variable names separated by commas.

What Does a Decision Involve?

It is important that we clarify what happens when we make a decision in ordinary life as we broach the subject of decision making for a computer. We need to develop a model of decision-making that is consistent with the way a computer "makes" a decision. If we practice developing and applying this model in everyday decisions, then we will be better able to adapt our thinking to write the code that allows the computer to "make" a decision.

Developing a Model for Making a Decision

There are many situations in ordinary life where we make a decision, which is a choice from two or more options. Once the decision is made—an option is chosen—then we may have a resulting course of action associated with that choice. Let's review the structure of a decision in everyday life, and later we will apply this structure to programmed decisions.

When you make a decision you must choose one of at least two things. Once the choice has been made, you may be required to follow a specific course of action for that choice. We will call each resulting course of action an *outcome*.

Consider the decision of whether to buy tickets to a concert. The decision is a choice between two options: buying the tickets or *not* buying the tickets.

Decision	Option 1	Option 2
	Buying tickets	Not buying tickets

Now what do we mean by an outcome? An outcome is a resulting course of action associated with each option. What is the resulting course of action of choosing option 1?

The resulting action could be that you work overtime to make extra money, you get an evening off from work for the night of the concert, you then go to the ticket agency, and you spend the money on the tickets. The resulting action of choosing option 2 could be nothing. You don't have to do anything if you decide not to buy tickets to the concert.

Outcome 1	Outcome 2
Work overtime	Nothing
Get a night off	
Go to ticket agency	
Buy the tickets	

Consider another decision from everyday life that involves two options and two outcomes. Your parents are going away for the weekend. They ask you whether you would like to go away with them to the mountains. If you go to the mountains, you can go hiking or sailing on a nearby lake. If you stay home, you'll be all alone, but your mother wants you to paint the porch while they are away. So your decision is whether to hang with your parents for the weekend or work like a slave while they are away. Let's consider the decision, the options, and the outcomes associated with this situation.

Decision	Option 1	Option 2
	Go away with parents	Stay home alone

Outcome 1	Outcome 2
Ride in the car with parents	Wash porch
Eat dinner with parents	Sand porch
Go hiking	Paint porch
Go sailing	Have friends over if you can stay awake

Depending on which option you choose, an outcome will follow, if it exists for that option. The important thing to notice about decisions is what your options are as well as the outcomes for each option. Decisions always involve a choice between at least *two* options. Once you decide, you then branch off to follow the outcome associated with that decision. See Figures 6.1 and 6.2.

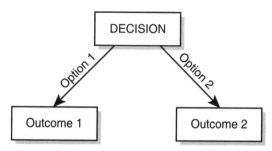

Figure 6.1
A decision involves a choice leading to two outcomes: outcome 1 and outcome 2. Outcome 1 leads to the left branch, and outcome 2 leads to the right branch.

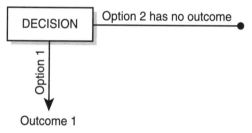

Figure 6.2
A decision involves a choice leading to only one outcome. The other choice has no resulting action.

Let's look at some other examples from everyday life. Put each decision in the context of our model using outcomes. Consider what the decision is in each situation—what your options are—and whether each option has an outcome.

Example 1
If you go to the early showing of a movie, you will be home in time to watch a program you like on TV. If you choose the later show, then you should set your TiVo to record the program. See Figure 6.3.

Example 2
Another decision is how you wish to spend your allowance. If you spend it on a shirt you like, you will not have money for a CD. So you must make a decision. See Figure 6.4.

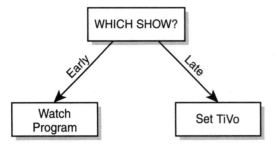

Figure 6.3
The choice of the earlier or later show involves two outcomes: watching the program when you return or programming your TiVo now.

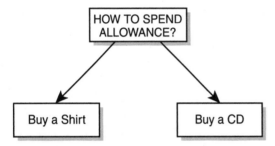

Figure 6.4
The decision about how to spend your allowance shows two options (choosing the shirt or the CD) and two outcomes (purchasing the shirt or purchasing the CD).

A decision, by its nature, always has a choice between at least two things—this or that, yes or no, true or false. A decision must involve at least two options; otherwise, it's not a decision. This is true in our ordinary experience, and computer programs simulate that process.

Remember, this is a machine—not a thinking being. It has a limited ability to decide. This is a machine that only understands two things—current "on" or "off," which can be associated with integer 1 or integer 0. And now we take this to a higher abstract level where the integers 1 and 0 are used to represent the boolean values true and false, respectively. Don't worry about how this is done— that's done by low-level programmers. The computer will make a decision based on whether it gets a boolean value of true or false. For us, as programmers, we need to develop boolean expressions that model our decisions. So we have to make certain adjustments in our intuitive processes to fit this model of a decision with its options and outcomes *clearly stated*.

As you might imagine, the computer has a limited capacity in how it makes decisions. When a computer makes a decision, it evaluates a boolean expression.

We use the boolean type because of its values: true or false. The computer will choose between true and false—and that's it! The computer *always* chooses true. Through the use of a special programming statement, the computer can be manipulated to execute an outcome.

Applying the Decision Model

Let's examine situations where decisions are made by a computer. In each example, we will look at the decision, the options, and the outcomes. As you read each situation, try to identify the decision and the outcomes. The decision will be framed so that a boolean expression can be used.

Entering a Password at an ATM

Initially, this may not seem to involve a decision, but for the computer, it involves a lot of decisions. When you enter a password at an ATM, the computer must match your entered password with the information obtained from the magnetic strip on your bank card. The password you type after inserting your card should match the password obtained from the strip. If there is no match, then a message will be printed to the effect of "Your password is incorrect: please enter it again." See Figure 6.5.

Decision: Does the password entered equal (==) the actual password?

Outcome 1: Grant access.

Outcome 2: Print message saying try again.

Counting the Number of People with Last Names Beginning with L

If we want to keep a tally or count of people whose last names begin with the letter L, we need to program the computer to look at the first letter of a name to

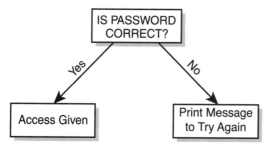

Figure 6.5
A password is evaluated for accuracy. If the password is correct, access is given. Otherwise a message is given to try again.

see if it is the letter L. Every time a name is entered at the computer, we either increase the count of the names or ignore the name because it does not satisfy our condition. So a decision has been made, and two outcomes are possible: to count or to ignore. See Figure 6.6.

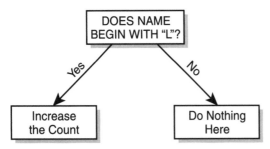

Figure 6.6
The name is entered, after which a decision is made by the computer to see whether the name begins with an L. If it does, the count of names beginning with the letter L is increased. If not, no action is taken.

Decision: Does the first letter of the name equal (==) the letter L?

Outcome 1: Increase the number that keeps track of the count of last names beginning with L.

Outcome 2: Nothing.

Heads or Tails

Another example of a decision is the one involved in "heads you win, tails you lose." If you flip a coin and the head appears, then you have won. The other option is that the tail appears and you have lost. See Figure 6.7.

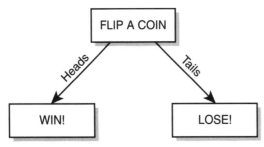

Figure 6.7
The outcomes after flipping a coin are shown: winning or losing.

Decision: Does the coin face equal (==) a head?

Outcome 1: You win.

Outcome 2: You lose.

Tip

Decisions always involve a choice between two or more options. Each choice may have an outcome associated with it.

Controlling Where the Compiler Goes

It is important to remember that the compiler moves through a program and executes statements in the order in which they are written. If you want to alter that order—and this is important for decision-making—you need to understand how to control the compiler.

Program Flow

Program flow is an important concept. It is based on the idea that the translator of any program we write in a high-level language will *sequentially* carry out the instructions we write unless programmed otherwise. What does this mean? This means your programming statements are executed in order—one after the other.

Look at this example from the programming language BASIC. Notice how the program has line numbers to the left of each statement. This numbering of lines emphasizes the *order* of translation of each statement. It helps the programmer to remember that what is on line 10 is executed before what is on line 40.

```
10    LET x = 7
20    LET m = 2 * x
30    PRINT "The answer is "; m
40    END
```

Everything is done sequentially unless we direct it otherwise. (The translator here is actually an interpreter, translating one line at a time.) So in the BASIC program, the interpreter goes from line 10 to line 20, and from line 20 it goes to line 30, and finally to line 40.

The *compiler*, another type of translator, is really similar to a large ball at the top of a hill. Once you give the ball a little push (or start to *run* a program), it will come down the hill and just roll over everything in its way. The compiler is similar in that it won't stop for anything unless it is *programmed* to do so because at a lower level it is programmed to go to the next statement. It automatically goes there unless the programmer controls the compiler through a *control statement*.

Control Statements

A *control statement* in a programming language is a statement that allows the compiler to alter its normal execution of line-by-line execution of code. Certain control statements allow the compiler to skip over one or more lines of code to get to another line or lines of code. Some control statements allow the compiler to repeat certain lines of code. The ability to skip a line or block of code is very important when you write a decision because you want to be able to execute *one* outcome from all the outcomes that follow the decision. You don't want to execute *all* the outcomes, but rather you would like the compiler to go to the outcome that it should execute and skip all the others.

Our first control statement will allow the compiler to evaluate a boolean expression and then either go to the next line or skip that line. In order to understand how a control statement works, we need to look at a specific control statement—the if statement.

The If Statement

The if statement is our first example of a control statement in a programming language. An if statement has two parts: a boolean condition followed by a conclusion.

The Boolean Condition

A *conditional* statement (you might have seen one in a geometry class) is a statement that begins with the word "if." A *boolean condition* is a conditional statement containing a boolean expression. Another name for a conditional statement is a *hypothesis*. In computer programming languages, a hypothesis is formed by using the word "if" with a boolean expression. The boolean expression can be evaluated as true or false. When the boolean expression within the hypothesis is true, then the conclusion occurs. The conclusion will not happen unless this hypothesis is *satisfied* (i.e., the boolean expression is true). So the if statement uses the boolean expression as a way of deciding whether the conclusion that follows is executed. If the boolean expression is true, the conclusion is executed.

The Conclusion

The *conclusion*, another name for the *outcome*, is a statement that follows the hypothesis. If the hypothesis is true, then the computer executes the conclusion. The conclusion represents one outcome you would like to have happen when the hypothesis is true. In the examples that follow, each bolded statement is a conclusion.

If it rains today, **we won't go outside**.

If I have enough money, **I will order tickets**.

If the password is correct, **I will get access to my account and withdraw money**.

Examples of If Statements in Everyday Circumstances

Hypothesis/Boolean Condition	Conclusion
If it rains tomorrow,	we won't go.
If you win the game,	you advance to the next round.
If they get home by 9,	we can leave by 10.

Let's rephrase each hypothesis with its boolean expression bolded. In order for any of these conclusions to occur, you need to ask whether the boolean expression of the hypothesis is true. In a sense, each statement can be rephrased like the following:

Boolean Condition	Conclusion
If **it's true that it will rain tomorrow**,	we won't go.
If **it's true that you won the game**,	you advance to the next round.
If **it's true that they'll get home by 9**,	we can leave by 10.

Examples of If Statements for a Computer

Here are some examples of if statements. Remember the boolean expression is contained within the part that begins with "if." The boldface part is the conclusion.

Examples

If amount of the check is less than the balance,
> boolean expression

subtract the amount of the check from the balance.
> conclusion

If password entered at the keyboard is the same as the true password,
> boolean expression

provide access to the account.
> conclusion

If your age is greater than 16,
> boolean expression

apply for your driver's license.
> conclusion

In each example, the hypothesis can be rewritten using a boolean expression. Boolean expressions, if you recall, come from using the *relational operators*: < (less than), > (greater than), <= (less than or equal to), >= (greater than or equal to), == (equal to), and != (not equal to). So let's take each of these conditions and rewrite them using relational operators to create a boolean expression. In each example, we will declare any variables we need so that we can write a boolean expression.

Examples Using the Relational Operators

I.

```
double check_amount, balance;
```

If amount of the check is less than the balance
> boolean expression
> **subtract the amount from the balance.**

```
if (check_amount < balance)
```
> boolean expression
> **subtract the amount from the balance.**

II.

```
string entered_password, real_password;
```

If data entered at the keyboard is the same as the actual password
> boolean expression

provide access to the account.

```
if (entered_password == real_password)
```
boolean expression

provide access to the account.

III.

```
char my_char;
```

If the first letter of the name is an L
boolean expression

increase the number of these names.

```
if (my_char == L)
```
boolean expression

increase the number of these names.

IV.

```
int age;
```

If your age is greater than 16
boolean expression

apply for your driver's license.

```
if (age > 16)
```
boolean expression

apply for your driver's license.

The compiler through the if statement makes a decision based on the value obtained from the boolean expression. A value of true allows the compiler to execute the *conclusion* of the if statement. A value of false allows the compiler *to skip the conclusion* to go directly to the next statement. The important fact to remember is that the line *immediately following* the if statement will be executed *no matter what*. The only alteration for the compiler is whether it *skips over the conclusion* after the hypothesis.

What the if statement allows you to do in terms of the decision model we discussed earlier is to put *one outcome* as the conclusion of the if statement. See Figure 6.8.

Note

The if statement needs a boolean expression to work properly.

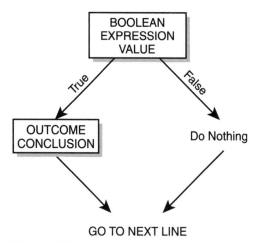

Figure 6.8
A model of the `if` statement with one outcome.

If there is more than one outcome from a decision, you need to use another control statement. There is no place for a second outcome to be executed when using the `if` statement. The only second outcome that works in the `if` statement is to do nothing.

A Block of Code

At this point, we need to introduce how to create a *block* of code—a group of programming statements that should be executed as a group. We use braces to block off a group of programming statements: { }. The first time we saw these braces was when we introduced the `main` section of a program in Chapter 4. Braces are a way of instructing the computer that we are *sectioning off* some lines of code.

With the control statement we just studied—the `if` statement—we needed to be able to write code for an outcome that has more than one instruction. Let's say you wanted to ask a person playing a video game whether she wishes to continue playing the game. If she says yes, you need to start the game again *and* reset the score.

`If answer == yes`

Outcome: `{start game again and set score to zero}`

In another example, you will access your bank account only if your password is correct. If it is correct, you'll be granted access *and* asked what you would like to do next—make a deposit, get cash, and so on.

`If password entered at keyboard == password obtained from magnetic strip`

Outcome: `{provide access, ask what user wishes to do, and get input from her}`

Note

Whenever more than one statement is used in the context of a control statement, use the braces to make a block of code.

The If...Else Statement: The Two-Outcome Decision

The `if...else` statement is another example of a *control statement*. Like the `if` statement, it uses a boolean expression followed by two conclusions (two outcomes). These two conclusions are executed according to the value of the boolean expression. Let's first look at some examples of the `if...else` statement in everyday life.

Examples

If Tom has to work tomorrow, I'll see him tonight; otherwise, I'll see him tomorrow.

If the repairs cost more than $2000, I'll buy a new car; otherwise, I'll get it repaired.

Each example, upon analysis, has a boolean condition and two outcomes. Let's identify the decision and outcomes for each example.

I.

Decision	Option 1	Option 2
	Tom works tomorrow	Tom doesn't work tomorrow
	⇓	⇓
	Outcome 1	**Outcome 2**
	see him tonight	see him tomorrow

II.

Decision	Option 1	Option 2
	repairs cost > $2000	repairs cost < = $2000
	⇓	⇓
	Outcome 1	**Outcome 2**
	buy a new car	repair the car

Now let's take each example and fit it into the `if...else` statement structure. Depending on the value of the boolean condition, one of the two outcomes will be executed.

`If` Tom has to work tomorrow, I'll see him tonight `else` I'll see him tomorrow.

       boolean expression   outcome 1   outcome 2

`If` the repairs cost more than $2000, I'll buy a new car `else` I'll get it repaired.

       boolean expression   outcome 1   outcome 2

Boolean Expression	Value	Which outcome is executed?
Tom works tomorrow	True	Outcome 1: I'll see him tonight.
Tom works tomorrow	False	Outcome 2: I'll see him tomorrow.
The repairs cost more than $2000	True	Outcome 1: I'll buy a new car.
The repairs cost more than $2000	False	Outcome 2: I'll get it repaired.

The value of the boolean expression *determines* whether outcome 1 or outcome 2 is executed. Whenever the boolean expression is true, outcome 1 (always placed first) is executed. When the expression is false, outcome 2, placed after the word `else`, is executed.

`If` the hypothesis/boolean expression is true

execute

Outcome 1

`else`

execute

Outcome 2

If the outcomes have multiple programming statements, then you need to use the braces around each *block* of instructions.

```
If (        expression        )
       boolean expression is true

       execute
       Outcome 1's {first statement,
                 second statement,
                 third statement, etc.}
```

```
else
      execute
      Outcome 2's {first statement,
                   second statement,
                   third statement, etc.}
```

Some Examples in Code

To save time, often we will examine only portions of a program—these are called *program fragments*. Rather than show the compiler directives and the main section for every example, we will just show a portion of the program that we need to study.

Here is a fragment from the programming language C++; an example of the if statement is written this way:

```
if (x > 12)
cout << "The variable is greater than 12." << endl;
```

Note that parentheses are used to surround the boolean expression in this language. Consider the following examples.

Examples

I.

```
If a number > 0 then inform the user the number is positive
else
inform the user that the number is not positive.
if (number > 0)
cout << "The number is positive." << endl;
else
cout << "The number is not positive." << endl;
```

II.

```
If your age > = 16 then inform the user she is old enough to drive
else
inform the user that she is not.
if (age >= 16)
      cout << "You are old enough to drive." << endl;
else
      cout << "You are not old enough to drive." << endl;
```

Using a Boolean Condition to Determine Whether a Number Is Even or Odd

In Examples 1 and 2 that follow, we will let the computer evaluate whether a number is even or odd. In order to do this, we need to use the *mod* operator (gives a remainder in division) from Chapter 3. Let's first review a few examples with the *mod* operator (%).

18 % 2 produces 0 since 18 divided by 2 is 9 with no (0) remainder.

15 % 2 produces 1 since 15 divided by 2 is 7 with a remainder of 1.

As you recall, the *mod* operator allows you to look at only the remainder from a division problem. 18 is an even number. *All even numbers will have no remainder when they are divided by 2.* So we write a boolean expression using the equality relational operator, ==. If a number is even, dividing the number by 2 gives us 0. If a number is odd, dividing the number by 2 gives us 1. Consider these examples using the variable x that has been assigned a value.

```
int x;
x = 24;

x % 2 == 0 // is 24 % 2 == 0?
  ⇓
24 % 2
  ⇓
      0 == 0
        ⇓
      true
```

(Therefore, x is an even number.)

```
int x;
x = 17;
x % 2 == 0 // is 17 % 2 == 0?
  ⇓
17 % 2
  ⇓
      1 == 0
        ⇓
      false
```

(Therefore, x is not even and so must be odd.)

Note

If number % 2 == 0 then the number is even.

If number % 2 == 1 then the number is odd.

So now we are ready to use the *mod* operator (%) in the context of an if statement. Both fragments accomplish the same thing—one uses a boolean variable (a holder for the boolean value) and the other does not.

Example 1

If a number is even, print a message saying it is even.

Program fragment with a boolean value:

```
int number;
cin >> number; // let the user give us the number
if ( number % 2 == 0)
    cout << "The number is even."<< endl;
```

Program fragment using a boolean type variable:

```
int number; boolean answer; //both variables are declared

cin >> number; // let the user give us the number
answer = number % 2== 0;// answer holds true or false
if ( answer)
    cout << "The number is even."<< endl;
```

Notice that the last statement uses a boolean variable in place of a boolean expression. This is possible because the value inside the variable, answer, will determine whether the conclusion is executed.

Example 2

If a number is even, print a message saying it is even; otherwise, print a message saying it is odd.

Program fragment with a boolean value:

```
int number;
cin >> number; // let the user give us the number.
if ( x % 2 == 0)
    cout << "The number is even."<< endl;
```

```
else
    cout << "The number is odd."<< endl;
```

Program fragment using a boolean type variable:

```
int number; boolean answer; //both variables are declared

cin >> number; // let the user give us the number
answer = number % 2 == 0;//answer holds true or false
if ( answer)
    cout << "The number is even."<< endl;
else
    cout << "The number is odd."<< endl;
```

The Switch/Case Statement

Decisions are generally made between two options. If you want to decide among more than two options, you can use a switch statement, as it is called in C++. Other languages use a different name. Once you understand what this statement does, you will be able to recognize it no matter what it is called in any programming language.

A switch statement works in this way. Think of this analogy. You are standing in a huge room that has three doors in it. Each door has a number on it. If you open door #1, outcome 1 is behind the door. If you open door #2, outcome 2 is behind the door. The same thing is true for door #3. Behind each door is a different set of instructions that makes up the outcome.

The switch statement evaluates an *integer* variable—that is, it looks at its value. Then it examines a list, looking for that value. When it finds the value in the list, it executes all the instructions that are associated with that value. This type of control statement always has *two* elements. One element is where an integer variable is examined to see what value is inside it. Then the value is found among a list of integer values, and the statements (the outcome) next to that value are executed. Here is a diagram using our door analogy:

switch	Door_Number
Door #1:	statement 1; statement 2; statement 3;
Door #2:	statement 1;
Door #3:	statement 1; statement 2;

The actual switch statement would need to "know" that the variable used to control it is an integer, so we first declare an integer. Also, it uses the word case of instead of Door # to list the integers. Let's do an example from a program that could be used at an ATM machine. The user will be asked whether she wishes to make a deposit, get cash, or check the balance of an account. If she inputs a 1, then she will expect to make a deposit. If she inputs a 2, she will be able to get cash, and if she inputs a 3, she will be able to examine the balance of one of her accounts. In the program fragment that follows, the numbered statements represent *undisclosed* programming statements.

```
int your_choice;

cout << "Please choose your option by typing the number 1, 2, or 3." << endl;
cin >> your_choice;


switch (your_choice)
{
case 1: statement 1; statement 2; statement 3;

case 2: statement 1;

case 3: statement 1; statement 2;
}
```

Not all outcomes for an integer have the same number of statements. One outcome might be just one statement. Another outcome might have three statements. The switch statement is a clean way of choosing among more than two things.

As you learn more about decisions, you will see that they can be more involved than the models we examined here. There are interesting ways to handle more complicated decisions. It just takes some practice to use the statements we have already mentioned in the correct way. The if statement with the if...else statement and some variations on those two statements—including using them together or one or both of them repeatedly—will allow any programmer to handle very complicated decisions of more than two choices and two outcomes.

Summary

The boolean type is another type of variable in addition to those we have already studied—the integer, character, string, and real. It is used to store the result of evaluating a boolean expression. It always holds the value true or the value false.

We examined how a decision can be modeled on options and outcomes. If you choose one option, it leads to one outcome. If you choose another option, it leads to another outcome.

Control statements are programming statements that allow the compiler to alter the usual order of execution of statements. In our case, we want to skip over one line of code to get to another. One example of a control statement, the `if` statement, has two parts—a hypothesis or boolean condition followed by a conclusion. It is used, ideally, for a decision that has only one outcome.

The `if...else` statement has three parts—a hypothesis containing a boolean expression followed by two outcomes—only one of which will be executed, depending on the value of the boolean condition. If the boolean expression is true, the first outcome is executed. If the boolean expression is false, the second outcome is executed.

The `if` statement can be used to determine whether a number is even or odd. This useful algorithm is done through the *mod* division operator (%). Finally, a `switch` statement is a statement that is best applied to decisions that involve more than two choices.

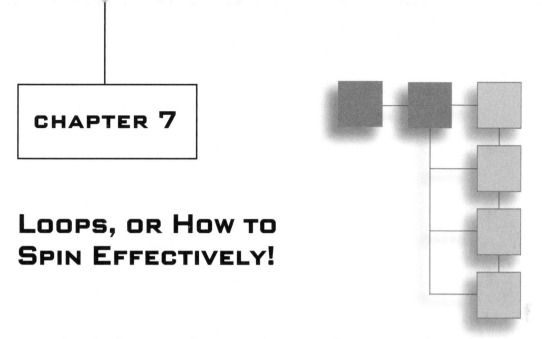

CHAPTER 7

LOOPS, OR HOW TO SPIN EFFECTIVELY!

Many times in the course of programming, you will want to use the computer to do some task over and over again. This involves constructing a *loop*. In this chapter, we examine how a loop encloses a group of lines and repeats them a certain number of times. There are different kinds of loops, and we will explore each type.

In This Chapter

- The loop
- The counter statement
- Fixed iterative vs. conditional loop
- The for loop
- The while loop
- The do...while loop
- Examples with loops

What Is a Loop?

Think of a cowboy using a rope to lasso a horse's neck, visualize a circus ring, or the balloon that encloses a cartoon character's thoughts. Each of these is a loop. A loop *always encloses* something. When you think of a loop, you might have some of these images. See Figure 7.1.

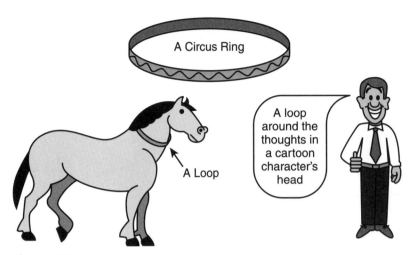

Figure 7.1
A loop around a horse's neck, a circus ring, and a loop around the thoughts in a cartoon character's head are all shown.

A *loop* brings to mind a circular image. What does the term *loop* have to do with computer programming? We use the term to describe a part of a program that you execute over and over again until you are permitted to leave that part to get to another programming statement. In a sense, you continuously loop back through statements that you just executed, and you execute them again.

Another image of the loop is one of going back to where you once were. Let's say you leave your house and go to your friend's house, but your friend is on her way to your house. You'll loop back to pick up your friend. In this sense, a loop means to go back to a place where you once were. To loop back to something means to go back to where you were and start again. See Figure 7.2.

Figure 7.2
A person drives a car back home ("loops back") to pick up a friend who is standing next to the house.

Loops in Programs

In a program, a loop describes a group of one or more lines of code that must be repeated some number of times. Consider this example. We are going to write a program to get 10 numbers from the user and check whether each number is even or odd. We need to get one number at a time from the user before checking to see whether it is even or odd. Then we go back to get another number to do the same thing. As we repeat each step, we go back to where we were in the program to repeat the same instructions. This is a loop. This loop encompasses two steps: getting the number followed by the second step—evaluating it as even or odd. See Figure 7.3.

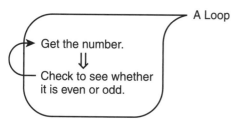

Figure 7.3
The first and second steps are shown. After the second step, we will go back to the first step—where we started—thus creating a loop.

Another way to envision a loop is to see it as a *circle* around a few lines of code. That way we have a clear understanding that everything within the loop (circle) will repeat as long as it should. I still have not mentioned anything about controlling a loop—for example, when does it end? How long does it last? These are natural questions that you should have when you first start learning about loops, and I will answer them shortly.

Another Control Statement

The loop is another example of a *control statement*. When you stay in one block of code (a group of programming statements) to do something over and over again, you are controlling program flow. Just as I mentioned in Chapter 6, normal program flow is *in sequence*—executing one line after another. A loop forces program flow to stay on a certain line or in a block until allowed to exit that place and proceed in sequence. I will shortly discuss how a loop is entered or exited.

Repeating Steps in a Loop

We make a decision to use a loop when we realize we want to do something over and over again on the computer. If you want to write the following sentence one thousand times—"I am sorry for chewing gum during class."—your best decision would be to write a program that will print that phrase repeatedly. If you want to add up 20 numbers, then you want to use a loop to get one number at a time and then add that number to the tally of all the numbers so far. See Figure 7.4.

There are many examples of situations that use loops. Every time you enter an incorrect password at an ATM, the machine asks you to enter it again. The machine is actually executing a loop, which, upon getting incorrect data, prints the message "Your password is incorrect. Please type it again." It will repeatedly print this message until you give it the correct password or it swallows your card. You can only get out of the loop by typing the correct data or if the machine puts a limit on your number of attempts. See Figure 7.5.

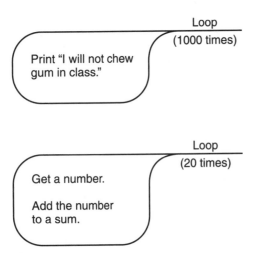

Figure 7.4
Each programming statement is shown enclosed by a loop.

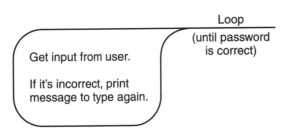

Figure 7.5
A loop is shown surrounding the body of instructions in the ATM situation.

A Counter Statement

In order to understand how loops work, we need to learn a preliminary statement that is used in most loops and that is called a *counter statement*. A counter statement is a statement that allows a variable to increase its own value—usually by 1. For example, if a variable x has the integer 3 inside of it, after a counter statement is used with x, x will contain the value 4.

How is this done? We write a statement to take the variable (in this case, x) and add one to its present value. Then the statement assigns the new value to the variable x. So the statement has two parts—one that increases the value of x by 1 and another part that assigns that value to x. This is what it looks like:

Think of the *right side* of the statement first. Adding 1 to x just gets the next integer greater than x. Assigning it to x gives x that new value. One is added to whatever is inside of x. If 3 is inside of x, then $3 + 1$ is 4. Now the value 4 is really what is meant by x + 1, so 4 is assigned to x.

x = x + 1;
 (3 + 1)
    ⇓
 x ⇐ 4

Another way to understand this statement is to consider the precedence of operators (refer to Chapter 2). The arithmetic operators $(+, -, *, $ and $/)$ have *higher* precedence than the assignment operator $(=)$. So 1 is added to x first, and then the result is assigned to x.

Using the Counter Statement

A counter statement is used frequently in the context of loops to count the number of times a loop spins. Let's see how this is done. This statement is used in the same way that a ticket taker works at the gate of a concert. Every time a person walks through the gate, the ticket taker clicks the clicker to keep a count of the number of people who pass through the gate.

Count = Count + 1;

new count = old count + 1

Another way to think of the counter statement is to think of the variable on the left side as being the newest Count. The newest Count we have is the most recent value of the variable. It should get what is inside of Count (now) with one more added to it. "New Count gets old Count plus one." See Figure 7.6.

Count

Count = Count + 1

5 + 1

6

Figure 7.6
Count is originally shown with the value 5. The addition (+) is executed before the assignment (=) so that 6 is assigned to Count, wiping out the old value of 5.

Two Different Kinds of Loops

There are two different kinds of loops in most languages. The main difference between loops is whether the loop is programmed to *spin* (a run through a loop) a known or fixed number of times. Some loops can be designed to spin 15, 30, or 100 times, for example. The programmer knows exactly how many times he wants to execute the loop. Other loops spin an unknown number of times at the time of writing the loop. These loops spin until something "happens" to stop them.

Fixed Iterative Loops vs. Conditional Loops

If you want to print a message 100 times on the screen, you use a *fixed iterative loop*. The term "fixed" implies that the number of times the loop spins (100 times) is known at the time the loop is written. The word "iterative" means "repeating." If you want to send a file to 50 people on a list, you know you will be sending the file out 50 times—that task should use a fixed iterative loop that will execute 50 times.

An example of a loop that spins an unknown number of times would be a loop that allows a player to play a computer game over and over again until he indicates he wants to stop playing. The programmer can't know ahead of time when the user will get sick of the game and want to stop playing. The player is always asked at the end of a game, "Do you want to continue?" Depending on the player's answer, the game playing ends—that is, the loop stops spinning. This is an example of a *conditional* loop. The loop spins until something happens—or, as we shall see shortly, until a boolean condition becomes false.

In another example, a loop controlling the number of times a game is played could depend on whether the player wins or loses. The loop stops when the player loses. As the programmer, you won't know ahead of time when the player will lose a game and be forced to stop.

In both cases, the loop was exited when an event *happened*—that is, the player didn't want to play anymore or he lost. The loop spun until something occurred to stop its spinning. We either know ahead of time how many times we want to do something or we don't. Depending on our type of situation, we choose the appropriate type of loop.

The first loop to examine is the for loop. The for loop should be used when you know how many times you want to do something.

The For Loop

The for loop is a fixed iterative loop. The loop will be used to do some task a predetermined number of times. Although its syntax varies from language to language, certain aspects of the for loop are the same. For one thing, it always has the word "for" mentioned at the beginning of the loop. The other characteristic of this loop is that you can figure out how many times it will spin before it is executed.

Before you construct a for loop you must decide what statement or statements you wish to *iterate*—that is, repeat. Then you need to know how many times you want to execute them. Once you decide, you can begin to construct the loop. You will need to declare a variable called a *control* variable that will aid you in the execution of the loop.

The control variable's value is changed while the loop executes over and over again. When the control variable's value reaches the number of times the loop was set to spin, the loop ends. So now let's examine how the loop is constructed.

The for loop has three key instructions in addition to the group of statements you wish to execute repeatedly—called the *body* of the loop. The first instruction is to *declare* a variable and assign it an initial value. The second instruction is to make sure that the variable is within range. (We will compare it with some limit.) The third instruction is to change the value of the variable. Before the third instruction occurs, the for loop executes the body of the loop.

As an example, let's use a loop to print a message five times on the computer. First, take a variable, *y*, and set its initial value to 1. Now compare 1 with the upper limit you have in mind—say, 5). Go into the loop and execute the body of the loop—printing the message. Next take *y* and increase its value from 1 to 2. Now you're on your second spin. Go back to the second instruction, which is to *compare* the variable with our upper limit, 5. Since 2 is less than 5, we continue and go into the loop to print the message again. Next, increase *y*'s value from 2 to 3. Compare 3 with 5 and continue because 3 is less than 5. (You are only on your third spin of the loop!) This process continues one more time as *y* increases and becomes 4. Just before exiting, the message is printed again and *y* becomes 5. Then the number 5 (the value in *y*) is compared with 5 (the upper limit). This comparison triggers an exit from the loop because 5 equals 5, but *is not less than* 5. The loop is exited. See Figure 7.7.

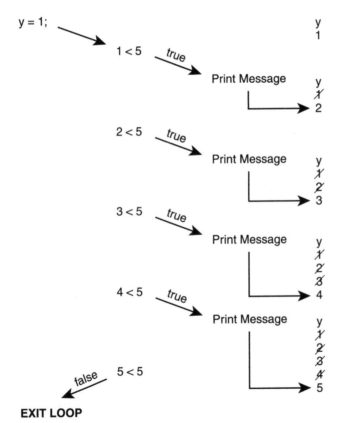

EXIT LOOP

Figure 7.7
The variable *y* is shown with its old values crossed out repeatedly and replaced by new values. The comparison statements are shown each time using new values in the boolean expression.

The `for` loop has the following elements: a *control variable* that facilitates the entire mechanics, or workings, of the loop, *a boolean expression* that checks to see whether the control variable is within range, and *a counter statement* to change the value of the control variable. We will examine each of these elements in order to understand the structure of the for loop.

The Control Variable

A control variable is a variable that does the work of the loop. (In the previous example, it was the variable *y*.) It must be declared first and then given an *initial value* before the loop starts to spin. The control variable is then used in a boolean condition to determine whether the loop spins or not. Just like other control statements, the if and the if...else boolean expression must be true for anything to happen. The loop will be exited when the boolean expression becomes false.

The general idea is that a control variable is compared with some limit—an upper limit or a lower limit. When it is compared with an upper limit, the control variable is checked to make sure that it is still less than the upper limit.

control variable < upper limit

As long as this is still true, the body of the loop is executed. After the body is executed, the control variable is *increased*.

Conversely, the control variable could be compared to a lower limit in the following manner. The control variable would be checked to see that it is still greater than a lower limit.

control variable > lower limit

As long as that is true, the body of the loop is executed. Then the control variable is *decreased*. See Figure 7.8.

Part of the structure of the syntax of a for loop is assigning the control variable its initial value—that is, the value it should have at the *start* of the execution of the loop. Then during the loop's repeated executions, the control variable changes value. Finally, when it reaches the last value and the boolean expression becomes false, the loop is exited.

The Initial Statement

The first statement contained within the parentheses of the for loop is the initialization statement for the loop's controlling variable. You must *declare* the

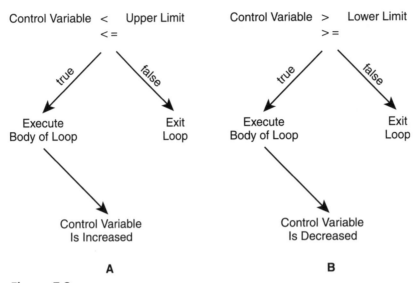

Figure 7.8
The control variable is shown in each example—compared to an upper limit or a lower limit, respectively. Depending on the value of the boolean expression, either the body is executed and the variable changed or the loop is exited.

variable before giving it its *initial* value in separate statements or in one combined statement. Notice that I have left the rest of the `for` loop's statement blank for now. This syntax (grammar) shows how to assign an initial value to the control variable.

Declared and Then Assigned	Declared and Assigned in the Same Statement
`int x;` `for (x = 1; ... )`	`for (int x = 1; ...)`
`int y;` `for (y = 100; ... )`	`for ( int y = 100; ...)`

Notice that in the first example, the initial value of the variable was 1. It is easiest to start counting at 0 or 1, and this is the reason why most `for` loop's will initialize the control variable to one of these integers. The second example uses a large number as its initial value—you will soon see why.

Note

The `for` loop's control variable is always an integer.

The Boolean Expression

The next statement used in a `for` loop is the *boolean expression*, which must be true in order for the loop to execute. We first examined boolean values in Chapter 6. Since a boolean expression has either the value of true or false, we can use that value for controlling whether a loop will execute or not execute. Think of the boolean expression as the permission granted or denied for the body of the loop to be executed. If the boolean expression is true, then we enter the loop and execute all the statements within its control. If the expression is false, then we exit the loop. To leave the loop means to go to the first line of code immediately following the `for` loop block.

```
for ( int count = 0; count < 25; count = count + 1)
{// body of loop is here: for example
cout << "I will not chew gum in class." << endl;
}
// program continues here after loop is executed.
```

Let's examine each of the previous examples and write a boolean expression using the control variable. In our first example, we initialized x to be 1, and now we will set the expression to show that x should be less than 5. As long as x is less than 5, we want to execute the loop. It will look like this:

```
for (int x = 1; x < 5; ...)
```

Here's another example. We will initialize the variable y to 100 and use a boolean expression that shows y greater than or equal to 0. Notice the use of the $=$ sign in the condition. This means that when y reaches 0, it will still spin one more time because 0 equals 0. In that case, it will execute the body of the `for` loop one last time.

```
for (int y = 100; y >= 0; ...)
```

Note

The body of the `for` loop is entered only when the boolean expression is true.

The Counter Statement

The counter statement we mentioned previously is the third statement used in the `for` loop. There are two types of counter statements: one that *increases* the value of a variable and one that *decreases* the value of a variable.

Increases the Variable	Decreases the Variable
x = x + 1;	y = y − 1;
count = count + 1;	answer = answer − 1;
age = age + 1;	sum = sum − 1;

Using our previous examples, we insert the third statement, the counter statement, into the for loop syntax. The third statement will be executed *after the body* of the loop is executed. Imagine that there are four parts to the entire for loop—these three statements and the body of the loop. Let's number them in the order in which they happen.

```
for (x = 0;
     1st
                ⇓
           x <= 100 ;
             2nd
        ⇓
{
// body of the loop
      3rd
}
              ⇓
           x = x + 1 )
            4th
```

So the for loop executes the first two steps, the 1st and 2nd, and then enters the loop as its 3rd step and executes the body. Lastly, it executes the 4th statement, the counter statement. Keep in mind, too, that the initial statement that sets the control variable's first value happens only once. The second time you loop back for instructions, the computer will only execute the 2nd, 3rd, and 4th steps. See Figure 7.9.

Here is another variation on the syntax of a for loop. The declaration of the control variable is outside the for loop.

```
int y;
for (y = 0; y <= 100; y = y + 1)
```

Example 1

Let's start with an example of a problem that would utilize a for loop. These problems are usually ones where you know ahead of time how many times you

```
x = 0;        // happens once
  ⇓
x < = 100;
  ⇓
body of loop
  ⇓
x = x + 1;
  ⇓
x < = 100
  ⇓
body of loop
  ⇓
x = x + 1;
  ⇓
x < = 100
  ⇓
body of loop
  ⇓
 etc.
```

Figure 7.9
The 2nd, 3rd, and 4th steps are shown in sequence repeating each time the loop spins.

wish to do something. In our example, let's print the numbers 1 through 10 on the screen. The first thing to notice is that we know we want to do something 10 times—printing those numbers on the screen.

```
for (x = 1; x <= 10 ; x = x + 1)
{
cout << x << endl;
}
```

Now let's step through the for loop one line at a time—just like a compiler would do. First x gets the value 1, then that value is checked to see whether $x <= 10$ is true. Because this is true, the body of the loop—only one statement, the printing statement—is executed. The next statement $(x = x + 1)$ changes x's value from 1 to 2. After that—recall that the initial statement is not executed again—we go directly to the boolean expression to see that $x <= 10$. (Yes, because $2 <= 10$.) It is true, so we execute the body of the loop and print the number (2) on the screen. After that, x changes from 2 to 3. This pattern continues. See Figure 7.10.

Example 2

In a second example utilizing a for loop, let's look at a list of 20 numbers, and for each number we will print a message on the screen indicating whether that

Control Variable	Boolean Expression	Value	Resulting Action
x			
1̸	1 < = 10	true	1 is printed
2̸	2 < = 10	true	2 is printed
3̸	3 < = 10	true	3 is printed
4̸	4 < = 10	true	4 is printed
5̸	5 < = 10	true	5 is printed
6̸	6 < = 10	true	6 is printed
7	7 < = 10	true	7 is printed
8̸	8 < = 10	true	8 is printed
9̸	9 < = 10	true	9 is printed
1̸0̸	10 < = 10	true	10 is printed
11	11 < = 10	FALSE	EXIT LOOP

Figure 7.10
The sequence of events in the for loop are shown as the control variable's values are repeatedly changing.

number is even or odd. Here, we will use the if statement from Chapter 6 to help the compiler decide whether the number is even or odd.

```
int x;

for ( x = 0; x < 20 ; x = x + 1)
{
if( x % 2 == 0 )
    cout << x << " is even. "<< endl;
else
    cout << x << " is odd. "<< endl;
/* We were able to use the if ... else statement from Chapter 6. See how useful it
is.*/
// Did you notice the syntax for the extended comment above?
```

Here is the output from running the preceding code fragment. Each number will be printed with the appropriate tag, is even. or is odd.

```
0    is even.
1    is odd.
2    is even.
3    is odd.
4    is even.
5    is odd.
6    is even.
7    is odd.
8    is even.
9    is odd.
```

```
10    is even.
11    is odd.
12    is even.
13    is odd.
14    is even.
15    is odd.
16    is even.
17    is odd.
18    is even.
19    is odd.
```

You will *not* see 20 on the screen because the loop is exited before 20 is used in the body of the loop. Recall that the boolean condition was $x < 20$. Once x hits 20, or becomes 20, the boolean expression becomes false, and the loop is exited.

On the CD

The complete program that prints even or odd next to a list of numbers.

The Conditional Loop

A *conditional* loop is a loop that does not spin a fixed number of times. It spins only on the condition that some boolean expression is true. You do not know beforehand how many times it will spin. While the boolean expression is true, the loop spins. Once the boolean expression changes from true to false, the loop, upon finishing the body, stops.

The While Loop

To understand the `while` loop, first we need to look at an analogy. Imagine that you enter a large office room where you must get all this work done. You need to get into the room and clean each desk in the room. You are a very methodical worker, so you only clean one desk at a time. This means that you wipe off the desk, sweep under it, and empty the waste barrel *for each desk* rather than empty *all* the barrels at once or sweep under all the desks first.

Another stipulation about how you work is that you can only work in the room *if the light is on.* (It's on an automatic timer.) You go to the door and check to see if the light is on. If it is, you enter the room and start to work. You will work in the room as long as the light is on. At some point you expect the lights to go off, since they are on an automatic timer that someone else set. When the lights go off, you finish the work at the desk you are at and then leave the room. In a sense, you work *while the lights are on.* You do each task as outlined in the following description.

```
while (lights are on : check the lights here! )
{ // Enter body of loop to do your work.
Clean the top of one desk.
Pull out the chair.
Sweep under the desk.
Push in the chair.
Empty the barrel next to the desk.
}
```

You have to finish all the steps at one desk even if the lights go off while you're still doing one of the tasks—like sweeping under the desk. Once the lights go out, and you have finished all the work at one desk, you leave the room. However, if the lights are still on, you go on to the next desk. (They actually might have gone off while you were sweeping under the desk. Remember—because of your odd work habits—you can't leave the room until you finish all the work at one desk.)

Now back to our while loop. The while loop will spin as long as some boolean expression is true (analogous to our lights being on). Inside the body of the while loop are the statements you wish to execute. Within the body of the loop there must also be a programming statement that triggers the boolean expression to change (like the lights going off with an automatic timer). When that happens, and control passes to the top of the loop, the boolean expression will be false, and we will leave the loop. Notice the sequence of arrows indicating how the loop is controlled. Once the last statement in the body of the loop is executed, we bounce back up to the top of the loop to see whether the boolean expression is true.

```
⇒      while (boolean expression is true)

       ⇓      {
⇑                    // the body of a loop
       ⇓      statement 1;
⇑                    statement 2; etc.
       ⇓             ...
⇑
   ⇐                 }
```

To expand on this loop structure, we need to add some key statements. A counter statement in the body of the loop will allow both loops to function like for loops. That is, the number of times they spin can be counted *as they are spinning*. Let's use the analogy to draw a picture of the while loop's structure. See Figure 7.11.

```
while (lights are on)              while (boolean expression is true)

  {                                  {
  Work at one desk.                  Execute the steps.
    .                                  .
    .                                  .
    .                                  .
  Did the lights go out?             Did the boolean expression change?
    .                                  .
    .                                  .
    .                                  .
  Finish work at one desk.           Finish all steps within { }.

  }                                  }
```

Figure 7.11
The while loop is shown both in the analogy of the office worker and in a programming context.

Let's continue to refine the analogy. When you are in the office, you only work *while* the lights are on. However, you can only check the automatic timer after you finish the work at one desk. The while loop operates the same way—you can only check the boolean expression at the top of the loop.

This analogy is used to emphasize how the while loop does its work. It only checks the boolean expression at the *top* of the loop. For this reason it is called *a pre-test loop*.

A pre-test loop is where the boolean expression is checked first, before entering the body of the loop to execute its instructions. At some point inside the loop, some statement will cause a future evaluation of the boolean expression to be false. After the body of the loop is executed, the control goes back up to the boolean expression, and since it is now false, the compiler exits the loop and goes to the next line after the loop.

The Do...While Loop

With the do...while loop, the same analogy can be applied. In the office room analogy for the do...while loop, you walk inside the room and start cleaning right away whether the lights are on or off. After you've done the work (all the tasks for one desk), you look up to see if the lights are on in the room. If they are, you stay in the room (in the loop) and do the same work on the next desk.

```
do
{
// Enter room to do your work.
Clean the top of one desk.
Pull out the chair.
Sweep under the desk.
Push in the chair.
Empty the barrel next to the desk.
}
while (lights are on );
```

The analogy is a little different from the one used in the while loop in that you only look up to check the light situation at the end of the loop—*not* at the beginning. At the end of the work done at one desk, you look up to see if the lights are still on. If so, you will move to the next desk. For this reason, the do... while loop is called a *post-test loop*. You test the condition (i.e., the lights) *after* the body of the loop.

```
do
{

execute the body of a loop

} while (boolean expression is true);
```

Two Examples from a Programming Perspective

The best way to understand these loops is to start using them. Let's look at an example using each loop. In each example, try to identify the boolean expression used to control the loop. Although there are many situations where any of the three loops could be used, each example uses a loop, which works particularly well in the context given.

Example 1

A good example of the while loop is when you use it to get some specific input from the user. Let's use it to verify a password entered by a user at an ATM. This is a good example, since we do not want to grant access to an account unless the password is correct. We also want to give the user a chance to correct his password. The while loop would test the password initially to make sure it is correct. Once it is correct, the user would be allowed to leave the loop. The while loop would spin as long as the password was incorrect. Here is an algorithm for verifying the user's password. Then the code fragment that executes the algorithm follows.

The Algorithm

1. Ask the user for his password.

2. Check to see if his password is correct.

3. If it is correct, go to step 6.

4. If it is not correct, ask the user to type it again.

5. Go to step 2.

6. Allow the user access to his account.

```
string response, password;
.
.
.
//password would be assigned before we get to this
//section.
cout << "Please type your password."<< endl;
cin >> response;
while ( response != password )
{
/* The loop will spin when the password is incorrect.
Once it is correct, the user will be "released" from the loop. */
cout << "Your password is incorrect."<<endl;
cout << "Would you please type it again ?"<<endl;
cin >> response;
}
```

Example 2

Here's an example where we simulate the game-playing scenario we spoke of earlier in the chapter. Let's surround code for a game with a loop that depends on the player's willingness to play the game. We will use the do...while loop in this example.

The Algorithm

1. Play the game.

2. Ask the user if he would like to play again.

3. Check to see whether his answer is yes.

4. If answer is yes, go back to step 1; otherwise, stop.

```
do
{
/* here is where all the code for the game belongs.
It is probably several pages long. You do not need to know that. */

cout << "Would you like to play the game again?"<<endl;
cin >> response;
}
while (response == yes);
```

The user plays the game at least once because of the way the loop is designed. You enter the loop no matter what because the boolean expression, which is controlling execution, is at the bottom of the loop. Then we ask the user whether he wants to play again. Only if he says yes do we execute the do loop a second time. Then he must say yes *again* in order to play the game a second time. He'll have to say yes before he can play the game again. You have probably experienced this kind of loop when you played a game.

```
Would you like to play the game?
yes
    game is played in here

then again ...
Would you like to play the game again?
yes

and again ...
Would you like to play the game again?
yes

one more time
Would you like to play the game again?
no
```

Then it stops. In fact it would stop for anything that did not look like yes, which encompasses a lot of responses—No, NO, N, Yes, YES, Y, MAYBE, okay, and so on—would all cause the loop to stop because the boolean expression (response == yes) would be false. Remember, the conditional statement is case-sensitive and computers have no intelligence—unless you provide it programmatically.

Using a Conditional Loop with a Counter Statement

Any while loop or do...while loop can be used to simulate the action of a for loop. What that means is the while loop is set up so that it has all the elements of a for loop. That is, it has a control variable, a counter statement, and a boolean condition dependent on the control variable. Unlike the for loop, which has these three statements at the beginning of the loop, the control variable is initialized *before* the while loop and the counter statement is *within the body* of the while loop. The boolean condition is at the top of its loop, however.

```
int x;
x = 1;
while ( x < 10 )
{
//body of the loop
cout << x << endl;
// counter statement to increase x
x = x + 1;
}
```

As this loop spins, x increases and gets closer to the upper limit, which is 10. Look at the output from executing this loop.

```
1
2
3
4
5
6
7
8
9
```

You will not see 10 on the screen because, once the control variable becomes 10, the boolean expression at the top of the loop is false (10 < 10 is false), and we exit the loop. Thus we never see the 10 on the screen.

When a while loop is used with a counter statement, the counter statement acts as a clicker and counts the number of times the while loop spins. Since the boolean expression is used to control the while loop, it must depend on the variable used in the counter statement.

We can do a similar example with the do...while loop. Recall that the boolean expression will be at the bottom of the loop. Like the while loop, we need to set the control variable before we enter the loop and put the counter statement within the body of the loop.

```
int x;
x = 1;
do
{
//body of the loop
cout << x << endl;
// counter statement to increase x
x = x + 1;
}
while ( x < 10 );
```

You will get the same output as you had in the while loop. Again, you will not see 10 in the output because the loop is exited before 10 can be printed on the screen.

```
1
2
3
4
5
6
7
8
9
```

Summary

I introduced the *loop*, which surrounds one or more programming statements referred to as the *body* of the loop. The loop is used for repeating steps in a program. It is another example of a control statement, since the compiler is forced to stay in a loop rather than go to the next line.

Another useful statement is the *counter statement*, which has this syntax:

```
var = var + 1.
```

Some variable gets its present value plus one. This statement is used to increase the value in a variable and it is also used in the context of loops. When a counter statement is used in a loop, it allows the variable to become bigger (or, conversely, smaller) so that the boolean expression controlling that loop can be altered.

We examined two kinds of loops—*fixed iterative* and *conditional* loops. The fixed iterative (repetitive) loop executes a known or fixed number of times. The conditional loop will spin as long as a boolean expression is true.

The `for` loop is a fixed iterative loop. It spins a known number of times. The loop has three parts besides the body of the loop: a statement initializing a control variable (assigning it a first value), a boolean expression, and a counter statement using the control variable.

Two conditional loops are the `while` loop and the `do...while` loop. The `while` loop is an example of a *pre-test* loop. A boolean expression is tested (examined to see if it is true) *before* the loop is entered. The `do...while` loop is an example of a *post-test* loop. The condition is tested *after* the loop is executed. Both the `while` loop and the `do` loop can be used to replace a `for` loop by inserting a counter statement into the body of either loop.

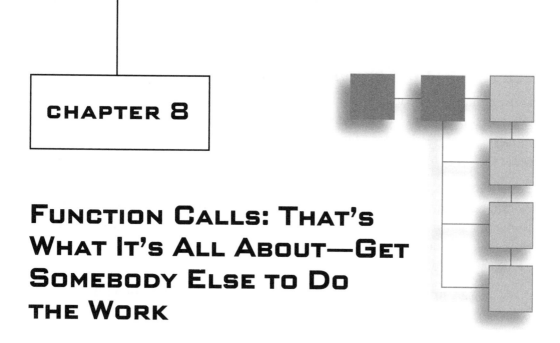

CHAPTER 8

FUNCTION CALLS: THAT'S WHAT IT'S ALL ABOUT—GET SOMEBODY ELSE TO DO THE WORK

In this chapter, we examine a way to separate a block of code from the main part of a program. This is a useful thing to do because, as programs become larger, the code gets more cumbersome unless it is organized in some manner. When we looked at design in Chapter 5, we considered why it was useful to organize a program. A *function* is a separate block of code within a program. Beyond organization considerations, it is useful to have functions for other reasons. If you have a task that you need to do repeatedly, then putting that task into a function will save you the problem of repeating that code throughout your program. In order for a function to execute, it needs to be called. We will look at how to call a function and also how to send and retrieve data from a function.

In This Chapter

- What is a function?
- What needs to be sent into a function (helpers or parameters)
- What comes out of a function—return values
- Two kinds of parameters: value (copy) parameters and variable (reference) parameters
- How to call a function
- Inside the `main` when you make a call
- Inside the function when you get called

What Is a Function and Why Use One?

In this chapter, we define functions and look at all the programming concepts addressed by them. *Functions* are separate blocks of code that appear before or after the main section we learned about in Chapter 4. A program will appear separated into blocks. See Figure 8.1.

Functions are a way of *organizing* a program into separate blocks to accomplish certain tasks. Imagine that you were writing a program to simulate all the tasks that a calculator could do on a number or pair of numbers. This program would be ideal for using functions because there are so many separate tasks that need to be programmed.

A calculator program would do many different things. Think of all the separate tasks that such a program would execute:

- Adding two numbers

- Subtracting two numbers

- Multiplying two numbers

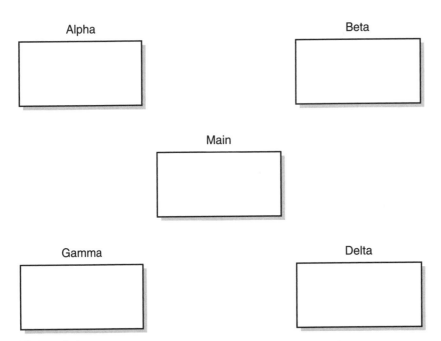

Figure 8.1
A *schematic* of a program shows a visual representation of each separate block with its name above it. Each block represents a separate block, or module, with its own code.

- Dividing two numbers

- Converting an answer to scientific notation

- Changing from degree to radian measure when working with angles, and so on.

Now we could have a large program with a separate function for each of the tasks we listed. See Figure 8.2.

Using functions on a complex problem allows the programmer to separate her code into separate blocks. By organizing code in this manner, it will be easier for someone else to read and understand her code. Functions are usually isolated in this manner—they appear outside of the main section, and they are called from the main, when needed, to be executed. Another reason for using a function is to separate code that you know you will use *repeatedly*.

Example 1

Suppose you write a program to maintain a savings account. The program should print out balances after each transaction. So, ideally, you would write a

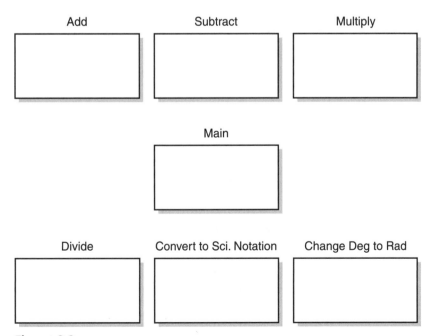

Figure 8.2
A schematic of a program is shown with each task as a separate block that would contain code to execute that task.

function to print the balance in the savings account. Every time you do something to the account—like make a deposit or a withdrawal—your program calls one of these functions to do the task. Here are three functions that would be included in your program:

```
Print_Balance
```

```
Make_A_Deposit
```

```
Make_a_Withdrawal
```

Example 2

Let's say you want to write a program that will keep track of all the music CDs you have. You might want to write a program that allows you to add a new CD to your collection, alphabetizes your list of CDs, and prints all the titles. Here are functions for each of these tasks:

```
Add_New_Title
```

```
Alphabetize_list
```

```
Print_all_titles
```

By using functions, you are organizing the program in a way that a reader will be able to better understand what you are doing. Furthermore, your code will be easier to debug because you can find your error in a function more easily than examining an entire program.

Along the same lines, you could write functions that access data without changing it. For example, if you write a function that keeps track of how many songs you have on your iPod, it would be useful as well as reusable. You could use the function over and over again every time you update the iPod.

What Is a Function and What Does It Do?

A *function* in mathematics is a set of directions to manipulate a variable. It is really a collection of operations on a variable. Think of what an adding function would do to two numbers like 3 and 5—3 + 5 produces 8. We could use other operators with four numbers (3, 2, 18, and 7) to produce a more complex result—3 + 2 * 18 − 7 produces 32. In each case, when using a function, think of the numbers that *go into* the function and the answer that *comes out* of the function.

In computer programming terms, a function is a separate body of code that performs some task. Think of it as a machine that has certain instructions to perform usually on a variable or variables that are being sent into it. Along with doing the instructions posted inside of it, a function "machine" will probably have some values or variables that come out of it. See Figures 8.3A and 8.3B.

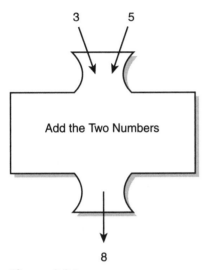

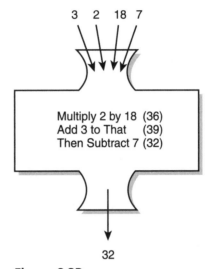

Figure 8.3A
A function is shown as a "sum" machine, where two numbers are sent into it and a sum comes out of it.

Figure 8.3B
Another function is shown, where four integers are sent into it and a result comes out of it after the operations are performed on them.

Example 1

A function finds the square of a number. Notice that in the squaring function, the number to be squared is sent into it and the result comes out of it. See Figure 8.4.

Example 2

A function prints a message the number of times specified. The number of times specified will be sent into the function, and there will be no values coming out of the function once it has finished. See Figure 8.5.

In the last example, we considered a function that has nothing going into it and nothing coming out of it. It is simply a function that does some task for the programmer. An icon or picture drawn by a computer is a separate task that is

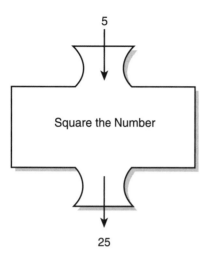

"Squaring" Machine

Figure 8.4
One function is shown as simply squaring the number sent into it.

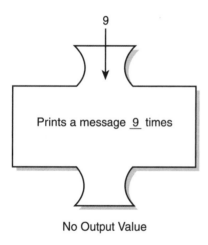

"Printing" Machine

Figure 8.5
The "Printing" function is shown with a number going into it so that a message can be printed that number of times. Once the function is complete, there is no value coming out of the function.

ideal for a function to do. The programmer does not have to write the code herself to draw the picture she wants. Look at the function "Draw Circle." See Figure 8.6.

In the previous examples, we spoke of values going into the functions and results coming out of them. This is the case most of the time. In the "Printing" function,

NOTHING GOES IN

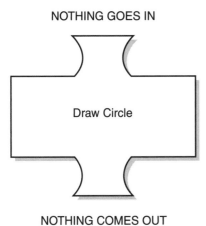

NOTHING COMES OUT

Figure 8.6
The "Draw Circle" function is shown with no value going into it and no value coming out of it.

a value went into the function (9), but no value came out of the function, since our task was simply to print a message. Compare this function with the "Squaring" one. The "Squaring" function accepts a number and then executes code to produce the square of the number.

Values (usually stored in variables) both going into and coming out of the function are two key concepts of function use. It is important that we stop to address all the issues that surround these aspects.

How Functions Interact with the Main

When a programmer wishes to go to a function to complete some task, she must write a command to *call* the function. Before we examine all the details associated with calling functions, let's examine some analogies from everyday life. Calling a function is like calling up a friend to help you complete a big project—like painting the interior of a house. You call your friend, Ingrid, to ask her to paint one room and give her what she needs—the paint, sandpaper, and some brushes—to do you the favor. When she is done, she tells you she finished it. This is an analogy of interacting with a function.

In another example, your DVD player is broken and you call a friend, Jack, who is really good at fixing broken DVD players. You call Jack on the phone to ask him if he can help you. He says yes but that he'll need some tools and a replacement part for the broken part. When Jack is done repairing the machine, he calls you back to say he finished it, and he returns the player to you.

Let's review our two examples to see what happened in each situation. By analyzing each case, both from a general and specific point of view, we will better understand how function calls work.

General	Specific
Call your friend.	Call Ingrid.
Give your friend something.	Sandpaper, brushes, and paint.
You are called back.	Ingrid calls you to say she finished.
You're given something (yes/no)	No.

General	Specific
Call your friend.	Call Jack.
Give your friend something.	Broken DVD player replacement part.
You are called back.	Jack calls you to say he is finished.
You're given something (yes/no)	Yes. Jack gives you back the player.

When Ingrid or Jack did us a favor, they first got something from us to do the work. Then they called us back to say they had finished. In Jack's case, he returned the DVD player to us. In Ingrid's case, she didn't return anything to us, but she accomplished the task—painting the room.

Functions work *almost* the same way. The programmer writes a command that is a *call*. In the call, she includes variables that the function needs to complete its work. The function executes its code, and after that the compiler leaves the function to return to the place that called it in order to continue executing the rest of the program. At that point, the compiler *may* return something to that place—but only if necessary.

Let's take four examples of functions that we discussed in the previous section and give them names so that we can call them—the Sum, Fun_With_Nums, Print, and Draw Circle functions.

General	Specific
Call the function.	Call Sum.
Give the function something.	Two integers.
Compiler "goes back."	Compiler moves from Sum to main.
A value is returned (yes/no).	Yes. Sum returns an integer.

General	Specific
Call the function.	Call `Fun_With_Nums`.
Give the function something.	Four integers.
Compiler "goes back."	Compiler moves from `Fun_With_Nums` to `main`.
A value is returned (yes/no).	Yes. `Fun_With_Nums` returns an integer.

General	Specific
Call the function.	Call `Print`.
Give the function something.	An integer.
Compiler "goes back."	`Print` calls `main` when done.
A value is returned (yes/no).	No. `Print` returns nothing.

General	Specific
Call the function.	Call `Draw Circle`.
Give the function something.	Nothing.
Compiler "goes back."	Compiler moves from `Draw Circle` to `main`.
A value is returned (yes/no).	No. `Draw Circle` returns nothing.

Notice that in the last example—the call to `Draw Circle`—nothing was sent in and nothing came out of the function.

Both Ingrid and Jack called us back to say they had completed the favor. In the first example, Ingrid simply called us to tell us she had finished the favor. In the second example, Jack called us to tell us he had finished the work and was returning something to us—the DVD player.

Functions behave the same way. The compiler will leave the function when it finishes executing its code and go back to the next line of code following the call. We need to know whether a function returns something after executing its code. This is called *returning* a value. Later in this chapter, we will look at the specifics of how to call a function. For now, it is only important that you understand what is meant by calling a function.

```
int main ( )
{
    .
    .
    .
```

```
//insert call to function here
//compiler will return to this line.
    .
    .
    .
}
```

Note

After executing a function, the compiler will return to the part of the program where the call was made.

Function Name and Parameter List

In most languages, a function has a name and a parameter list. The *name* is used whenever the function is called. Once the function is called, the compiler goes to the function to execute it. Here again, we see another example of controlling the compiler. The compiler leaves the line it is on and goes to the code of the function to execute it.

The *parameter list* is a list of all the variables and their types sent into the function. It appears to the right of the function name and gives us information about what kinds of values we can expect to see sent into this function.

Note

Think of the word "parameter" in English. It usually means a boundary or restriction. In computer programming, we are restricting *how* a function will operate. What is sent into a function through the parameter list determines what the function will produce most of the time. So the parameter list is like the boundaries of the function.

Return Values

Functions return values usually back to the main—the part of the program where the call was made. They produce a result in the form of some specific *type* of variable and that result is sent back to the main function after the called function has been executed.

Let's examine the previous examples to see which results were sent back. In the first example, where we added 3 + 5 to get 8, 8 (an integer) was the result. In the second example, which involved more operators, 3 + 2 * 18 − 7, 32 (also an integer) was the result. In the squaring function where 5 was sent into the function, 25 (an integer) was the result. In the last function we examined—the print message function—there was *no result*—only the actions taken by the function.

Let's start by reviewing what each function did:

Function	What the Function Did
Sum	Added two numbers
Fun_With_Nums	Took four numbers and performed three operations on them
Square	Squared a number
Print	Printed a message

Now we need to check what type of result is produced. If a function has no result, we use the term "void" to indicate that nothing is produced.

Function	Did It Produce a Result	What Type
Sum	Yes	A number
Fun_With_Nums	Yes	A number
Square	Yes	A number
Print	No	Void

Now we need to check to see whether the number produced is an integer or a real. Consider these examples with each function and the values that result from sending different numbers into each function.

Example	Send In These Numbers	Result	Type
Sum	5, 12		
What the function does:			
(adds the two values)			
5 + 12	$\Rightarrow$	17	$\Rightarrow$ integer
Sum	14, 17.2		
What the function does:			
(adds the two values)			
14 + 17.2	$\Rightarrow$	31.2	$\Rightarrow$ real
Fun_With_Nums	6, 3, 5, 8		
What the function does:			
(adds, multiplies, and subtracts—multiplication will be first!)			
(6 + 3 * 5 − 8)	$\Rightarrow$	13	$\Rightarrow$ integer

Fun_With_Nums
What the function does:
(adds, multiplies, and
  subtracts—multiplication
  will be first.)
12.4 + 5 * 8 − 4.2)
12.4 + 40 − 4.2
52.4 − 4.2
	12.4, 5, 8, 4.2
	
	⇒
			48.2	⇒ real

Square What the function does: (squares a number) 6 * 6	6 ⇒		36	⇒ integer
Square What the function does: (squares a number) 4.2 * 4.2	4.2 ⇒		17.64	⇒ real
Print What the function does: (prints a message 5 times)	5	void	void	

The value that is returned after the function is executed will depend on what types are sent into the function and what the function does to those types. Keep in mind that sometimes the same type comes out as it went in. You also want to remember that there are functions that do not produce anything to be sent back to the main section. In this case, we use the term *void* to indicate that nothing is coming back to the main function.

How to Write a Function Heading

A *function heading* is a line of code that tells the compiler all the important information it needs to know about the function. There are three parts to the function heading. First the *return type* is listed to tell the compiler that this function will produce an integer, for example, when completed. The term void will signal the compiler that nothing will be returned by the function. The next part of the function heading is the function *name*. If you are the compiler and you need to call on a function to do work, you need to call it by name. The third part of the function heading is the parameter list—the list of variables and their types sent into the function.

Return Type	Function Name	Parameter List
`int`	`Sum`	`(int x , int y)`
`double`	`Fun_With_Nums`	`(double a, int b, int c, int d)`
`double`	`Square`	`(double x)`
`void`	`Print`	`(int num_times)`

Combining return types with the name of the function and its parameter list creates function headings like the following:

`int Sum ( int x , int y )`

`double Fun_With_Nums (double a, int b, int c, int d)`

`double Square (double x)`

`void Print ( int num_times)`

Parameters: Two Different Types

Parameters (variables sent into functions) are boundaries or restrictions on a function's behavior. When you examine a parameter list, you learn a lot about how a function behaves. Does the function need one integer and one real? Does it require two integers? Or maybe it needs three doubles and one string. By reading a parameter list, you get a sense of the restrictions on the function's work. A parameter list tells us the requirements of the function, much like the analogy of what our friends needed when they did us a favor. Ingrid needed the materials to paint the room, and Jack needed a part for the broken DVD player.

In addition to the type of variable being an important aspect of a parameter sent to a function, there is one other aspect of a parameter list, that is, how the variable is sent into the function. Is it a copy of itself or itself being sent? This question gives rise to the two different types of parameters. As we examine these two types, notice how each variable gets sent into the function. You will learn about two different kinds of parameters: the value (copy) parameter and the variable (reference) parameter.

Value (Copy) Parameters

When variables are sent into functions, they can be sent in two different ways. One way is that the function sees a variable is coming into it, and it generates its own copy of the variable without altering the original variable.

Think of it this way. We will go back to our analogy of Ingrid painting a room for us. Instead of Ingrid taking the sandpaper, paint, and brushes from us that we want her to use, she talks to us on the phone to find out *exactly* what type and color of paint we want to use, what kind of sandpaper—coarse or fine—as well as the type and size of brush. Then she buys her own exact copies of what we would have given her. We keep our brushes, sandpaper, and paint, and she uses the ones she bought.

She copied everything we provided and used her own stuff. The only advantage of her buying her own stuff is that maybe she didn't have to carry our stuff over to the house. She just called us on the phone to check all the parameters—the required materials—for the task.

Value (copy) parameters behave the same way. They get all the values of the original variables, but they make their own copies of those variables for the function with the exact same values inside of them. See Figure 8.7.

Note

A function can do anything to these value parameters, since the original variables of the `main` *will not be touched.* This aspect is one of the main reasons that programmers use value parameters.

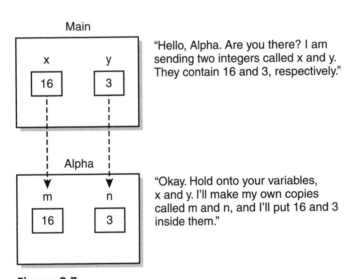

Figure 8.7
A conversation is shown between a `main` function and a function called `Alpha`. `Alpha` does not want to be responsible for `main`'s variables (x and y), so it generates its own copies (m and n) of those variables.

Variable (Reference) Parameters

Variable parameters (also called *reference* parameters) are the second type of parameter. Here the parameters do not create new copies of the original variables, but instead refer back to the original variables. In a sense, the function has full access to the original variables used in the main function. The reason these parameters are called variable is because the word "variable" (in English usage) means "changeable." A variable parameter has the power to change or alter an original variable back in the main function.

The intention of the programmer when she uses a variable parameter is that she wants to let the function manipulate the original variable. The function "works on" that variable and alters it. See Figure 8.8.

Note

> With the variable parameter, the function gets its hands on the original variable and not a copy of it. This aspect of parameter passing can be useful if the variable takes up a lot of memory and you do not want to waste more memory by generating a copy of it for the function. You decide to use the original.

The reason it is called a *reference parameter* is because the parameter *refers back* to the original variable—not a copy of it. A reference book is a useful comparison

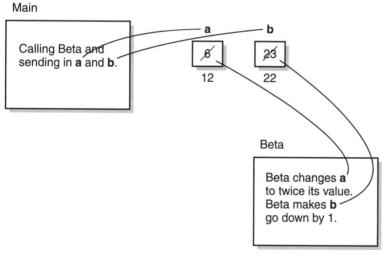

Figure 8.8
A main function is shown with its own variables, *a* and *b*, and their values. Another function, Beta, is shown affecting the values in those variables. Beta doubles *a*'s value and makes *b*'s value drop by 1. Since *a* started out as 6, it ends up being 12. Since *b* started out as 23, it ends up being 22.

because, in a reference library, you cannot walk off with this book or take it back to your own room—you can only look at it there at the library.

The difference with a variable parameter is that it can do whatever it wants to the original variable—including change its value—from inside the function. In our comparison with the reference book, the variable parameter has more privileges than you do. When you use a reference book, you cannot write in it or alter it, while a variable parameter can do whatever it wants to the variable it references (the variables in the main).

The Symbol for a Variable (Reference) Parameter

Variable parameters are designated by a symbol used in front of the name of the parameter in the parameter list of the function heading. In C++, the ampersand (&) is the symbol used. The symbol (&) is the only way to indicate that a parameter will refer back to an original variable (in the main) rather than generate a copy of that original variable.

Example

Int	Alpha	(int & x, int & y);
return type	function name	var type with reference symbol and parameter name

Note

If there is no symbol in front of a parameter name, then the parameter is a *value parameter*, and it will be a copy of an original variable.

How to Call a Function

When you call a function from the main function, you direct the compiler to go to the function, bringing with it any variables you are sending into the function. When you write a call, you use the syntax of the function heading as a guide. For example, if a function heading has a return type and a parameter list containing two variables, it might look like this:

`double Find_Average ( int first_num, second_num);`

A function call will look exactly like the heading *without* any of the variable types mentioned. Let's practice developing the syntax for a *call*—the command to get the compiler to leave where it is and go to a function. We'll do this in stages, since there is a lot of detail in this process.

Where the Calling Begins: Inside the Main Function

The first part of the call is to use the function name:

```
Find_Average
```

The next step is to follow the restrictions of the parameter list by examining the parameters that `Find_Average` has. That is, we need two integers from the `main` to match those in the parameter list.

```
Find_Average (             ,                )
                  ⇑                ⇑
               an integer      an integer
```

But wait! Now comes the tricky part. `first_num` and `second_num` are actually variables that belong to the function `Find_Average` because those were the names used in the heading. They *do not belong* to the `main` function. So the `main` needs to have its own variables whose values will be passed into the `Find_Average` function. Let's declare some variables of the exact same type given in the parameter list. We need two integers. Let's declare them and assign them values.

```
int x, y ;
x = 5;
y = 7;
```

Now we can insert them into the call itself. (We're almost done.)

```
int x, y ;
x = 5;
y = 7;
Find_Average ( x, y); // this is an incomplete call!
```

Remember that `Find_Average` (which uses value parameters—there is no & symbol!) will copy the values of x and y, but, ultimately, leave those variables alone. `Find_Average` looks at x and y and generates copies of those variables and calls them by its own designated names of `first_num` and `second_num`.

The last stage of developing a call is to handle the return type. When `Find_Average` is done with its work, it will send back a variable of type `double` to the `main` function, which called it. So we need to be ready to "catch" what it sends back. We declare a double variable and use it in an assignment statement, like this:

```
int x, y ;
double avg;
x = 5;
y = 7;

avg = Find_Average ( x, y); // the call is now complete
```

Now we can analyze the syntax of a correct call.

avg	=	Find_Average	(x, y);
return type	assignment operator	function name	variables from the main that will be copied by function

The Receiving End: Inside the Called Function Find_Average

Once the call has been made, the compiler enters the function but now is doing its work—that is, executing code with the copies of the variables and their new names—here, first_num and second_num.

```
double Find_Average ( int first_num, second_num);
{

// developing an average for two things
// add the two variables like this:
// first_num + second_num
// then divide that answer by 2 for the average.

// (first_num + second_num ) / 2

// I need parentheses to do addition first.
}
```

We're almost done! We just need to handle the part about returning values. We use a return statement as the last part of the function. When the function has finished its work, it needs to return a value that is of the double type, as specified in the heading. (Remember when Jack *returned* the DVD player when he had finished repairing it?) We do the same in a function. We return the value. Before we do that, we will declare a variable of the double type.

```
double Find_Average (int first_num, second_num)
{
double the_average;

the_average = (first_num + second_num ) / 2 ;
// I did the same thing I did in the "main."
// I assigned the result to the variable.
// Now I can return it.

return the_average;

}
```

In order to avoid confusion about the different variable names, let's look at it this way. Imagine two rooms—one called the Main room and another called the Find_Average room. Each room has its own variables. These variables can't leave the room they're in—they are only recognized in their respective rooms. When the main makes a call to a function, it uses its own variables to do this. On the other end, the function receives the call and "catches" these variables with its own variables of the exact same type. Variables in calls must match variables in headings *type for type*. See Figure 8.9.

Each variable is only recognized in its own room, so we need to have different names for the call and the heading.

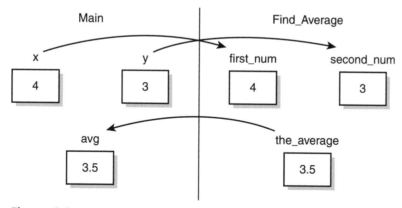

Figure 8.9
Variables as they appear in their own room. Each variable has its own box to show that it contains a certain value. In this example, we will send the numbers 4 and 3 into the function and get back the value 3.5 after the average of 4 and 3 is computed. Note the direction of the arrows to show which variable "sent" its value back to the other.

The Main Room	The Find_Average Room
x , y	first_num, second_num
avg	the_average

Note

Using functions in your program is a great idea because it allows you to reuse parts of the code without rewriting it. Every time you want to compute an average, for example, you just have to call the function that computes averages instead of writing that code again. Reusability is how we describe the kind of code that contains functions for repetitive tasks.

Summary

In this chapter, we covered the topic of functions. Functions provide a way of organizing code in a program so that any reader of the program will be able to understand it easily. Calling a function to do a task (like printing a chart) whenever you need it done is easier than repeating a block of code in your program. Your program will be shorter and more organized through the use of functions.

I gave some examples of different kinds of functions—both those that produce a value as well as those that execute a task, like printing some message repeatedly. Functions have very specific syntax (grammar) requirements. You need to write a function heading that includes a function name, parameter list, and a return variable type, if necessary.

Parameters are the names of variables that the function needs from the main function (the calling place) of the program. There are two types of parameters: *value* (also called *copy*) parameters and *variable* (also known as *reference* parameters). The variable parameters are designated by the ampersand (&) symbol in front of them.

When you *call* a function, it is important to match the variables from the main *type for type* with those in the function heading. It is also a good practice to use *different* variable names in the function heading so there will be no confusion between the variables used in the call (in the main function) and those used in the heading of the function.

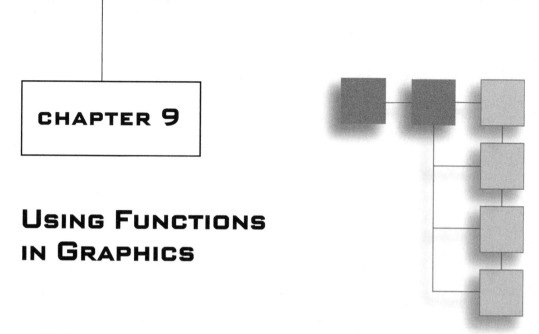

CHAPTER 9

USING FUNCTIONS IN GRAPHICS

In this chapter, we examine how to display graphics on the computer using *vector* graphics. With vector graphics, you draw images using lines and position the lines on the screen using coordinates that determine where the resulting image goes. You will also learn how to move an image on the screen by manipulating the *forecolor* of the image. The functions you learned in Chapter 8 will be very useful in programming graphics.

In This Chapter

- Defining graphics
- Vector graphics
- How graphics work
- Drawing lines and points
- Examples of functions that generate graphics
- Typical graphic moves
- Making a drawing "disappear"
- Moving a drawing
- Delaying the computer
- How to call a function

151

Graphics: How Did You Do That?

One of the coolest things you can do when you first learn how to program is to draw an image on the screen. The topic of graphics brings to mind anything from complicated 3D games, like *Halo* and *Final Fantasy*, to the simplistic graphics used on highway notification signs.

In this chapter, we will look at some of the techniques involved in creating and displaying images. By examining older graphics methods, you can feel confident that you will be able to handle whatever newer languages offer in the way of graphics. The method of graphics we will learn is called *vector* graphics, which derives its name from the meaning of the word *vector*: a directed line segment. If you can design an image in terms of a sequence of lines, you will be able to show it on the screen using vector graphics. This is not a difficult thing to do. You will then learn how to move that image—something even more impressive.

Vector Graphics

The word *vector* implies magnitude and direction. Think of a vector as an arrow that has a *length* and a *direction*—is the arrow pointing down or up or sideways? Imagine drawing a picture with the following restrictions on your drawing. First of all, you can only draw an image with straight lines. What could you draw if someone restricted you in this manner? See Figure 9.1.

Figure 9.1
A house is drawn that has only one door and two square windows. Grass on the front lawn is depicted through lines.

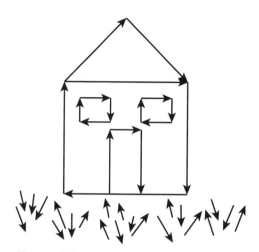

Figure 9.2
A house is drawn as a sequence of arrows joined head to tail to create the final image of a house.

What if someone forced you to draw your pictures sequentially? You would draw one arrow, and then the next arrow would begin where the previous arrow left off. The third arrow would begin where the second arrow left off, and so on. See Figure 9.2.

Creating an image from line segments that touch each other is an example of *vector graphics*. In reality, you do not need to have each new line touching the previous one. However, it is helpful to remember where lines begin and end.

Drawing Lines and Points

To draw lines and points, you first need to understand that you are drawing onto a "piece of paper"—the screen—that has been marked as a grid that has rows and columns. The rows are numbered beginning in the top left at row 1 and column 1 and continuing down to row 2, 3, 4, and so on, to row 150, for example. The columns start at the top left and continue to the right for columns 2, 3, 4, and so on, all the way to column 250, let's say. See Figure 9.3.

The actual number of rows and columns will depend on your computer screen. Once you understand how the screen has been delineated into these blocks, then you can start to draw. The way to draw is to decide *where* you would like to start drawing a line.

Imagine that you are holding a pen in your hand, and you want to put the pen down onto the paper. Where do you want to put it? Let's start by putting the pen

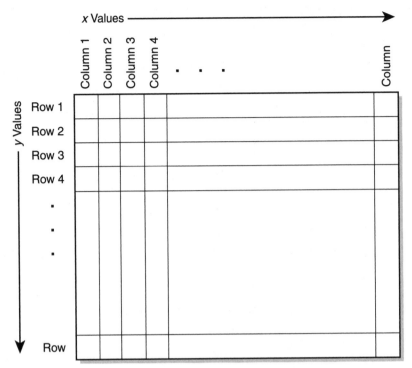

Figure 9.3
The screen is shown with an imaginary grid imposed over it to show the positions on the screen.

onto the block marked 40,5. That means we have put the pen down onto the paper at row 40 and column 5. We haven't drawn anything until we call on a function to help us draw something. See Figure 9.4.

Example 1

Let's look at some headings of functions that will be useful for our drawing. Our initial position (40, 5) is a location on the grid. Let's call those two integers taken together a *point*. The first function is called MoveTo, and we will use it to move to a different point from the one we are currently on (40, 5). Because it is a function, we need to examine its parameters so that we can call it properly. The value parameters of the function MoveTo are *two integers*—one for the row and column positions of the new point where we intend to move.

```
MoveTo (45,50); /* this call will cause us to move to row 45 and column 50 on
the grid.*/
MoveTo (5,5); /* this call will cause us to move back up to the upper left
corner of the screen. */
```

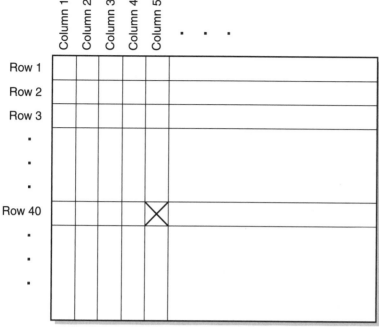

MARKS THE SPOT 5, 40

Figure 9.4
An "X" is shown on position 40,5 on the superimposed grid on the screen. (You cannot see the grid on the screen.)

Note

Recall that nothing is drawn by the MoveTo function. We simply are moving to a new position on the screen.

Example 2

The second function, LineTo, takes two integer parameters, as well, to represent the two coordinates (the row and the column) of the point on the grid where you wish to draw a line. LineTo will draw a line from your present position on the grid to the new position sent into the function.

```
LineTo (20,25);
```

In the example, a line will be drawn from our present position (5,5) to the new position (20,25) as specified by the call to the LineTo function. Here are the headings for each of the functions:

```
void MoveTo ( int row, int col );
void LineTo ( int row1, int col1 );
```

Both functions have the word void in the return type position. This indicates that *no values* will be sent back to the calling place after the functions have been executed.

So let's practice using these functions so you can see how they work. The first thing we will do is draw a huge capital letter M. We'll draw this by using the following algorithm.

Algorithm for drawing an M

1. Move to the lower-left corner of the letter.

2. Draw a line straight up (|).

3. From that position draw a diagonal line down to the middle of the M.

4. From there draw another diagonal up to the top-right corner of the letter.

5. Draw a line straight down to finish the letter.

The algorithm involves moving to where we want to position the M, and then drawing the four line segments that make up the M. The difficult part about making the letter will be judging where the two diagonal lines should meet in the middle of the letter.

M

Find the middle of this letter.

The column should be halfway between the left and right columns.

Step 1. Move to 45,10 position.

Step 2. Draw a line up to 25,10.

That means that our line is 20 units long. That is, it stretches from row 45 up to row 25. (Remember, we are moving in a direction as we draw this letter. We are trying to draw in sequence and not just any way that we want. Otherwise, we would constantly have to reposition ourselves by calling the MoveTo function.)

Step 3. Draw a diagonal line down to row 40 (not as deep as 45) and at column 30.

Step 4. Draw a diagonal line up to row 25 (same height as left vertical line) but at column 50.

Notice that these last two steps position the top tips of the M 40 units apart. (The left tip is at column 10, and the right tip is at column 50.) The middle point of the letter (let's call it the vertex) is at column 30. By adding or subtracting 20 columns from this vertex we get *symmetry*—a natural mirror-like quality where one side of the letter is a mirror image of the other.

Step 5. Draw a line from the right tip down to the bottom (from the point 25,50 to 45,50).

Let's look at each of these steps as a connection of points on a surface. Consider that you map the points first, then afterward you connect them to create the letter M. See Figure 9.5.

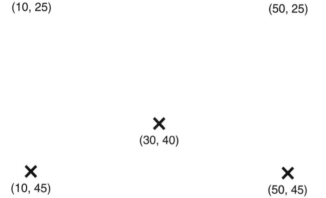

Figure 9.5
The outline of the letter M is shown as a group of unconnected points on a surface.

Now let's list the sequence of steps to draw the letter M that would be used in a program.

The first part of the program is to include the *library* (group of files) that contains these functions. If you recall, we have already seen the iostream library (which has the functions that facilitate showing output and receiving input) and the string library (which has the functions that manipulate strings). A graphics library will include these functions that I have mentioned. So let's examine a small program to draw the letter M. The program is not complete because some of the initial commands to open a window on which to draw will vary from machine to machine.

```
#include iostream.h
#include graphics.h
```

```
int main ()

{.
 .
 .

MoveTo (45,10);/*we position ourselves at the lower-left corner. Nothing is
drawn yet.*/
LineTo (25,10);// a line is drawn up to the top left
LineTo (40,30);// a line is drawn to the middle of the M
LineTo (25,50);// a line is drawn up to the top right
LineTo (45,50);// a line is drawn down to the bottom right
return 0;
}
```

So we have just drawn the letter M by moving to a point on the grid and then drawing a sequence of lines from that first point through the other points we saw in Figure 9.5.

Some Helpful Hints When Drawing

In addition to some of the functions we just examined, we need to consider additional functions that help us draw. One of the understood features of drawing when using these functions is that you draw with an imaginary pen. The pen's thickness and color can be controlled by the programmer through functions that we will examine next.

Using the "Pen" to Draw

Before using the pen, we will want to set the size of the pen tip. Imagine that the tip of the pen is a rectangle rather than a point. How big that rectangular tip is will determine the thickness of the lines we can draw. Imagine the differences among pens whose tips are rectangles with these sizes:

2×2

4×6

8×10

The smallest tip will be the 2×2 tip, and it will not be as big of a tip as the 8×10. See Figure 9.6.

A line segment drawn with a "tip" that is
4 units wide and 6 units high.

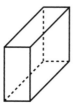

A line segment drawn with a "tip" that is
8 units wide and 10 units high.

Figure 9.6
Lines drawn with pen tips of varying sizes.

We set the size of the pen tip through a function called PenSize. This function takes two integers as parameters—one to set the height of the rectangle and one for the width. Here is the heading of the function followed by some calls to the function.

```
void PenSize ( int height, int width);
PenSize (2,2);
PenSize (4,6);
PenSize (8,10);
```

Later in the section titled "Using Functions to Draw," we will look at a function that allows us to change the color with which we draw. For now, you may assume that we are drawing black lines on a white background.

Background vs. Foreground

It is important to define two terms in graphics, and these are the background and foreground. The background represents the window onto which we are drawing. Usually it is white. The foreground represents anything we draw onto the background. In the section titled "Using Functions to Draw," we will look at the functions that allow us to control the foreground color.

Note

It is important to familiarize yourself with the graphics functions that are available to you. These functions will be dependent on the hardware of your computer and its operating system.

How to Make an Object Move

A nice thing to do after creating an image is to make the object move—that is, appear in a new position. Making an object move uses an interesting algorithm. We begin by displaying the object in some foreground color, called the forecolor. (The *forecolor* is the color with which we draw against the background color—usually white.) Then we "erase" it by drawing it again in the same color as the background. This has the effect of making the object disappear. After that, we draw the image again in its new position. It will appear to have moved!

By manipulating the colors with which we draw the image, we can make the image, drawn in some forecolor, either match the background color or contrast with it. When the image is drawn in a contrasting forecolor, it is visible on the screen. When the image is drawn in the same color as the background, it will not be visible. This has the effect of "erasing" the image.

Once you practice drawing an image in either the forecolor or the background color, you will start to understand how a programmer gets an image to move on the screen. She will change the image's forecolor to match the background color. Then she will draw the image in a new position with a contrasting forecolor. The image will appear to have moved.

But there is another thing to consider. Computers process instructions so quickly that any programming statements used to display images will execute so rapidly that you may not recognize what happened on the screen. So to slow down, or *delay*, the computer so that you can see the images as you intended them to look, we add a loop.

Let's look at the algorithm that accomplishes movement:

1. Display the image (using the code that creates the image).

2. Change the color of the pen to the same color as the background color that you are drawing on.

3. Redraw the image in the background color. (The object will have seemed to disappear.)

4. Delay the computer.

5. Change the pen back to the original color.

6. Redraw the image using new points for positions

Every time you move the object, you need to match its color to the background color to "erase" it, and then redraw it in a new position.

Delaying the Computer

Nowadays, most computers' microprocessors are so fast that the computer will be able to execute your program very quickly. In the case of moving an image, the computer will execute your instructions perhaps too quickly, to the point that a viewer will not recognize what you are trying to do.

Before you are able to give the appearance of movement, you will need to control the speed of that movement. What we want to do is *delay* the computer, or slow it down. One of the easiest ways to do this is give it an empty for loop to execute. This is the name I give to a for loop that spins but does nothing. (Think of the analogy of lifting the back bicycle wheel and then turning the pedal. You see the wheel spin, but the bike can't go anywhere because the wheel is not on the ground.)

So you write the code for the for loop, but the loop itself is empty—that is, the body of the loop has no programming statements. The compiler then spends time setting the initial variable, checking the boolean condition using that variable, and then increasing the value of the variable. It repeatedly does these three steps, but because there is nothing to do inside the loop itself, the user does not see anything happen on the screen. The computer is, in effect, spinning its wheels and being kept busy. After delaying the computer, we can allow the computer to do the next thing.

Examples

Let's look at the syntax of an empty for loop. We will set the control variable to 1 in each example, but we will change the upper limit used in each boolean condition. The higher the upper limit, the more times the loop spins.

```
for ( int x = 1 ; x < 1000 ; x = x + 1 );

for ( int x = 1 ; x < 100000 ; x = x + 1 );
```

In the first example, the loop spins 1,000 times. (That's a lot.) However, in the second example, the loop spins 100,000 times. (That's really a lot.) Notice in each example that a semicolon (;) follows immediately after the statement to show that the loop ends right away. This design shows that the loop is not controlling any other statements—it has no statements (called the *body* of the loop) to spin.

The best way to see the results of using an empty `for` loop is to run your program without this loop. If what you see appears to be happening too fast, then maybe you will need to slow down the program. This loop can be helpful for you.

When you become a more experienced programmer, you can also write code to access the clock function, which will return the time elapsed, in number of tics, from the beginning of the processing in the program. Accessing this time will allow you to more accurately occupy the processor. There is a constant called `CLK_TICS`, which tells you how many tics occur per second. (On many computers, this number will be 1,000).

If you take the number of ticks per second and multiply by the number of seconds you wish to delay the processor, you will get a new number that can be used with the elapsed processor clock time of the CPU.

Look at this example:

```
Clock_t firstTime = clock();// the present elapsed tics of the processor
double m = 3 * CLK_TICS ;// the number of tics needed to equal 3 seconds
While ( clock() - firstTime < m ) ; /* the empty loop which will execute until
the present number of tics exceeds the number needed for 3 seconds.*/
```

Using Functions to Draw

Most applications of a programming language will provide some graphics capabilities in the form of a toolbox or a library of functions. You need to access that library and look at those functions. The *frustrating* thing, however, is finding out what functions have been provided for your use. Depending on what version of what language you purchase, your graphics functions will be specific to that version and the *hardware* on which you run your programs.

You need to look at the functions themselves and examine their headings—just like we did with `MoveTo` and `LineTo`. Once you understand what parameters (the variable types each function needs) and what each function does, then you can make decisions about how you wish to draw some object.

In this section, we will examine some *generic* functions that are simulated in languages that provide graphics capabilities. You might be able to use these exact same functions or something like them.

- `PenSize.` Takes the height and width of the pen.

- `ForeColor.` Allows you to set the color of the foreground.

- `SetRect.` Sets the coordinates of each of the corners of a rectangle, but does not draw it.

- `FrameRect.` Draws the outline of the rectangle.

- `PaintRect.` Paints the rectangle with the forecolor you choose.

- `FrameOval.` Outlines the circle.

- `PaintOval.` Fills in the circle with a color.

First I'll need to explain how each of these functions work. Then you can use them to make whatever drawings you wish. A rectangle has four sides. It is a special type of variable whose syntax I will explain in Chapter 11, when you learn about a struct. (I won't forget!) Each side of the rectangle has a name that represents either a row or a column. See Figure 9.7.

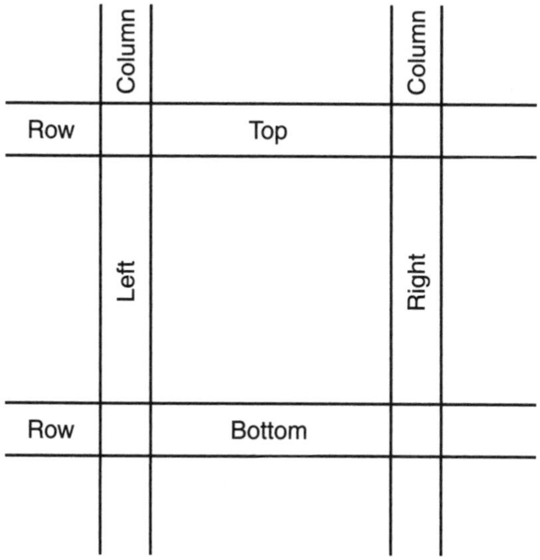

Figure 9.7
Each side has been named and drawn as either a row or a column.

Both the top and bottom of the rectangle are *rows*, which you need to estimate depending on the size of the screen on which you are drawing. Both the left and right sides of the rectangle are *columns* that you position. There are two things to consider when you construct a rectangle: its position relative to the screen and its dimensions (width and height).

If a screen is 400 rows by 600 columns, then you might want to position a rectangle in the middle of the screen. You would start to think about being at row 200 and column 300. If you want the rectangle to be 50 units wide and 100 units long, then you need to consider the following positions. The right side of the rectangle should be at column 350. If you want the rectangle to be 100 units long, then you should set the bottom of the rectangle to be 100 units below row 200 at row 300.

The difference between the two sides (left and right) of the rectangle is 50 units (350–300). The difference between the other two sides (top and bottom) is 100 units (300–200). Every time you construct a rectangle, you need to consider where you will position it and then how to adjust the sides of the rectangle so that they have the appropriate dimensions you want.

Once you decide which rows and columns you will use for your rectangle's sides, then you set their values by calling the SetRect function. You need to follow the heading given in SetRect, which might look like this:

```
void SetRect ( rect * R; int Top, Left, Bottom, Right );
```

Notice that the parameters of the function are all integers, except for the first parameter, which is a rect. But what is a rect? It is a special variable (called a *pointer* variable) which we will examine later in Chapter 17. For now, just think of it as a *rectangle* and follow the syntax used in the example.

We want to make a call to SetRect, but we don't have any name for the rectangle yet. So let's call it by this name (house), and we will declare it in the following manner:

```
rect * house;// use the '*' in between the rect and its name
```

Next we make the call by using the integers that comprise the sides of the rectangle:

```
top = 200;
bottom = 300;
left = 300;
right = 350;
```

Our call would be this:

```
SetRect ( house, top, bottom, left, right );
```

Notice that in the call, there are no types mentioned (i.e., int or rect *), only the names of the variables are used. After calling this function, the rectangle is ready to be drawn, since all its coordinates have been set. Now to draw it, we need to call another function, FrameRect. FrameRect has only one parameter, the rect itself, R. Let's look at its heading.

```
void FrameRect ( rect * R);
```

Now we will call FrameRect in the main program using our rectangle called house. Notice that since the function is a function that does not return anything (note the word void), the call looks like this:

```
FrameRect (house);
```

The next thing you should do is fill in the house with some color so that it is not just an outline of a house. We will call the function PaintRect next. Here is its heading and the call we should use with it. Notice the differences in syntax between the heading and the call. In the tables that follow, each part of the function heading is separated so you can understand the syntax better. First the return type of the function is listed, followed by the function name, and then what parameters it requires. Recall from Chapter 8 that all functions must indicate what they return as a value. If they don't return a value, the word void is listed. All functions have names so that they can be called, and usually they require some variable to work on. This variable is called a parameter.

```
void PaintRect (rect * R ); // function heading
```

Return Type	Function Name	Parameter Type	Parameter Name
void	PaintRect	(rect *	R);
		Parentheses begin here	and end here.

Next, the function call is listed in a table so that you can see the syntax is almost the same as the heading. Because the return type was void, as listed previously, the call is made with the function name only and the parameter it requires, which we saw was a rect type variable.

```
PaintRect (house); // function call
```

Return Type	Function Name	Actual Parameter
None Expected	PaintRect	(house);

Caution

Calls always differ from headings because the *type* of variable is not mentioned in the call, only the *name* of the variable. The compiler will "know" what type is being sent in because it has already translated the heading.

Now let's take care of some of the smaller details that we need to consider. Following is a list of typical colors from which you can choose. We will pick a color with which we will draw the house. Let's pick black.

- Cyan
- Magenta
- Green
- Red
- Yellow
- Blue
- Black
- White

Let's look back at the heading that set the color for the drawing. It was called `ForeColor`. It sets the color in the foreground—the area where we are drawing everything. For the second time, you will see an unfamiliar type. After the `rect *` type we saw in `SetRect`, we are now seeing the `color` type. Think of the `color` type as a built-in type that is independent of the language. It really was defined for the sake of the computer's hardware. Since we need to pay attention to syntax, let's follow the syntax given in `ForeColor`'s heading so that we can make an appropriate call. Here again, we list the elements in a table so that you can better understand the different parts of the function heading.

```
void ForeColor (color c );// function heading
```

Return Type	Function Name	Parameter Type	Parameter Name
void	ForeColor	(color	c);
		Parentheses begin here	and end here.

```
ForeColor (black); //function call
```

Return Type	Function Name	Actual Parameter
None	ForeColor	(black);
Expected		

One last detail is to set the size of the pen with which we are drawing. The pen tip size is measured in height and width. Let's set the width of the pen tip to be 4 units wide by 6 units long. Look at the following table to see the different elements of the function heading.

```
void PenSize ( int height, int width );//function heading
```

Return Type	Function Name	Parameter Type	Parameter Name
void	PenSize	(2 ints	Height, width);
		Parentheses begin here	and end here.

```
PenSize (4, 6); // function call
```

Return Type	Function Name	Actual Parameter
None	PenSize	(4, 6);
Expected		

Notice that in the call to PenSize, I did not use any variables—only the direct values 4 and 6. We can do this when we are using value parameters. Recall that the function just needs the values of the variables, not the variable holders themselves. Now we will put together all the separate parts into one program fragment in the main function:

```
rect * house;
int top, bottom, left, right;
top = 200;
bottom = 300;
left = 300;
right = 350;
PenSize (4, 6);
ForeColor (black);
SetRect (house, top, bottom, left, right );
FrameRect (house);
PaintRect (house);
```

That should draw a house that looks like Figure 9.8.

Figure 9.8
A black rectangle is shown representing a house.

So in your algorithm for drawing any object, you need to set the color of the objects being drawn. You will probably have to change the color each time you draw something new.

Drawing the Sun By Using the Oval Commands

Next if we wish to draw the sun in the sky, for example, we need to call a function that allows us to draw a circle. Circles are drawn through Oval functions, which are functions that can draw any oval of any size specified. The size of the oval is determined from a circumscribed rectangle—that is, a rectangle drawn around the oval. First the rectangle's size is set according to the previous sides mentioned (top, bottom, left, and right). Then the largest possible oval (one that touches all sides) is drawn to fit inside of the rectangle. See Figure 9.9.

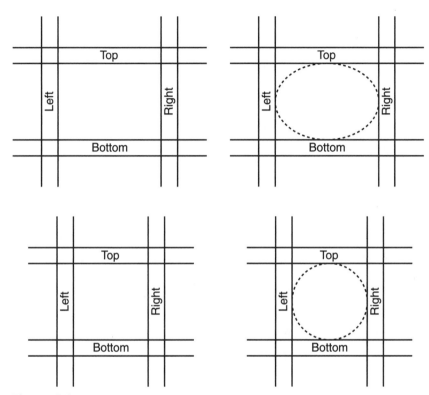

Figure 9.9
Two rectangles are shown empty and then with the largest oval that fits inside each. In the second example, the oval is a circle since the rectangle in which it is drawn is a square.

Here are the headings of a couple of oval functions. By using the SetRect function that you saw previously, you can set the coordinates for the sides of the frame of the rectangle and then call on the oval commands to actually draw the oval. Here are the headings of the oval functions:

```
void FrameOval (rect * r );
void PaintOval ( rect * r );
```

Before calling SetRect, we will set the coordinates of the rectangle in which we will draw the oval representing the sun. We will position it above the house and to the left of it by using the values that follow:

```
rect * sun;
int top, bottom, left, right;
top = 75;
bottom = 100;
left = 200;
right = 225;
//we will change the forecolor to yellow so that it looks
//appropriate.
ForeColor (yellow);
SetRect (sun, top, bottom, left, right );
FrameOval (sun);
PaintOval (sun);
```

Examining the rectangle's width, you can see that it is 25 units wide (100–75), and the length is also 25 units long (225–200). This demonstrates that the rectangle is really a square (25 units by 25 units). So the oval drawn inside that square will be a circle.

Just from these two examples, you can see that it is a lot of work to call on these functions to draw objects. You also need to work within the parameters specified by the function. Imagine that drawing a circle involves designing a rectangle that is really a square so that an oval drawn inside it appears to be a circle. That is complicated! The good part about these functions is that they are good practice for working within a function's parameters.

Summary

First we began by defining graphics as programming the computer to draw shapes. We introduced a type called *vector* graphics, where lines are drawn with direction in mind. A line is always drawn from an initial position to a new position where it ends and for this reason is an example of vector (directed) graphics. Most graphics will be drawn by calling functions that do the work for you. The only thing to be careful about is what type of parameters each function needs to operate properly. Functions will vary from language to language and will also be dependent on the operating system used.

The first two functions we examined were LineTo and MoveTo, used to draw lines from your present position to a new position and for moving to a new position.

There are certain tricks that allow the programmer to make a drawing disappear. The first point is to draw the shape and then redraw it in the background color.

That has the effect of erasing it. Then move the shape by drawing it in a new position. Every time you want to move, you have to draw it in the background color so that it can "disappear." If any of these tricks are executed too quickly by the computer, there is an additional tactic to be employed—*delaying* the computer. This is done by inserting an empty `for` loop to make the computer spin its wheels.

There are many graphics functions that allow the programmer to draw different shapes on the screen. By calling these functions properly, the programmer only has to decide where a particular shape should be drawn. The screen is divided into rows and columns. Depending on the number of rows and columns visible on your screen, you will position shapes accordingly.

Rectangles are used in many of these functions and consist of a top and a bottom (both of which are rows) and a left and a right (both of which are columns). Functions like `SetRect`, `FrameRect`, and `PaintRect` will set the size of the rectangle, then draw its outline and fill it in with the foreground color. The oval functions (`FrameOval` and `PaintOval`) are extensions of these rectangle functions that allow the largest possible oval to be drawn within a rectangle whose position is set by the programmer.

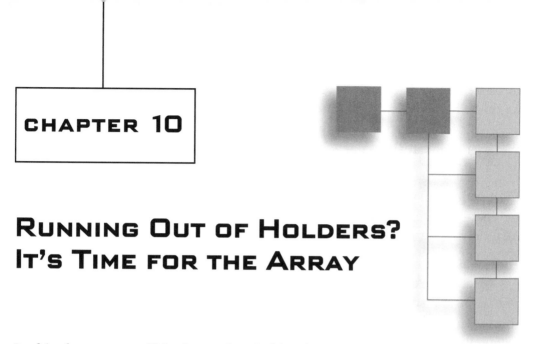

CHAPTER 10

RUNNING OUT OF HOLDERS? IT'S TIME FOR THE ARRAY

In this chapter, we will look at a data holder that is very useful in programming languages. It is called the *array*. The array is used to hold several values of the same type of variable. We'll start with some analogies before we look at the array itself.

In This Chapter

- The array—keeping what's alike together

- Members bound by their type

- Loops work well with arrays

- Programming with arrays

- Assigning an array

- Printing an array

- Copying an array

An Analogy for the Array Holder

The array is designed to hold a collection of data. When we deal with a large collection of data, we need to put each piece of data into a separate variable holder. If you have, let's say, 50 data items, you would have to sit and think of 50 variable names—one name for each data item. That can be difficult, since there are only 26 letters in the alphabet. You could certainly use a, b, c, d, and so on, but what would you use after that? The array type holder provides a useful technique for holding large quantities of information. In order to understand the array, let's look at an analogy.

Think of a large chest of drawers. Most bureaus have only three or four drawers. Imagine if you had a bureau with 50 drawers. You could refer to each drawer by a number—drawer 1, drawer 2, drawer 3, and so forth. You would put clothes in each drawer, but the clothes would differ from drawer to drawer.

Socks would be in drawer 1. Shirts would be in drawer 2. In drawer 3, you would put sweaters for spring. In drawer 4 you could put shorts. In drawer 5 you could put jeans, and so on. Each drawer has different items—socks, shirts, sweaters, shorts, jeans—but each of these items is an item of clothing. All of these items belong in the bureau because they are clothing items.

An array is similar to a bureau—it has many different drawers (or slots) called *members*. Each member is identified with a number. The array is used to hold different values that are of the same type. You could have an array of integers. Let's look at a bureau that has a different integer in each drawer. Compare it with the bureau of clothing we just discussed. See Figure 10.1.

Caution

In the programming language C++, the array "drawers" (members) are numbered beginning with 0 instead of with 1. So if you are trying to reference the 7th member of the array, you will need to use slot 6 because the numbering started at 0. If you wanted the 3rd member you would use slot 2, and so on.

An Array Is Used for a Collection

An array is used for a collection of items. Each item is unique, but it does belong to a common *type*. Think about a collection of MP3s. If you were really organized, you might make an excel file with a number for each MP3 you own. Then you could generate a list of MP3s like the following:

- MP3 1: My Chemical Romance's *The Black Parade's All Time Hits*

- MP3 2: Radiohead's *In Rainbows*

- MP3 3: U2's *How to Dismantle an Atomic Bomb*

- MP3 4: *The Best of Beethoven*

- MP3 5: Evanescence's *Fallen*

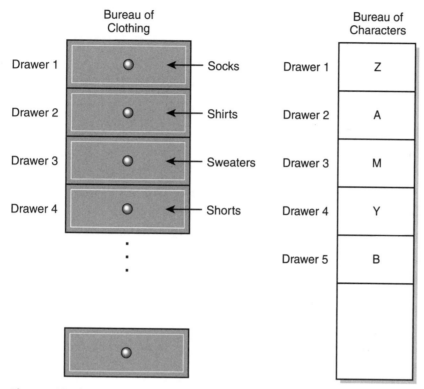

Figure 10.1
Two bureaus are shown—one with different clothing items and another with different integers in each drawer.

The collection is a collection of MP3s, and each MP3 is unique. Rather than referring to each MP3 individually by its title, we refer to each MP3 by its number in the collection, MP3 1, MP3 2, MP3 3, and so on. What we have created is an array of MP3s—a collection of MP3s.

Why Is the Array Used?

The array is used to group together variables of the same type but differing in values.

As you learn to program, you may need to deal with large quantities of data. For example, if you know that you will have to store 50 names of people you know, then the array is a good choice of holder for this information.

The array would allow you to put each name into a drawer of a bureau, so to speak. Instead of calling each drawer a drawer, we'll call it a *name*—name 1, name 2, name 3, name 4, and so forth. Otherwise, you would have to come up with a list of unique variable names like first_friend, second_friend, third_ friend, and so on. When we get to array syntax, you will see how much easier it is to create 50 variables that are unique without having to type a variable name for each.

Array Syntax

When you *declare* an array to the compiler, you are telling it to create a large bureau with each drawer of the bureau numbered. After you declare the array, you can start to load the array by assigning each member (or "drawer") a value. The key thing about array syntax is letting the compiler know how many drawers it should set aside in memory and what type item should it expect to store in each drawer.

So far we have used the int, char, double, string, and boolean types. We could make an array of each of these types if we wanted.

Example

Let's look at a declaration of an array of 50 members where each member is an integer.

Just as we did with the collection of MP3s by naming each MP3, MP3 1, MP3 2, and so on, we need to come up with a name for the collection. Let's use the term group.

```
int    group    [50];
```

int	group	[50];
Type	**Name**	**Number of Members**

Notice that brackets [ ] were used to let the compiler know it should create 50 integer holders. If the brackets had been missing, the declaration would have looked like a straightforward integer declaration.

```
int          group;
```

That would have meant we were declaring one integer called group. The array defined earlier, however, enables us to create 50 integers, all with the common name group. Here's how these integers would be named. I need to forewarn you that in C++, the array members are numbered *beginning with zero*. Let's look at how each variable is named—first in English and then in a programming language.

English	Programming Language
group 1	group[0]
group 2	group[1]
group 3	group[2]
group 4	group[3]
. .	
. .	
. .	
group 48	group[47]
group 49	group[48]
group 50	group[49]

There is no group[50] in the programming column because group[49] is the 50th member of the array. (That's because we started at group[0] instead of at group[1].) The brackets are used to identify the member number ("drawer number") of the array. See Figure 10.2.

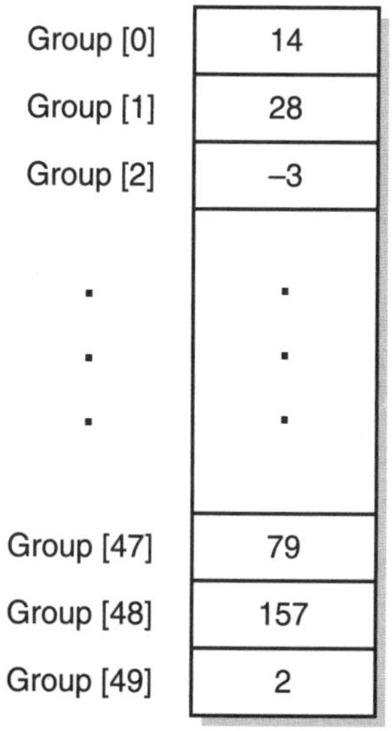

Group [0]	14
Group [1]	28
Group [2]	-3
.	.
.	.
.	.
Group [47]	79
Group [48]	157
Group [49]	2

Figure 10.2
Each member of the array is shown with its value inside of it.

Caution

Note that values have no correlation with the number member where they are stored.

Different Types of Arrays

Let's declare some other arrays using of different variable types. We'll start with an array of strings to hold a collection of phone numbers. We'll declare an array of 35 strings.

```
string   phone_book   [35];
```

Look at this table, which indicates each part of the declaration:

Type	Array Name	Number of Members
string	phone_book	[35];

Another example of an array would be one used to hold a collection of real numbers. Imagine that you were trying to store the checking account balance for a group of 40 individuals. Each person would need a slot, or drawer, in the array for her balance. Consider this declaration followed by a table that clarifies each part of the code.

```
double   account_balance   [40];
```

Type	Array Name	Number of Members
double	account_balance	[40];

Assigning Values to an Array

Now that we have declared a couple of different arrays, it is time to *load* an array. What that means is we will assign each member of an array a value. Let's start with the phone_book array we declared previously. Consider this list of members and the value each slot contains.

Member	Value
phone_book [0]	"555-2222"
phone_book [1]	"555-4567"
phone_book [2]	"555-2345"

```
phone_book [3]        "555-4567"
phone_book [4]        "555-1234"
   .                      .
   .                      .
   .                      .
phone_book [31]       "555-5678"
phone_book [32]       "555-6789"
phone_book [33]       "555-9876"
phone_book [34]       "555-4567"
```

We have only used 18 slots in the array; the other 17 are empty and have nothing in them—not even blanks. The compiler considers them to be *uninitialized*. This means that they have not been given any value. Remember that if you try to work with a variable that has no value, the compiler will have problems.

Note

If you try to use a value that has not been initialized—such as the 36th member in a 35-element array—the compiler will use whatever value it finds in that memory location, which could be anything. At best, your program will have seemingly random errors, and at worst, your program will crash your computer.

Now another point to notice about the array values in phone_book is that integer values have been mixed with the dash (-). Yet we know that this array has been declared as an array of strings. A string type is useful because you can mix characters with numbers and still store them in one variable holder.

The next point to consider is how we will assign values to members of an array. Of course, you could use several assignment statements to load (assign) the array like this:

```
phone_book [0] = "641-2222";
phone_book [1] = "123-4567";
phone_book [2] = "654-2345";
phone_book [3] = "234-4567";
phone_book [4] = "890-1234";
   .
   .
   .
phone_book [31] = "345-5678" ;
phone_book [32] = "567-6789";
phone_book [33] = "345-9876";
phone_book [34] = "432-4567";
```

But that seems to be a tedious way of assigning values to several variables. You might also start to think "what is the point of the array?" because we don't appear to be saving any time at all. The answer to this tedium is found in the application of a loop to our problem; a loop is ideally suited for accessing members of the array efficiently. The real power of the array is using it in conjunction with a loop to save time.

How to Use Loops with Arrays

In order to understand how a loop can be used in conjunction with an array, let's start by comparing the members of the array with a control variable from a for loop. (If you recall, the control variable is the variable that is increased or decreased during the loop.) We'll start by declaring an array of 10 members, each of which is an integer. Next to it we'll declare a control variable that will be used in a for loop.

```
int    list [10];
int    x;
```

The first step in understanding how a control variable might be useful with an array is to think of the control variable as a variable that moves through the members (slots or drawers) of an array. The control variable changes during a for loop. If we use it to move through the array members—one at a time—we can use a loop to access the members more efficiently. Consider this list of array members, slot position, and the control variable's values.

Member	Slot #	Control Variable Value
list [0]	0	0
list [1]	1	1
list [2]	2	2
list [3]	3	3
list [4]	4	4
list [5]	5	5
list [6]	6	6
list [7]	7	7
list [8]	8	8
list [9]	9	9

Designing a For Loop with an Array in Mind

A for loop can be set so that its control variable spins through a range of numbers that corresponds with the slots of the members of an array. In the array we just declared, we have 10 members that are numbered 0 through 9. Now we need to set up a for loop whose control variable will spin from 0 through 9, inclusive. (The term *inclusive* just means that we will hit the numbers 0 and 9 in addition to the numbers in between.) Our for loop would look like this:

```
for ( int x = 0; x <= 9; x = x + 1)
```

This for loop will spin 10 times and hit every number from 0, 1, . . . , 7, 8, 9. The next part of the problem is to address how to use the for loop to access members of the array. Consider each array member's name:

```
list [number]
```

The number is the only part that changes as you move through successive members in the list. Each array member has the name list followed by the brackets with the slot number inside. We'll use the control variable to represent that number. That way, each time the for loop spins a different member of the array is accessed.

If the variable *x* has the value   then list[x] refers to

⇓   ⇓

0   list[0]

If the variable *x* has the value   then list[x] refers to

⇓   ⇓

1   list[1]

If the variable *x* has the value   then list[x] refers to

⇓   ⇓

2   list[2]

If the variable *x* has the value   then list[x] refers to

⇓   ⇓

3   list[3]

.
.
.

If the variable x has the value	then list[x] refers to
⇓	⇓
8	list[8]

If the variable x has the value	then list[x] refers to
⇓	⇓
9	list[9]

Let's start with an example where we use the for loop to print out all the members of the list array.

```
for ( int x = 0; x <= 9; x = x + 1)
{
cout << list[x]<< endl;
}
```

Recall that the statement, x = x + 1, will cause the value in x to increase by 1. This statement allows the for loop to spin. In this case, it allows us to look at each slot of the array during each spin of the for loop.

First list[0] is printed, then list[1], list[2], and so on. Let's consider some other examples using the for loop to move through the array. In the next example, we will let the user assign the members of the array. We'll put a message to the user inside the loop, as well as an input statement. It will look like this:

```
for ( int x = 0; x <= 9; x = x + 1)
{
cout << "Please type an integer." << endl;
cin >> list[x];
}
```

In order to understand everything that happens in the loop, let's consider the dialogue between the screen and the user:

What the User Sees on the Screen	What the User Types at the Keyboard
Please type an integer.	5
Please type an integer.	18
Please type an integer.	22
Please type an integer.	−1
Please type an integer.	98
Please type an integer.	12

Please type an integer.	100
Please type an integer.	24
Please type an integer.	16
Please type an integer.	31

As a result of the `for` loop's execution, the array looks like a chest of drawers with each of these values in the appropriate box. See Figure 10.3.

Note

Notice that the values in the array appear in the order they were entered by the user. The array simply stores the data—it does not order it in any way. Unless you create code to process or sort the array in some way, the values remain in the order they were entered.

Caution

There is no correlation between the array slot and the value in the slot. It would be unusual to have the value 10 in `list[10]` for example. That would be a coincidence.

`for` loops are the easiest way of moving through an array because you can set the control variable's values to match those used for the array's members. Following are some other examples of using `for` loops with the array.

Some Short Examples Using the Array

It is important to look at different examples that you will encounter when working with an array. You will want to be able to load (assign) an array, print its values, and initialize an array, for example. In this section, we consider some fragments of code that will accomplish these tasks and others.

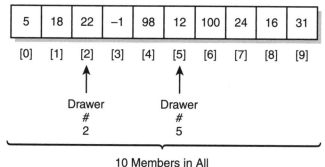

Figure 10.3
The `list` array is shown with its values—each in the appropriate drawer of the array. There are 10 members in all.

Initializing an Array

If you recall, when you *initialize* a variable, you give it its first value. When you initialize an array, you put a value (usually 0) into each slot of the array. For that reason, the drawers of the array are never empty, and the compiler does not experience any problems when it accesses these members.

In the first example, we declare an array of integers and set all the members to 0. (Usually when you initialize an array of numbers, you assign each member 0.)

```
int ages[15]; // declaring an array of integers

for ( int count = 0; count <= 14; count = count + 1)
{
ages[x] = 0;//zero is being assigned to each slot
}
```

In the second example, let's declare an array of characters and initialize each member to the blank character, the space. Here's a fragment to do this:

```
char name[20]; // declaring an array of characters

for ( int x = 0; x <= 19; x = x + 1)
{
name[x] = ' ';//the blank is being assigned to each slot
}
```

Printing an Array

When using the for loop to print the members of an array that has already been assigned its values, decide how you want your output to look. If you wish the array members to be listed horizontally, look at Example 1. Example 2 shows the array with its values listed on separate lines. Note that in each version, we put the value in *x* to indicate which member of the array we are printing.

Example 1

```
char friend [20]; // declaring an array of chars

for ( int count = 0; count <= 19; count = count + 1)
{
cout << x << " " << friend[x]<< " "; //info will be put on one line
}
```

Example 2

```
char friend [20]; // declaring an array of chars

for ( int y = 0; y <= 19; y = y + 1)
{
cout << y << " " << friend[y]<<endl;//info will be
// put on separate lines.
}
```

On the CD

A program that initializes, prints, and then lets the user assign the members of the array.

Counting the Number of Negative Values in an Array

Imagine an array of 100 real numbers, where each real number stands for the balance in a checking account for one individual. If you work at the bank, you would probably want to keep track of the number of people who have overdrawn their accounts. In this fragment, we will count the number of people (array members that are negative) who have negative balances. If an array of doubles has already been assigned its values, we can use an if statement inside a for loop to accomplish our task.

```
double balances[100]; // declaring the array
int total_count = 0;// initializing a variable
// to keep track of the negative numbers

for ( int count = 0; count <= 99; count = count + 1)
{
if ( balances[count] < 0)
  total_count = total_count + 1;
//total_count is increased each time a negative value in a
//member is recorded.
}
```

Imagine that the array already has its values and that a small arrow is running down the right side of the array. The arrow will count the number of negatives it finds in the array. This total will be stored in the total_count variable. See Figure 10.4.

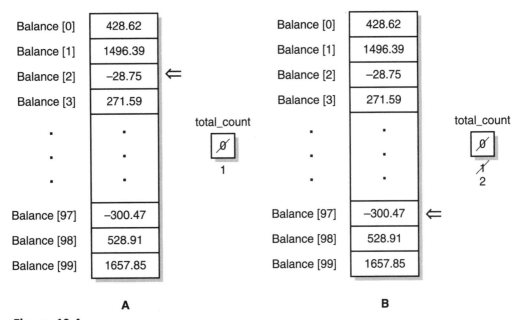

Figure 10.4
The arrow is shown to the right of the only two negative numbers it encounters. As a result, total_count has the value of 2.

Copying One Array to Another

Let's say you are given an array that you wish to copy. First you need to declare another array, for example, called copy_array, of the same type and size. Then you can use a for loop to copy each member from the original array into the copy array, one member at a time. See Figure 10.5.

Now consider the code that will execute this problem. Keep in mind we are assuming that orig_array has already been assigned its values.

```
int orig_array [50];
int copy_array [50]; // declaring two arrays of ints
.
. // code to assign orig_array goes here
.
for ( int y = 0; y <= 49; y = y + 1)
{
copy_array[y] = orig_array[y];
/* each member of orig_array is copied, one at a time, into the new array. This
section presumes that orig_array was assigned already. */
}
```

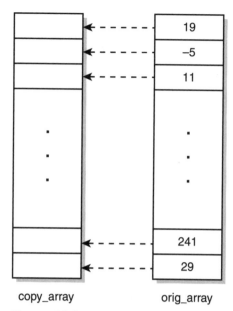

Figure 10.5

orig_array is shown passing copies of its values into the empty array, copy_array.

On the CD

A program to swap all the members of one array with another.

Summary

In this chapter, I introduced the array as a collection of holders for the same data type. An array could be a collection of integers, reals, booleans, strings, or characters. An array is like a collection of drawers where each drawer contains a separate value, but all values are of the same type. I explained the array through the analogy of a bureau where each drawer of the bureau contains different kinds of clothing—socks, sweaters, shirts, and so on—but they are all of the same type: articles of clothing.

When declaring an array, state the type first, then the array name followed by brackets [ ], with the number of members indicated. The array declaration differs only slightly from other declarations by using these brackets. All arrays have members (like slots or drawers) that are numbered beginning with 0, then followed by 1, 2, 3, and so forth. Take an array called group, for example. The members are called group[0], group[1], group[2], and so on.

Loops, especially the for loop, work well with arrays. Whenever you want to work with an array, such as assigning it values or printing its values on the screen, using a for loop to access the members of the array is quite useful. The for loop should be declared so that its control variable spins through the array members. For this reason, most for loops that are used in conjunction with arrays start spinning at 0, since arrays are generally numbered 0, 1, 2, and so on.

In the last section of the chapter, I covered different examples using the for loop with an array. We printed, initialized, and then copied one array into another array.

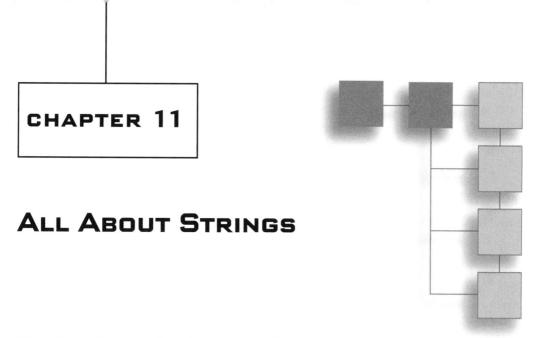

CHAPTER 11

ALL ABOUT STRINGS

Now that we have studied the array and the string type, it's time to see the string data type for what it really is—an array of characters. In this chapter, we will look at some of the standard string functions that most languages provide. We will practice calling those functions so that we can understand what they can do for us.

In This Chapter

- The string as an array

- Concatenation

- The plus sign (+) as an overloaded operator

- A preview of objects

- length and substring

- find and charAt

- The brace set [ ] as overloaded operators

The String as an Array

I bet you did not figure that the string would appear as an array. It is ideally suited to be an array structure because it is a group of one type—a group of characters. Look at the word "hello." These five letters could be each of the five slots of an array of characters. Let's call the array myWord.

```
char MyWord[5];
```

Now let's assign each of those slots manually rather than through a loop.

```
myWord[0] = 'h';
myWord[1] = 'e';
myWord[2] = 'l';
myWord[3] = 'l';
myWord[4] = 'o';
```

Recall that we have to use the zero (0) index in C++ for the first slot in the array. Alternately, we could declare myWord as a string.

```
String myWord = "hello";
```

That was a lot easier! The only problem with the string declaration is that you lose the understanding of what is really going on when you work with strings in a programming language. In the next few sections, we will look at the typical string functions and practice using them in examples. After this, you will be happy to use the string type and let the computer do all the work. But I think you will appreciate how these functions work, since they operate on an array.

The first thing we will do is *concatenate* two strings—that is, add two strings together. Watch how this is done.

```
String myWord = "hello";
String name = "James";
String greeting = myWord + name;
```

If we look at each of the strings as arrays, this is what they look like. See Figure 11.1.

You should also notice that greeting does not insert any space between the other two words:

```
greeting contains helloJames
```

```
myWord[0] h
myWord[1] e
myWord[2] l
myWord[3] l
myWord[4] o

name[0] J
name[1] a
name[2] m
name[3] e
name[4] s

greeting[0] h
greeting[1] e
greeting[2] l
greeting[3] l
greeting[4] o
greeting[5] J
greeting[6] a
greeting[7] m
greeting[8] e
greeting[9] s
```

Figure 11.1
Each of the strings is viewed as an array, and the array greeting is seen as a composite of the other two strings.

If we want to add an intervening space, we need to explicitly add it, as in this example:

```
greeting = myWord + " " + name;
```

The addition (+) operator has been programmed to add two strings as well as two numbers. We say that this operator has been *overloaded* to do this additional operation. That means the language has two built-in functions for the addition sign—one that works for numbers being added and another that works for strings or characters being added. When the types of the arguments on either side of the + sign are read, the appropriate function for the + sign is executed. As you advance in your programming skills, you can learn how to write your own overloaded operators.

Remember that the computer will know which function to use—it will use the one that corresponds to the data types that match it. See Figure 11.2.

The workload that the plus sign normally has is to add two numbers. To overload it is to add another job to its workload—that of concatenation.

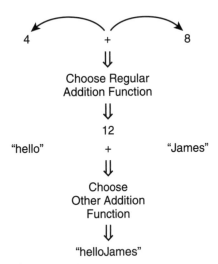

Figure 11.2
A plus sign is shown with arguments on either side of it. Depending on the arguments present, the appropriate function will be used.

Here is another example of concatenation:

```
String sentence = " My" + " name" + " is" + " John.";
```

Notice that I added a space before each word so that the string will look good when it is printed.

```
cout << sentence << endl;
```

```
My name is John.
```

String Functions

In this section, we will use some of the typical string functions in C++: length, substring, and find. length is a useful function because it tells you how long your string is. Of course, you could just count the letters in the word, assuming it is not user input, and you would have the answer. But strings behave a little differently than the array. There is often a special character called a *null* character, which is put on the end of the string. I think of it as a stop sign, keeping the programmer from looking for any other letters in the string.

Consider Figure 11.3 where one part shows an array loaded with characters, and the other shows a string with the same characters but also with the appended null character.

T		T
H		H
E		E
Blank		Blank
C		C
A		A
T		T
Blank		Blank
I		I
S		S
Blank		Blank
F		F
A		A
T		T
.		.
		Null

Figure 11.3
Both strings appear as arrays, but the string on the right shows the terminating null character.

Length and Substring

Most languages have some kind of length function that returns the number of letters, including any other characters, like blanks, punctuation, and so on. Since you learned about functions in Chapter 8, we can practice calling that function.

Except for some early languages, like Pascal, strings are treated as objects in C++ and Java. Although you will read about objects in Chapter 15, we will have to make some minor adjustments in the way we call functions.

With regular functions, you make a call by matching the parameter list with the appropriate types in your call. Consider the following example.

The heading of a length function could be as follows:

```
int  length ( String m );
```

So in order to call the length function, we would need to send in the appropriate parameter—a string argument. Here would be the call to the function:

```
int m = length ( greeting);
```

Notice that greeting was passed *into* the function so that length could work on it to find the length.

Objects use a different way of calling a function, and this is how it would look:

```
String greeting = "Hello James." ;
cout << greeting.length( );
/* notice that greeting (the object) is followed by the function name, rather
than being contained in the parentheses. That is the main difference in the
call.*/
```

So let's practice calling the length function again.

```
String firstString = "My cat is " ;
String secondString = "really cool.";
String thirdString = firstString + secondString;
cout << firstString.length( )<< " " << secondString.length( )<< endl;
cout << thirdString.length();
// 10 followed by 12 then 22 (on the next line) are printed.
// remember to count the blanks and punctuation.
```

Once you know the function heading and more about object syntax, you can easily call other string functions that the language has. However, we will delay calls made by objects until we learn more about objects. So all of the functions that follow have different headings from the exact ones you find for the String object. However, the most important thing for you to understand is *what* each function does.

Following is an example of a string function that can be useful: substring. A substring function will return a section of the string depending on what parameters are provided. Taking a subsection of a string is called *extracting* from the string. Here are some typical substring headings:

Note

This code is for illustrative purposes so that you will know about the kinds of string functions you can call. However, you have not learned all of the grammar of C++, so I am presenting them in this way so that you can understand string functions even though we are not ready to look at the actual code in C++.

```
// Warning: not Standard C++ code!
String substring ( String m, int start );
String substring (String m, int start, int length);
String substring ( String m, int start, int firstIgnored );
```

Notice that both functions have the same name, but their parameters differ. This is another example of overloading, specifically, function overloading. Here we are overloading a given function rather than the arithmetic operator.

There are a couple of ways the extraction works. The first way is to take the string and find the first position where you want to start your new string, and then you extract everything both including and after that position. This is pretty easy to do. Let's put objects aside for the moment and look at the following example where we call the first function:

```
// Warning: not Standard C++ code!
String m = "headhunter";
String result = substring (m, 4);
/* result will contain "hunter" since the 'h' of "hunter" is in the 4th slot of the
array.*/
// Recall that all arrays in C++ begin with slot 0.
String word = substring (m, 6);
// word will contain "ter" since t is in slot 6
```

In the second example, there are two parameters besides the string m: the start and the length. This function behaves a little differently from the previous substring function. The start position still refers to the place where the extraction should begin, but length tells how long that new string should be from the starting place.

Here are a couple of examples to demonstrate how this substring function works.

```
// Warning: not Standard C++ code!
String m = "headhunter";
String result = substring ( m, 4, 4);
// result will contain "hunt" since the starting position is 4 followed by
// the length of 4, meaning 4 characters are stored in the new string.
```

In another example, let's extract the first part of headhunter, namely, the string head. This is how we would do that:

```
// Warning: not standard C++ code!
String m = "headhunter";
String result = substring ( m,0,4);
```

```
// since 0 is the starting position, we extract the h at the beginning and
// show 4 characters.
```

You can even extract a string of one character. Look at this example:

```
// Warning: not standard C++ code!
String m = "headhunter";
String result = substring ( m,3,1);
/* since the 3rd slot is the letter d followed by a length of 1, we extract only the
letter d */
```

The third function has two parameters in addition to the string. The third parameter, instead of indicating the length of the newly extracted string, indicates the first slot that will *not* be part of the extraction. That's a mouthful! Let's look at an example to clarify how this works:

```
// Warning: not standard C++ code!
String m = "headhunter";
String result = substring ( m,4,8);
/* since 4 is the starting position, we extract from slot 4 through slot 7 because 8
is the first slot we wish to exclude. Result will contain "hunt" */
```

Here's another extraction using this same substring function:

```
// Warning: not standard C++ code!
String m = "headhunter";
String result = substring ( m,2,9);
/* since 2 is the starting position, we extract from slot 2 through slot 8 because 9
is the first slot we wish to exclude. Result will contain "adhunte"
*/
```

Strings are objects in C++, so it is easier to wait until you learn something about objects to address how the syntax changes.

Find and CharAt

Just like the previous functions, we can't really use the precise C++ code to call them, but at least we can look at what each of these functions does.

The find function will take a string, call it firstString, and look for the occurrence of another string, called otherString, within it.

If it finds otherString within the firstString string, it will return the slot (the index) where that string begins. If it does not find the string, it will return −1.

Look at this typical find function heading:

```
// Warning: not Standard C++ code
int find ( String firstString, String otherString);
```

Let's look at an example to see how it works.

```
// Warning: not standard C++ code!
String firstString = "foolhardy";
String otherString = "hard";
int x = find(firstString, otherString);
cout << x << endl;
/* 4 will be printed on the screen. */
```

In another example, let's pass in a string that is not in firstString.

```
// Warning: not standard C++ code!
String firstString = "foolhardy";
String otherString = "day";
int x = find(firstString, otherString);
cout << x << endl;
/* -1 will be printed on the screen. */
```

Obviously, "day" is not contained in the word "foolhardy", so the negative 1 passed into the x is clearly not an index value, since those values begin at zero.

Note

Negative 1 is a typical value used to indicate that something unusual has happened to an array, and likewise, a string. Arrays usually start with the 0 index and continue through the positive numbers. The negative 1 as a return value is a clever way of signaling that a problem has occurred.

String functions are very *precise*. Words like day and Day will not be considered the same because of the difference in the d's. Nor will day be found within Day.

charAt is a simple function that allows you to extract a character from a string. It behaves like the substring function where the length is always 1. Let's look at an example:

```
// Warning: not standard C++ code!
String m = "foolhardy";
char letter = charAt(m,6);
cout << letter << endl;
/* r will be printed on the screen. */
```

charAt is easier to use than the substring function we used previously. Even easier to use is the following overloaded operator: the brace set.

The Brace Set Operator

The last function we will examine is the brace set, which works directly on a string. The brace set represents another overloaded operator. We have seen the brace set before in accessing array elements—list[5], for example. By over-loading this operator, we are making the string as accessible as the arrays we studied. Look at how simple it is to use:

```
// Warning: not standard C++ code!
String m = "foolhardy";
cout << m[5] << endl;
/* The letter a will be printed on the screen. */
```

Here's a better example of the braces at work:

```
// Warning: not standard C++ code!
String m = "foolhardy";
String otherString = "hard";
for( x = 0; x < m.length( ); x++)
cout << m[x] << endl;
/* Each letter is printed on a separate line. */
```

Of course, it is easier to just print out a string all at once. But the brace operator allows you to treat the string like the array type.

Summary

The string is like an array of characters. In any language, there are string functions available to you. In C++ and Java, the string is an object, so objects call functions differently from the way we have studied function calls. We examined typical string functions like length, substring, find, charAt and two overloaded operators: + and [ ].

The + allows two strings to be combined or concatenated. The substring function extracts a string from another string. length will find the length of the string—this is the number of characters in the string, including any blanks or punctuation. find allows you to find the first occurrence of one string within another. If the string is not found, a value like –1 will be returned. charAt extracts a single character from a string. Finally, the brace set allows the string to be manipulated in the same way as an array.

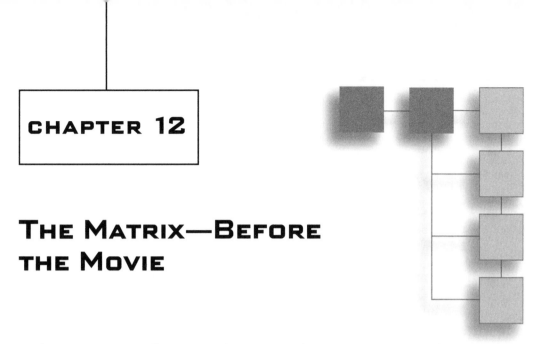

CHAPTER 12

THE MATRIX—BEFORE THE MOVIE

In this chapter, we will examine the *matrix*, which is an interesting data structure. It is a two-dimensional holder for variables and is best understood as a grid or table. You will learn how to assign values to each spot in the matrix as well as learn how to retrieve values already stored in it. The last thing we will examine is the diagonal—an important part of the matrix.

In This Chapter

- The grid of rows and columns

- Loading one row at a time

- Nested `for` loops

- Manipulating a matrix

- The diagonal of a matrix

The Matrix as a Grid

Now that we have studied the array, it would be good to examine the *matrix*, which is the name given to any multi-dimensional array. You might recall from an algebra II class the word "matrix." Matrices look like grids. See Figure 12.1.

Figure 12.1
A two-dimensional grid with three rows and four columns.

Each slot in the grid has a numbered location, and this is why matrices are a good place to store data. See Figure 12.2.

Each of the locations is unique because of the row and column, which vary for each slot. Look at slot 1,1 and think of it as the first member in the first row and first column. If you look at the slot just to the right of it, it is numbered 1,2. You can think of this as the second member in the first row. Slot 1,3 is the third member in the first row. If you skip down to slot 3,1 you can think of this member as the first member in the third row.

Now let's give a name to this matrix, just as we gave a name to the arrays we examined. We could call it Student. See Figure 12.3 for one interpretation of the grid. Note that the grid serves to illustrate how the values in a matrix are organized.

Each student is identified by the two numbers, which could represent where they sit in the class. Student 1,1 is the first student in the first row while Student 2,1 is the first student in the second row. Then Student 3,2 must be the second student in the third row. See Figure 12.4.

As mentioned earlier, computers lack imagination. It's easier to use numbers to identify elements than individual names.

1,1	1,2	1,3	1,4
2,1	2,2	2,3	2,4
3,1	3,2	3,3	3,4

Figure 12.2
Each slot has a unique location: its row followed by its column.

Student1,1	Student1,2	Student1,3	Student1,4
Student2,1	Student2,2	Student2,3	Student2,4
Student3,1	Student3,2	Student3,3	Student3,4

Figure 12.3
The grid is shown filled with different students identified by their row and column.

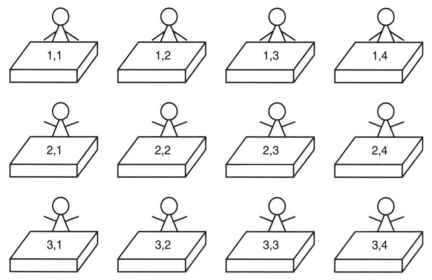

Figure 12.4
Each student is sitting at a different desk and identified by location instead of name.

When we studied the array, we looked at each part of the array as a separate numbered slot with a common name. Do you recall how we called one array group? Each of the members were named group[1], group[2], group[3], group[4], and so on. The nice thing about the array was that we could easily distinguish among the different group members because of the subscript attached.

Think of all the friends you have with the same name Mike, for example. I have a lot of friends named Mike. The way I think of each Mike in my head is to distinguish each one: I think of the Mike who takes the same math class as I do, the Mike I work with, the Mike who is my cousin, and the Mike I met over the summer. In computer programming, these distinctions are made as a matter of fact and with less description: Mike1, Mike2, Mike3, Mike4, and so on, and these would be written as follows:

```
Mike[1]
Mike[2]
Mike[3]
Mike[4]
```

So the array we talked about previously in Chapter 8 is a nice way of recognizing that there is a common name for the variable holders, but each holder is also unique.

Before we look at the matrix in computer terms, let's examine it from the perspective of algebra.

The Matrix

The *matrix* is a grid where each slot has a unique location, and the location is numbered according to where it is in the grid. A matrix is a really nice holder for data. It allows several values to be stored in one place under a common name that reminds us that the data is grouped together.

In algebra II, matrices are often used to store coefficients of variables in equations. The matrix is a great storage facility. It can be used to calculate the determinant. Whether you have learned this yet or not, the neat thing is that understanding what a matrix is in computer programming will make it easier for you to understand its use in algebra.

Let's revisit the Student matrix we talked about.

Note

In most computer languages, a matrix has a row 0 and a column 0. We have ignored that to simplify the discussion. See the programs on the CD for examples of those matrices.

Let's look at how each member would be named in a computer language.

Name	Computer Name
Student 1,1	Student[1][1]
Student 1,2	Student [1][2]
Student 1,3	Student [1][3]
Student 1,4	Student [1][4]

As you can see, the first subscript is 1 and the second changes from 1 to 4. As a matter of uniformity, the first number represents the *row* number while the second number represents the *column* number. So when you declare a matrix to the computer (compiler), you tell the computer how many rows and how many columns your matrix will have using the same brackets we used when we declared an array.

[3][4]

So now the matrix has three rows and four columns, like we discussed.

In each of the examples that follow, we will make different declarations for different matrices. It requires a special declaration, just like the array we studied previously. If you recall with the array, we had to state the name or identifier and then how many members it would have and what type of data it would hold:

```
int list [10];
```

This array is a declaration of 10 members holding integers and all with the common name of list. The matrix will follow a similar syntax:

```
int group [6][4];
```

Here we have a 6 by 4 matrix that will hold integers and will have the name group.

Here's another example of the Student matrix we discussed previously:

```
String Student [3][4];
```

So the Student matrix has three rows and four columns, and each holder will contain a string. Think of the string as the name of each student sitting in the class at the assigned seat.

Consider this example:

```
double Prices [5][5];
```

This represents a 5 by 5 matrix with the name Prices and containing doubles (real numbers).

How Does Storage Work?

So with the previous examples, we have informed the computer what kind of data holder we need and how many slots of memory we need as well. In the example with the Student matrix, the computer has to set aside enough storage to hold 12 different strings. Each string will take a fixed number of bytes for storage, so 12 of those strings will take 12 times that number bytes of memory. Recall that that is the most important reason for declaration of variables: we need to tell the computer how much memory it should set aside, or *allocate*, for the data we have.

In the other example, where we declared the group matrix, we needed to have 24 slots, all with the common name of group and each holding an integer. If each integer needs 2 bytes for storage, then 24 of those integers will take 48 bytes of storage, and the computer will look for 48 sequential free bytes once the declaration has been made (and the program starts to compile).

Loading One Row at a Time

Consider this example where we will load the following:

```
int group[6][4];
```

We know we have six rows and four columns. Let's start by loading the first row only. And, to make things easier, let's put the same number into each member of the first row, like this:

	Col 1	Col 2	Col 3	Col 4
Row 1	group [1][1]	group [1][2]	group [1][3]	group [1][4]
Data inside	5	5	5	5

If we were to load the row manually, we would have to write this code:

```
          Row Col
group[1][1] = 5;
group[1][2] = 5;
group[1][3] = 5;
group[1][4] = 5;
```

So instead of typing each member separately, let's use a for loop to hit each of the members in row 1.

Here is the for loop that will do that.

```
for (int x = 1; x <= 4; x++ )
{
group[1][x] = 5;
}
```

I have only used one for loop just so that we can see that we are only loading row 1 across. Notice that I referred to the row as group[1][x]. The reason I did this was because I wanted to stay in row 1, and then move across each of its columns to load each member in that row. The x represents the changing column.

It is helpful to keep the classroom seating plan in mind as we work with the matrix. Let's try to load all the members who are sitting in row 2, and let's load those members with the same number. Let's put the number 10 into each member of the second row.

	Col 1	Col 2	Col 3	Col 4
Row 2	group[2][1]	group[2][2]	group[2][3]	group[2][4]
Data inside	10	10	10	10

If we were to load the row manually, it would look like this:

```
        Row Col
group[2][1] = 10;
group[2][2] = 10;
group[2][3] = 10;
group[2][4] = 10;
```

We can now use the same code as before with only a couple of alterations: changing the row we are interested in loading, as well as the number we want to store into the matrix.

```
for(int x = 1; x <= 4; x++ )
{
group[2][x] = 10;
}
```

On the CD

See each of these examples written in Java, which uses the 0 subscript.

Nested For Loops

Before we examine the array further, let's look at nested for loops, which will prove very useful in working with a matrix. There are two loops in a nested for loop: the inner loop and the outer loop. To understand the two loops better, let's examine a bicycle and its gears.

The Bicycle Gear Analogy

Think of the outer and inner loops as gears in a bike. On a 10-speed, you have two outer gears and five inner gears. You set the outer gear to one of two choices. The smaller one is for hills, and the bigger one is for flat riding. You have a choice of five different speeds for the inner gear and two different speeds for the outer gear.

Let's say you want to test all 10 speeds that the bike has. You decide that you will methodically test them in an organized sequential manner. So you decide to set the outer speed to the hill setting, and then try each of the inner gears with that hill gear.

This is a list of the speeds that you are testing:

The *hill* gear with the inner gear #1

The *hill* gear with the inner gear #2

The *hill* gear with the inner gear #3

The *hill* gear with the inner gear #4

The *hill* gear with the inner gear #5

Notice how the hill gear does not change, while the inner gear does change. This will be important when we look at nested loops. We have methodically exhausted all of the inner gears with one of the outer gears set. Now if we change the outer gear to the flat surface gear, we can do the same process again and test five more speeds on the bike.

This is a list of the rest of the speeds you are testing:

The *flat* surface gear with the inner gear #1

The *flat* surface gear with the inner gear #2

The *flat* surface gear with the inner gear #3

The *flat* surface gear with the inner gear #4

The *flat* surface gear with the inner gear #5

Notice how the flat gear doesn't change at all as we change the inner gears. So for each outer gear, we used five different choices for the inner gear.

Let's summarize what the different possibilities for each gear were:

Outer	Inner
hill	1,2,3,4,5
flat	1,2,3,4,5

For each outer gear, the inner gear had five different choices. As we test each choice of the inner gear, we make a complete "spin" through the options. What do I mean by this? For example, the outer gear was in the hill setting, while the inner gear spins from 1 through 5.

Applying the Loops

Let's write some pseudo code to represent the gear settings on the bike. Recall that pseudo code is not real code—just an approximation of real code.

```
for ( x = hill setting; x <= flat setting; x++)
for ( y = 1st gear; y < 6; y++)
     Test gear.
```

Look at the preceding code. The outer loop with the variable x will be set to the hill gear, and then the compiler will enter the inner loop because that is contained within the body of the x loop. But there is another loop inside the x loop, and that is the y loop. Since the y loop is completely contained within the x loop, the y loop will spin completely from 1 to 5. Once the y variable hits 6, the y loop will stop executing and control will bounce back up to the last statement of the x loop, x++, where x's value will change from hill gear to flat gear.

Once the x variable changes and is checked to be valid (that is, the boolean statement is true), then the y loop is entered again and the y value is set to 1 as it was the first time.

This is how the other five speeds get set. So now all five speeds will be paired with the x value of flat gear.

Our next step is to examine a matrix and to use what we call *nested* for loops to load the matrix. The term nested means that we will put one for loop inside the other. Before I explain what this does, look at this code:

```
for ( int x = 1; x <= 5; x++ )
    for ( int y = 1; y <= 4; y++)
      {
      group[x][y] = 5;
      }
```

The loop that we see first is called the *outer* loop. The loop that is second is called the *inner* loop. The way I like to think of the outer loop is that it is the driver of the inner loop. The outer loop engages the inner loop in the same way that a driver engages the shift to cause the gears to engage. So let's watch the computer step by step to see what I mean when I say that the outer loop controls the inner loop.

```
for ( int x = 1; x <= 5; x++ )
// the outer loop sets x to the value of 1
//then the inner loop starts to spin:
    for ( int y = 1; y <= 4; y++)
```

```
{
group[x][y] = 5;
// remember that x has the value of 1.
}
```

So the outer loop sets x to 1, and then the inner loop starts to spin. The inner loop will spin, and y will go from 1 to 4. Look at this chart of values of the variables:

x	y
1	no value
1	1
1	2
1	3
1	4
2	

On the last line, we see that x becomes 2, and the inner loop that controls y will start to spin again. Now look at the chart with the variables:

x	y
1	no value
1	1
1	2
1	3
1	4
2	no value
2	1
2	2
2	3
2	4

So what happens is the outer loop holds its value, while the inner loop spins through all its values. The entire execution of both loops looks like this:

x	y
1	no value
1	1
1	2
1	3
1	4
	5

y becomes 5, and so the value is too big for the loop condition to be true. The y loop stops. The x loop then changes its value from 1 to 2 and executes again.

Because the y loop is inside the x loop, the y loop starts to spin again.

x	y
2	1
2	2
2	3
2	4
	5

Notice that y again changes its value to 5, and its boolean condition is not true.

Also notice that, while the y variable is changing its value, the x value is not changing at all. This is because the end of the x loop has not been reached. Its value cannot be increased until all its statements within are executed. Notice that the statements inside the x loop are the body of the y loop.

x	y
3	
3	1
3	2
3	3
3	4
	5
4	
4	1
4	2
4	3
4	4
	5
5	
5	1
5	2
5	3
5	4

How to Store Data in a Matrix

Now that our declarations have been made, let's consider how we might store data into each slot of the matrix. When we worked with the array, we used a for loop to load each slot of the array. We will do the same thing with our matrix, except that we will need *two* for loops to load all the members of the matrix.

```
for ( int x = 1; x <= 5; x++ )
{
// the outer loop sets x to the value of 1
//then the inner loop starts to spin:
    for ( int y = 1; y <= 4; y++)
      {
      cout << << Please type a value for each slot.";
      cin>> group[x][y];
      // remember that x has the value of 1.
      } // closes the y loop
}// closes the x loop
```

How to Retrieve Data from a Matrix

Now that we have loaded a matrix, let's check to see that everything we put into the matrix got sent in correctly. Let's start by checking row 1 of the group matrix to see if the first row contains 5s.

We want to print out the contents of row 1. These four statements will show row 1.

```
cout << group[1][1] <<"   ";
cout << group[1][2] <<"   ";
cout << group[1][3] <<"   ";
cout << group[1][4] <<"   ";
```

It will look like this:

```
5   5   5   5
```

Let's follow the previous code with a line feed and the next four print statements

```
cout << endl;
cout << group[2][1] <<"   ";
cout << group[2][2] <<"   ";
cout << group[2][3] <<"   ";
cout << group[2][4] <<"   ";
```

So now all nine lines will produce the following output—the 5s from the first row, a line feed, and the 10s from the second row.

```
5  5  5  5
10  10  10  10
```

If we had not put the `cout << endl` statement in the code, all the numbers would appear on one line like this:

```
5  5  5  5  10  10  10  10
```

Now let's take the previous code and replace it with two `for` loops:

```
for ( int x = 1: x <= 4; x++ )
{
cout << group[1][x] <<"  ";
}
cout << endl;
for ( int x = 1: x <= 4; x++ )
{
cout << group[2][x] <<"  ";
}
```

Each loop spins through its row and prints each member. We could write three additional loops to print the other rows, but it will be easier to employ the nested loops we studied in the previous section. Look at this code:

```
for ( int x = 1; x <= 5; x++ )
{
    for ( int y = 1; y <= 4; y++)
      {
      cout << group[x][y]<<"  ";
      }
cout << endl; //This line feed puts each row on a separate line
}
```

Manipulating a Matrix

There are many ways to manipulate a matrix once it has been assigned values. We will look at some examples in this section. One of the main alterations you can make to a matrix is to change the values in one row or column. Another thing you can do is work with the diagonal of a matrix. These are a few ways you can manipulate a matrix.

The Diagonal

First we need to define a square matrix. As its name suggests, it is a matrix with the same number of rows and columns, so it looks like a square. The diagonal is the diagonal line running through it from top-left to bottom-right. See Figure 12.5.

The diagonal members of a matrix are also interesting because of their locations. Look at the same matrix, but this time look at the locations rather than the contents. See Figure 12.6.

1	0	0	0
0	1	0	0
0	0	1	0
0	0	0	1

Figure 12.5
Each member along the diagonal in this square matrix has the value 1, while the other members have 0.

1,1	1,2	1,3	1,4
2,1	2,2	2,3	2,4
3,1	3,2	3,3	3,4
4,1	4,2	4,3	4,4

Figure 12.6
All of the locations of the matrix are given. Notice how the diagonal locations have matching rows and columns.

If you want to access the values along the diagonal of a matrix, you insert a boolean condition inside the nested for loop. Consider this example:

```
for ( int x = 1; x <= 4; x++ )
{
      for ( int y = 1; y <= 4; y++)
        {
        If ( x == y)
        cout << box[x][y]<< "   ";
        }
}
```

Notice that both x and y have an upper limit value, which is 4, indicating that the matrix is a square matrix. The boolean condition, if x equals y, allows the programmer to select the member along the diagonal. The other members are ignored.

How to Change an Individual Row or Column of a Matrix

In order to alter a particular row or column, you need to spin a loop that holds that column or row "fixed." To see what I mean by this, let's return to a previous example where we loaded one row, row 1, of the group matrix. Recall that the group matrix was a 6 by 4 matrix of integers. This information will be useful when we change a column instead of a row.

```
for (int x = 1; x <= 4; x++ )
{
group[1][x] = 5;
}
```

Notice that the row index, always the first index, is fixed at 1. It is only the column index that is changing. The x is being used as the variable that controls the column position. Right now each member of row 1 is being assigned the value 5. Let's change the code so that we set all the values in row 1 to have the value 8.

```
for (int x = 1; x <= 4; x++ )
{
group[1][x] = 8; // we only had to change this line!
}
```

Let's say you wanted to change row 4 instead of row 1. We will change the fixed row from 1 to 4. Here is the code that accomplishes that:

```
for (int x = 1; x <= 4; x++ )
{
group[4][x] = 10;
}
```

As you can see, we are assigning the value 10 to all the members of row 4.

Look at the next example where we print all the members of row 5.

```
for (int x = 1; x <= 4; x++ )
{
cout << group[5][x] <<"   ";
}
```

The only thing remaining to do is to alter a column. Let's put the value 4 into all the slots in column 3. Think of it this way: we need to fix the column and move down the column from row 1 to row 6. In order to do that, we have to change the for loop we are using to one that will target all the rows. Remember it is a 6 by 4 matrix. Look at this example:

```
for (int x = 1; x <= 6; x++ )
{
group[x][3] = 4;
}
```

Notice that column 3, as the second subscript, does not change. Only the rows change, since we have to move down the rows in column 3.

Summary

In this chapter, we learned about the matrix, a two-dimensional grid, which has a certain number of rows and columns. The matrix is ideally assigned through the use of nested for loops—one for loop inside of another. By using nested for loops, we can move through every member of the matrix. We examined the analogy of the gears on a bicycle, since holding one gear while changing the other is very similar to the way nested for loops work. After practicing some examples of assigning and printing the contents of the matrix, we also manipulated individual rows and columns as well as the diagonal of a square matrix.

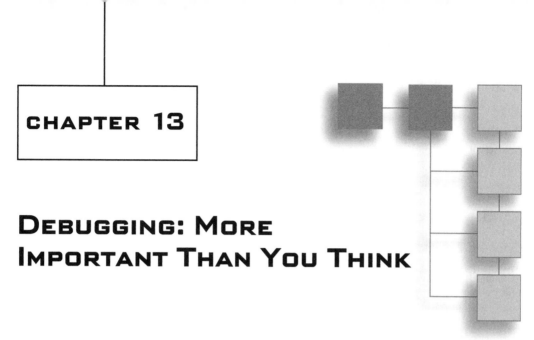

CHAPTER 13

DEBUGGING: MORE IMPORTANT THAN YOU THINK

Debugging is the name given to the process of finding errors in programs when they don't run. One of the most frustrating experiences in programming is to spend a lot of time writing a program, then having it run, but not get the results you expect and wonder why that happened. Before I talk about the necessary steps in debugging, let's start by classifying the types of errors that are typically found in programs. Once you understand the differences among these three errors, you will better understand how to find the errors associated with each.

In This Chapter

- Definition of debugging

- Syntax, run-time, and logic errors

- How to debug

- Tracing

Three Types of Errors

There are three types of errors you get when you run a program: syntax errors, logic errors, and run-time errors. Let's look at definitions and examples of each so that we can learn how to eliminate those errors through debugging techniques.

Syntax Errors

Syntax errors are the easiest errors to spot, since you will probably have the aid of a compiler to spot them. Even if you don't have a compiler, you'll probably have some aid in checking the syntax. A *syntax* error is a grammar error. Just as you can make a mistake when you misuse English grammar, you can make a mistake in the grammar of the language in which you are programming.

Let's look at the typical syntax errors that programmers make.

Spelling Errors

If you misspell a word in a computer language—specifically, a reserved word that has a built-in purpose in the language—you will get a syntax error. For example, look at the following misspellings:

nit instead of not

Lete instead of Let

newe instead of new

A computer has no innate intelligence. It will not examine your misspelled word and think you must have meant the word "new" instead of the "newe" that you wrote (unless you program it to do so!).

Punctuation Errors

Punctuation errors can be harder to spot, unless you like looking at small exacting code. Here are a few examples:

```
x = x + 1.
```

instead of

```
x = x + 1;
```

```
if (y < 6
cout << "hello";
```

instead of

```
if (y < 6)
cout << "hello";
```

In the first example, the final period (.) should have been a semicolon (;). In the second example, there should have been parentheses on both sides of the boolean condition (y < 6), instead of only on one side.

The compiler will help you to find these simple errors because it is easy for a machine to spot symbolic differences. It will be harder for the compiler to find other errors, though, like run-time errors and logic errors.

Tip

> It's best to correct the first error caught by the compiler and then test your program again (recompile) rather than trying to correct multiple errors all at once. Why? Any code later in the program that depends on data related to the earlier error will probably also generate an error.

Run-Time Errors

Run-time errors are errors that arise *while* a program is running, that is, they are discovered only as the program runs. They are not easy to spot because they are not syntax or grammar errors, which the compiler can spot easily. They are subtle errors and develop in the course of the program's execution.

The typical run-time error is the division-by-zero error. If you write a program, for example, where you are trying to calculate the average of some number of test scores, you might have a program fragment written like this:

```
x = x + 1;
y = sum / x;
cout << y << endl;
```

Notice how x was changed just before being used in the division statement. Unless you know that x is always positive (and, therefore, greater than zero), you can't assume that at some point x would not take on the zero value, causing this algebraic problem:

```
y = sum / 0
```

Yikes! Some compilers might even recognize this error, but you should recognize it first. Here is how you can amend your program code:

```
x = x + 1;
if (x != 0)
{
y = sum / x;
cout << y << endl;
}
```

A simple statement like if (x != 0) will go a long way in helping you to program more cleanly and efficiently.

Logic Errors

Logic errors are the most difficult to spot because programs that contain logic errors have no problems running and are never spotted by compilers. A logic error is the type of error that only the programmer can recognize. He runs his program, gets results, but knows that his program did not do what he wanted it to do. So the program did not execute his logic or his thinking. (It's really his fault, but he doesn't know that yet).

Let's look at a typical logic error and then address how we can fix it.

Here's a program fragment where you compute the average of three test scores, and then you print the result:

```
num_scores = 3;
cout << "Please type in your three test scores: ";
cin >> a >> b >> c ;
average = (a + b + c)/ num_scores;
cout << "The average is" << num_scores << endl;
```

So what's wrong with this fragment? There are cout and cin statements and the grammar is correct. What will happen when you run this fragment? You will always get a 3 printed on the screen. You might try typing in different values for test scores, but you will start to notice that you always see a 3 on the screen.

It might seem really easy to you and not worth mentioning, but the error is a very simple one to overlook. It is the last cout statement that causes the logic error. We should have printed the variable average, not the variable num_scores. That's where the logic error is. See Figure 13.1.

So how do we avoid the logic error? The easiest way to do so is to trace through your program by putting some output statements in judicious places. Output statements will allow you, the programmer, to see what is happening *while* it is happening to help you better understand what the error is. Look at the same program fragment, except this time you will see some additional output statements.

```
num_scores = 3;
cout << "The value of num_scores is " << num_scores << endl;

cout << "Please type in your three test scores: ";
cin >> a >> b >> c ;
cout << a << " " << b << " " << c << endl;
average = (a + b + c)/ num_scores;
```

```
cout << average << endl;
cout << "The average is" << num_scores << endl;
```

Figure 13.1
The programmer thinks of different test scores but notices that the screen always shows the number 3, which makes no sense to him.

The additional output lines will help the programmer realize that he made a mistake in the last output statement where he should have printed `average` instead of `num_scores`.

It's a good habit to use print statements to help yourself "see" what the computer is doing, in a sense. Of course, if the development platform you use (that is, Visual Basic) has a debugger, you'll want to use that as well.

What Are Debuggers?

Debuggers are an additional utility (or tool) that come with your programming language. They allow you to stop or halt program execution in progress. This is a very powerful tool because you can get a window into what the compiler is doing as it runs your program. You can often see what values are in your program, and you can watch them as they are changing. This proves to be very useful, since it is often the unexpected value of a variable that causes an error for a programmer.

So whether you have a debugger or not, you can simulate what a debugger does by adding a few output statements to your program. These statements act as windows into your program. They allow you to see the values of variables and how they are changing.

As you learn more about how to organize your program, and as your programs increase in size and complexity, it is important to know how to debug well. Otherwise, you will spend a lot of time and frustration trying to find out what went wrong.

Tracing Through a Loop

A lot of problems in programming arise when using a loop. A loop always changes the value of the control variable. One good idea is to put an output statement into a loop so you can watch the values of the variable as it changes during the loop's execution. Here is an example:

```
for ( x = 1; x < 25 ; x ++ )
{
average = sum / x;
cout << "x has this value: "<< x << endl;
cout << "The average is now "<< average << endl;
}
```

In the preceding example, the two output statements make it easy to see that both x and average are changing. It might seem like a trivial thing to do, but it helps a lot.

Here is another example of using a trace inside a loop (a while loop):

```
while ( x < 25 )
{
average = sum / x;
cout << "x has this value: "<< x << endl;
cout << "The average is now "<< average << endl;
x = x + 1;
}
```

Consider what would happen in this badly written fragment:

```
cin >> x; // x's value is set by the user.
while ( x != 25 )
{
average = sum / x;
cout << "has this value: "<< x << endl;
cout << "The average is now" << average << endl;
x = x + 1;
}
```

There are a few problems that you might have spotted. The value x was set by the user, and then it is used as the control variable of the loop. The programmer has no control over its initial value. Secondly, the boolean condition of the loop is too general—allowing the loop to spin simply when x does not equal 25 is not as specific as it should be. We need to stick with a more restricted comparison: x < 25, and so on.

Tracing Through a Function

As your programming becomes more complex, you will have to watch values of variables as they are being passed into a function. You might need to put some output statements before and after entering a function.

In Chapter 8, you learned about functions and how they are designed to do work outside of the main section of a program. Look at how we have used some output statements to clarify the values of the variables as we run the program:

```
int main ( )
{ int x, result;
cout << "Please type a number for which we will find the square. "<< endl;
cin >> x;
// cout << x << endl; We put this here to see x's value
result = square ( x );
cout << "The result of the function is "<< result << endl;
}

int Square ( int m )
{
// cout << m << endl; we check the value of m
int ans = m * m;
// cout << ans;
return ans;
}
```

By inserting these extra output statements, you can check your program each step of the way to make sure that it is working properly. We are simulating what a debugger does—it allows you to stop and view variables and their values at intermediate points.

Sometimes you have to clarify a variable's value if it is changing both *within* and *outside* of a function. Here is a suggestion of how to clarify those changes. If you have the same variable that you are passing back and forth, use descriptive statements that indicate where you are in the program. For example:

```
cout << "The value of x inside the alpha function is " << x << endl;
```

or

```
cout << "The value of x just after leaving the alpha function is " << x << endl;
```

A few statements like the ones in this chapter will be extremely helpful to you as you continue to program.

Summary

A debugger is a program that you can use to help you find *bugs*, or mistakes, in your program. There are three types of common errors in programming: syntax, run-time, and logic errors. Syntax errors are the easiest ones to find. The compiler will spot the grammar error right away. Run-time errors only develop as a program is running, so they are not found by the compiler. Logic errors are the most difficult to find because only the programmer knows whether she did the right thing or not as far as her intent. Adding output statements as a way of watching the variables' values is a good technique for debugging. Using the existing debuggers with your language application is the best.

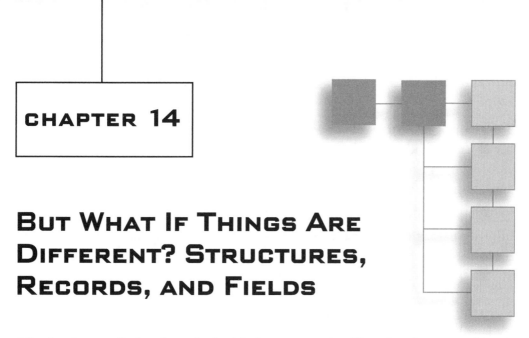

CHAPTER 14

But What If Things Are Different? Structures, Records, and Fields

After having studied and worked with the array, you will notice that something is lacking in our exploration of data structures. That is, we do not have any type that can hold *mixed* types (like something that could hold both an integer and a string at the same time). That is why we introduce the *record* in this chapter.

In This Chapter

- The limitation of the array

- What to do if you must mix data types

- Definition of the record and its fields

- The struct—short for structure

- Programming with structures and records

- What can you do now?

- One step further—arrays of records and structures

Beyond the Array: The Record

Once you have seen the standard data types—integer, real, character, string, and boolean—you are ready to design your own data types. This includes the array, whereby you can declare a collection of one type. Now we can introduce the *record*, which allows you to create a collection of different types.

The record is used to hold various data. If you want to keep track of information about an individual, such as her name, age, and grade point average (gpa), a record would be a good choice to hold this data. The name would be a string, the age, an integer, and the gpa, a real number (because of the decimal).

Think of the record as a box into which you throw different things. Unlike the bureau analogy (used for the array in Chapter 9) where you only put clothing items into the bureau, the box, an analogy we use for the record, can hold anything that we define for it.

How to Design a Record

The first thing to consider about a record is what types of data you would like to put inside of it. In our previous example, we grouped together a string, an integer, and a real number for a record that keeps information about an individual (probably a student). Let's give names to each of these types:

```
string   name;
int    age;
double g_p_a;   /*recall that variable names do not have any
periods in them. You will soon see why. */
```

The preceding declaration shows each of these variables declared separately. The purpose of the record, however, is to group these variables together into *one new variable* of the record type.

Defining a Record

Before you define a record, you need to think of a good name for the record's contents. Let's name our record individual for the information we just mentioned. The syntax for declaring a record will include braces { } to show where the record begins and ends. Here is an example of a declaration in the programming language C++. A record in C++ is called a *struct*, short for "structure," which suggests that you are building something—in this case, something unique.

```
struct individual
{

// the different data types go in here
}; // the semicolon ends the declaration
```

This is just a skeleton of a definition. We have not finished it yet. Inside the braces, we will *declare* the internal variables of the record—each of which is called a *field* of the struct (record).

```
struct individual
{
string name;
int age;
double g_p_a;
// the different data types go in here
}; // the semicolon ends the declaration
```

individual is the name of a box with three things inside of it—an individual's name, age, and gpa. See Figure 14.1.

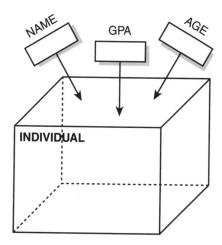

A Box Symbolizing a Record

Figure 14.1
A box is shown with the name "individual" on the outside. Inside it are the name, age, and gpa fields.

Reserved Words

Reserved words in any language (sometimes called *keywords*) are words set aside because they have special meanings in the language. When the compiler (or interpreter) encounters a reserved word, it will translate it according to the meaning already associated with it. Let's consider this brief list of reserved words that would be common to most programming languages: *for, do, while, and,* and *or.*

Because these words have been reserved, a programmer will avoid using them as a choice for a variable name. Now that you have the skills to create your own variable types as well as names, it is important you understand that you cannot use these words for variable names in your programs. The compiler, when it encounters a reserved word, will start to execute the command or commands associated with that word. If the compiler sees the word *for*, it will assume that there is a loop that must be executed. This is just one example, and it is the main reason why you cannot choose a reserved word as either a variable type or variable name.

Declaring One or More Records

Once you have defined the record, you are ready to declare one or more records. When you declare a record, you will be telling the compiler that a variable of type `individual` now exists. Remember—because of the declaration you made to the compiler—a new type, `individual`, now exists for the duration of that program (this is in addition to the standard types, `int`, `char`, `double`, and so on. Let's declare two variables of type `individual`.

```
individual first_person, second_person;
/* Individual is not boldfaced because we want to emphasize that it is not a
reserved word. */
```

Once you have declared these two new variables, the compiler will set aside memory for each variable, which includes memory for each of its fields. The name you give that `individual` is the variable name.

Distinguishing Among the Record's Type, the Record Variable, and the Fields

The most difficult part of dealing with records (called structs in C++) is the confusion that arises from all the variable names that are part of the definition. Let's take a moment to clarify what each variable name, struct (record) name, and type refers to.

When a record is *defined*, the compiler is informed what it will contain and, as a result, sets aside the appropriate memory for everything that it contains. Each internal variable (each *field*) has its own type and memory requirements. Each record has to be given a name to identify it as a new type. That way, a later declaration of the type is possible. Let's examine two different type records with similarities.

A `struct` that contains two strings and one character will be used to define a person's first name, middle initial, and last name. That `struct` will be given the name `identity`. `identity` represents a new type. (Recall that C++ is a case-sensitive language, so `identity` must begin with a small letter—even when it appears at the beginning of a sentence.)

```
"struct" indicates a new type      type name // like int, char, etc.
         ↓                                    ↓
      struct                         identity // struct definition begins here
   {
      string           first_name;
        ↑                  ↑
     field type      field variable name
      string           last_name;
        ↑                  ↑
     field type      field variable name
       char             mid_init;
        ↑                  ↑
     field type      field variable name
   };
```

Another `struct` will be defined with an integer and two strings—the integer for the apartment number and the strings for the street address and city. (We assume all these locations are for people who live in apartments.) This `struct` represents a new type called `location`. For the duration of the program, we have seven types available—an `int`, `string`, `double`, `char`, `boolean`, `identity`, or `location`.

```
struct location
{
int apt_no;
string street;
string city;
};
```

Defining a `struct` in C++ allows us to create a new type. This `struct` is really just a collection of variables—usually grouped together for clarity in the design of a program. In the `identity` type, two strings and a char are used to represent the full name of a person. The `location` type has an integer and two strings to represent a complete address. When you declare variables of these types, you declare them in the same manner that you declare any variables—you state the type first followed by the variable names. Let's declare some variables of type `identity` and `location`.

```
identity  first_individ, second_individ;
location address1, address2;
```

So four variables have just been declared, and all of them are, as yet, unassigned. These variables would be declared alongside other variables used in the program, as in this example:

```
int x;
char initial;
identity  first_individ, second_individ;
location address1, address2;
```

How to Assign Record Variables

When you assign any record variable, you need to assign each field of the record. The record is, essentially, a group of other variables—the fields. When you assign a record or struct, you are really assigning its fields. It is important both to recognize the field *name* and to distinguish it from the field *type*. In order to assign a record, we focus on the field name in the assignment statement. Consider this example where we *partially* assign three fields from an `identity` type.

```
first_name = "Mike";
last_name = "Smith";
mid_init = 'T';
```

In order to complete the assignment statement, we need to use the *variable name* of the `identity` type. In that way, we will be communicating to the compiler that we understand the connection between the field name and the new type. First we need to examine the meaning of a *delimiter*, which will allow us to make this connection for the compiler. Using a delimiter, we will access the field names through the variable name.

Using a Delimiter

A *delimiter* is a punctuation symbol used to get access to an internal part of a larger part. In the case of a record or struct, the record or struct is the larger part, and the field is the smaller part. The delimiter is used to connect the variable name to the field name. When you want to access the fields, you use the variable name that was declared, followed by a delimiter, and then the field name. You can use this sequence in an assignment statement or any other acceptable statement for the variable.

Let's look at an example using the variable name, first_individual, and one of its fields—first_name. We will use the period (.) delimiter between the variable name (the name used for the new type) and the field name.

first_individ.	first_name
variable name	field name

Notice that we have not used the "type" names in this example. Type names are only used for declarations and definitions. Consider the next example, which is a complete assignment statement.

first_individ.	first_name	= "Mike";
variable name	field name	assigned value

In this example we are really assigning the field of the variable. When all the fields of the record have been assigned, then the record is considered assigned, or *loaded*, as I like to say. Let's assign the other fields of this struct.

```
first_individ.last_name = "Smith";
first_individ.mid_init = "T";
```

Note

Periods are often used to separate larger parts from smaller parts. Just consider this fictitious Internet address: www.mycompany.com. Notice how the period is used to separate the company name "mycompany" from the "com," or the entire commercial group of companies on the Web.

Letting the User Assign a Record

The user can assign a struct by responding to the cin statement. We will follow the syntax used in the previous examples. Instead of using an assignment statement with the equals sign operator (=), we will use the cin statement. The user should be given some prompt so that she understands what input she should be typing. Here are some examples using the variable name address_1 followed by all the field names in the location type.

```
cout << "Please type the street address."<< endl;
cin >> address1.street ;
cout << "Please type the city." << endl;
cin >> address1.city;
cout << "Please type the apartment number."<< endl;
cin >> address1.state;
```

Now the record address1 has been completely assigned because all of its fields were assigned. (Remember that when you declared address_1, it acquired all the field names and types associated with the new location type.

The same thing can be done for address2—either the user or the programmer can assign it. Right now, only first_individ and address1 have been assigned; the other two record variables, second_individ and address2, are unassigned. See Figure 14.2.

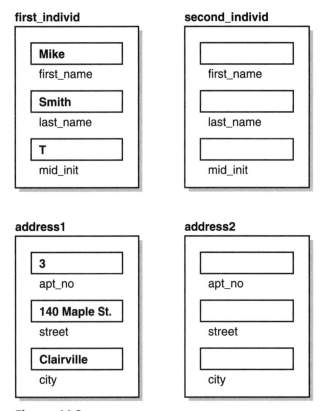

Figure 14.2
A diagram of the four record variables is shown. Either the fields have been assigned, or they have been left blank to show they have no values yet.

Examples of Different Records

Records are very useful for storing information about items with varied data. Think of the inventory in a store for each item sold. A piece of clothing, for example, could have the following fields to describe it.

```
struct item
{
string item_type;//pants? shorts? shoes? etc.
int floor;//floor where item is found
double price;//the price of the item
int percentage;//highest percentage discount allowed on //item
};
```

An item could be a pair of jeans, found on level two of the store, and priced at $48 but with an allowable discount of up to, but no higher than, 50%. Another example is a struct, which contains information about a CD in a music store.

```
struct CD
{
string name;//the name of the CD
string artist;//the artist's name
double price;//price of CD
int year_released;//year CD came out
};
```

An Array of Records

Usually when we define a record, we need it because we are anticipating a program, which requires variables for lots of data. Think about the problem of storing all the pertinent information in a collection of CDs, books, or DVDs. You are not really designing a record data structure because you have only one CD in mind. You are really contemplating storing the data for *all* of your CDs. What we need to define is an *array* of records, where each member of the array is a record. See Figure 14.3.

Defining an Array of Records

We define an array of records just as we would define any array. But first, let's review a definition that we saw previously—the definition of a CD. Let's start by restating that definition, which was a struct.

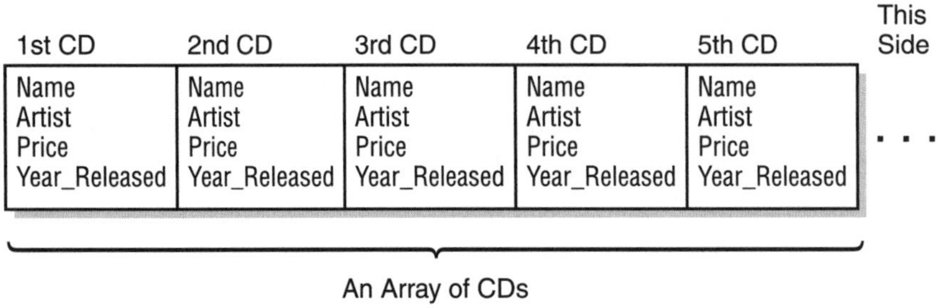

An Array of CDs

Figure 14.3
An array of records is shown where each slot of the array is a record.

```
struct CD
{
string name;//the name of the CD
string artist;//the artist's name
double price;//price of CD
int year_released;//year CD came out
};
```

Next we will declare an array of CDs. The first step is to state the type (CD) followed by the name we wish to give the array followed by brackets with the number of array members inside. Remember that the array declaration is like any other declaration, except that the brackets are used with the *number* of intended members inside.

CD	my_collection	[25];
type	array name	number of members

Each member of the group is a CD struct. Look at this list of variable names on the left and types on the right.

Variable Name	Type
my_collection[0]	CD
my_collection[1]	CD
my_collection[2]	CD
my_collection[3]	CD

Caution

Always define a record (struct) before declaring an array of that type. Otherwise, the compiler will not understand what the array contains.

Where to Place the Record Definition

You need to precede the array declaration by the record (struct) definition. Otherwise, the compiler will not understand what you are declaring. Since our example has been written in C++, we will refer to our record as a struct. Recall that you are creating a new type when you define a struct.

If you think that you will be writing functions that use the struct definition, you will need to put the definition in a place where everything can recognize it. For this reason, we place the struct definition at the top of the program.

Consider the following skeleton of a program. Notice that we have placed the struct definition at the top of the program—above the function headings and the main function.

```
#include <iostream.h>
#include <string.h>

struct book
{
string title;
string author;
int year;
char discount;
};

void Print_ALL ( book B);
void Change_Discount (book B);

int main ()
{
// declaring three variables of the book type
book my_book, your_book, x ;
.
.
.
return 0;
}
```

The `book`'s definition is placed above every other part of the program where a variable could be declared. The reason for placing it here, as opposed to placing it just before the declaration, is to allow all functions, including the `main` function, to recognize this new variable we have just created. Our next topic concerns the *scope* of a variable, and scope will help you to understand the placement of the definition.

Every part of the program should recognize the `struct` definition of a `book`. For this reason, we place the `struct` definition above all functions. By placing the definition here, we are making the struct definition *global*, that is, the definition is recognized globally, or everywhere within the program.

Global Variables, Local Variables, and Their Scope

There are other ways to classify variables other than what type they are. Variables can be classified according to the extent of their recognition. If the variable is recognized by every function, including the `main` function, then we say it is a *global* variable. Think of some of the most popular actors, rock stars, and politicians. Some are recognized only locally, while others are recognized everywhere, or globally.

Think of the example of a U.S. senator. She might not be widely recognized outside of her own state. Now take the Majority Leader of the Senate. Many people would recognize him because his popularity would extend farther than the state that elected him. However, he would probably not be recognized outside of the United States. Next consider the example of the president of the United States. Most people would recognize the name of the president of the United States.

Each of these individuals has a scope of recognition. The term *scope* refers to the largest possible place where that individual is known. We use the term local to describe a limited scope—one that is not global.

Individual	Recognized Where	Scope
A U.S. senator	The state that elected him/her	Local to the state
The leader of the Senate	Most/all states	Local to the U.S.
The president	Most/all countries	Global

Another example to consider is the scope of recognition for three soccer players. The first player is the best player in your town soccer league. Let's call him Joseph Thomas. Most people in the town recognize Joe because they have been watching him play since he was a child, and they know how good he is. He is recognized throughout the town but relatively unknown beyond there. Now take a well-known college player. He plays on a college team and is so skilled that most college players have heard of him. His scope would be the college teams, including the players and those who watch their games. Now take Mia Hamm. She has played in the Olympics, the World Cup, and professionally. Many people in many countries have seen her play and have heard of her. Her scope is much larger than the college player or the town player. We would consider it global.

Individual	Recognized Where	Scope
Town player	The town	Local to the town
College player	The college circuit	Local in the college circuit
Mia Hamm	The world	Global

Now consider a variable's *scope*. If a variable is defined within a function, it is a *local* variable because it will only be recognized within that function. A variable's scope refers to the largest possible area of recognition. For local variables, the scope is usually the function where it was defined.

If a variable is recognized everywhere, we call it a *global* variable. All functions recognize a global variable. A global variable must be defined at the top of a program, *outside* and *above* all the functions, including the main function. In our example using the struct, we put the definition of the struct before all the function headings, and so forth, to ensure that it would be a global variable. We also say that its scope (extent of recognition) is global because it extends throughout the entire program.

```cpp
#include <iostream.h>
#include <string.h>

int x;    // a global variable

struct book    // a global struct (another global variable)
{
string title;
string author;
int year;
char discount;
};
```

Notice the variable x; it is also a global variable. All functions will recognize x because it has been defined above everything.

All functions that follow can now use the book type. We do not need to redefine it inside of every function that would want to use a book type variable.

Note

Using the same name for a variable in different functions is okay because these functions are separate, and so there will be no confusion for the compiler. In more elaborate programs where functions call back and forth to one another, this may not be the case.

Caution

Global variables, although useful, can pose problems for programmers because all functions have access to the global variable *at any time*. Sometimes the values in a global variable will be inadvertently changed, and this may not be what the programmer intended.

Summary

We introduced the *record,* which is a data type designed to hold different data types. Each type within a record is called a *field* of the record. In C++, a record is known as a *struct.* When a struct is defined, it is given a name. This name refers to the new type of variable that has just been created.

Records can be assigned values just like any variable. To assign values to a struct, we assign each of the fields of the struct using the field names.

We introduced an array of structs. This is very useful, since we frequently need to hold data for several structs, not just one. Next the *scope* of a variable was introduced. The scope represents the extent to which a variable is recognized in a program. If a variable is recognized everywhere in a program, we say that the variable is *global.* If it has a limited scope, then the variable is *local.* Variables defined at the top of a program are global, since all functions, including the main function, can recognize them.

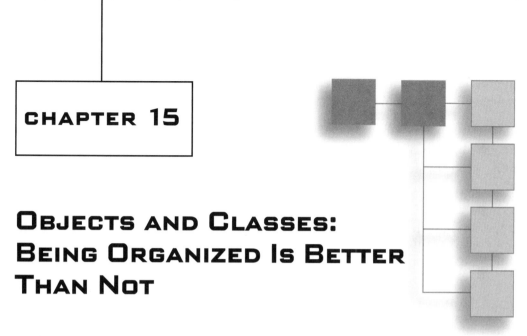

CHAPTER 15

OBJECTS AND CLASSES: BEING ORGANIZED IS BETTER THAN NOT

In the last chapter, we examined some interesting data holders: structures and records. These are the precursors to the *object*, which we will look at in this chapter. Perhaps you have heard the term *object-oriented programming*. If not, you will have a good grasp of what that means by the end of this chapter.

In This Chapter

- The object

- Classes and objects: public or private

- Fields

- Constructors, accessors, and modifiers

- Instantiating an object

- Calling a method from inside and outside the class

The Object

Object is a special term for a type of data structure that encompasses both a data structure and its behavior. This is a departure from all previous holders, which just store different kinds of data. The object is a more powerful structure because a programmer must consider both what kind of data it will contain and the *behavior* it will have. When we talk about behavior of an object, we are discussing what kinds of functions it will be able to carry out.

So an object is a data structure designed to execute certain kinds of behavior. When you consider an object, you think of two things: what you want to store in the object and what you want the object to be able to do. You write and design programs with an object and its actions in mind. This is a departure from previous considerations where data structures and the actions executed on them were considered separately. We call this *focus object-oriented programming*.

Example

Think of a student object that you might design for a school computer system. You would want the student object to have storage for a name, address, age, gpa, and so on, and you would want that object to be able to access all of that information as well as modify it. Look at this:

```
String name, address;
int age;
String gpa;
int yearofGraduation;
```

These are just a few of the possible data fields this object could have.

Now let's consider the behavior of the student object. All objects have to be able to load themselves—that is, assign all of their fields some data. We call this *constructing* the object or, a fancier word, *instantiating* the object—what I call bringing the object into existence.

Once the object has been instantiated, we should be able both to access its fields (attributes) and also alter them. So that means we are now starting to consider the behavior of the object. We need to write functions that will give us access to these attributes and allow us to modify them.

So some of the behavior of the student object would include assigning the name of the student, the address of the student, the age, the gpa, and the year of graduation of the student. But the word behavior suggests that the student object should be able to do something. What if the student object could change its address or update its age or even increase its gpa? These actions would constitute the behavior of the student object.

An object together with all the functions (methods) that make up its behavior is known as a *class*. You might have heard that word before. Hereafter we will use the terms *method* and *function* interchangeably.

Object-Oriented Programming

Object-oriented programming is a tidy way of designing a program and keeping everything organized. If you always have to consider an object and what it can do, you are keeping the object as the focus of your program. Programs (and languages, for that matter) that do not include objects can become unruly and disorganized because the programs are dependent on the programmer's design—whatever that may be.

Keep in mind that computer science is a relatively young discipline compared to mathematics, chemistry, or English literature, to name a few examples. Programmers have learned to become more organized through the development of languages that allowed them a systematic way to be organized. The original BASIC language (recall that the name was originally an acronym) did not allow a programmer to block off work, even into a function. Imagine a program without functions and how unruly that program might be.

The advent of objects and classes has allowed programmers to be even more organized than before, since they cannot consider functions or behavior separate from the data structure (object) involved.

If you keep this in mind as you study objects and learn how to program with them, you will start to see the benefits of this perspective.

Privacy of the Object

One of the first rules about handling objects is getting used to some of the restrictions in working with them. First of all, you have to create a place where the object lives, so to speak. This is the *class*.

At the top of the declaration of a class is the word `public` (see Figure 15.1). This is to notify other classes that they will have access to the objects in the class. After this declaration, the attributes of the object are listed next. Usually these attributes are *private*. One reason attributes of an object are private is because of the general rule that programmers try to protect objects from being inadvertently modified by other methods or functions within the program. The `private` tags used here mean that outside of the class, no one can touch these private attributes.

```
public class Student {
private String name;
private int age;
private String address;
private String gpa;
private int yearofGraduation;
public Student ( )  // constructors here
{

}
public int getAge ( ) // accessors here
{
}
.
.
.
.// modifiers here
} // class definition ends here
```

Figure 15.1
Notice that the word private is used before each attribute is declared. Braces also enclose all the fields
and methods.

Consider our student object. We would like a student's name, address, age, and gpa to be kept private. If another part of the program needs this information, we will force it to call a method to get that information rather than being able to know the gpa right away.

Figure 15.1 is an example of a class definition for a student.

The Class

The class consists of the fields of the object followed by the constructors, the accessors, and the modifiers.

Constructors

At the top of the class following the attribute listings are the constructors. These are the special functions that assign all the data fields of an object. You will notice that they have a heading that has no return type. This is the best way to recognize a constructor. The syntax of a constructor heading is as follows:

```
public    objectName    (parameter list, if necessary)
```

The main purpose of the constructor is to bring the object into existence and to assign all its data fields. There are different types of constructors: *default* constructors and *copy* constructors.

The examples that follow are written in Java, since it's a fully object-oriented language. It's easier to view these examples in Java because it was designed to handle objects.

Default Constructors

Default constructors load all the fields of an object with default values. So all integer and number fields would be assigned zero, and any strings would be assigned the null value. All classes are programmed to have a default constructor whether the programmer provides one or not. A default constructor is a safe-guard against a class that did not have its own constructor. Here is a default constructor:

```
public Student ( )
{
name = " ";
address = " ";
gpa = 0.0;
age = 0;
yearofGraduation = 0.
}
```

Other Constructors

Other constructors will assign the fields of the object with data passed in through the parameter list.

```
public Student (String name1, address1; double gpa1; int age1, yog)
{
name = name1;
gpa = gpa1;
address = address1;
yearOfGraduation = yog;
age = age1;
}
```

Each field has been assigned with values that were passed in. Notice that the data types match.

It is not necessary to assign all the fields from the parameter list, as in the preceding code. Look at the following example:

```
public Student (String OtherName)
{
name = OtherName; /* Only OtherName is passed into the constructor for the name
field. The other fields are assigned. */
gpa = 3.0;
address = "15 Larkspur Lane";
// etc.
}
```

When we call a constructor, we are really *instantiating* the object—that is, we are bringing the object into existence.

Note

> In Appendix B, you will see how constructors are handled in C++.

Accessors

Methods that access parts of an object are called *accessors*. Here is an example of an accessor. You want to find out a student's age. The way to do that is to write a method (function) called getAge. If you want to find out a certain student's name, you would write a function called getName. The same goes for finding a student's address or gpa. You would write methods called getAddress and getGpa, respectively.

Here are examples of two of those methods:

```
String getName ( )
{
return name; // returns the name of the object that called it.
}
int getAge ( )
{
return age;
}
```

Recall from Chapter 8 that functions often return a value to the calling place; otherwise, they return no values, and the word void would be used in the function heading.

Note

> Methods that begin with the word "get" are called get functions because they get information that you need about an object.

Modifiers

Methods that alter existing fields of an object are called *modifiers*. Modifiers allow the programmer to change the values of any of the fields of the object. As a point of organization, there is generally a modifier method for each field of the object. Look at these examples:

```
void setName (String otherName)
{
name = otherName;
}
void setGpa (String otherGpa )
{
gpa = otherGpa;
}
void setAddress (String otherAddress)
{
address = otherAddress;
}
```

In each of the examples, the return type is void because no values are being passed back to the calling function. Also each method contains only one statement—an assignment statement. The assignment statement has this form:

```
Field     ←     new value
```

The field of the object is being assigned the new value that came from the outside—the value being passed into the function as a parameter.

When the programmer wants to alter the value of an attribute of the object, she just calls that method and passes in the new value she wants there. Notice how the modifier forces the programmer to keep her hands off the object's fields. That's how the object stays private, in a sense. In the next section, we will talk more about who has direct access to the object.

Note

Methods that begin with the word "set" are called set functions because they set, or assign, the fields of an object after it has been constructed.

How an Object Calls Its Methods

As we saw in Chapter 11 on strings, objects call their own functions. Function calls are not made separately from an object. An object calls its methods either from within the class or outside of it. Let's start by looking at how an object calls methods from outside the class.

Calling from Outside the Class

Once a class has been defined and given its accessibility, objects can be instantiated and methods can be called. Let's assume all our classes are public so that we can make a call to the object's constructor outside the class but within our program. We will use the Student object, which we already defined.

```
Student firstStudent = new Student( );
// the default Student has been constructed


...

// get a name for the student
firstStudent.setName(newName);
```

In this program fragment from Java, firstStudent is instantiated with the default constructor. As we know, the default just assigns zeros and empty strings to any fields of the object. So we call a modifier method to assign firstStudent's name with a name that we get from the user or some other place. Let's examine the call to the default constructor:

```
Student firstStudent = new Student( );
```

We use the new word—always present in instantiating an object and, later you will see, in working with a pointer (see Chapter 17). Also notice that we called one of the three Student constructors; and since our parentheses are empty, the compiler will choose the constructor with the empty parameter list as the matching method to execute.

Next let's examine the call made to the modifier method:

```
firstStudent.setName(newName);
```

Look at the sequence of items: the object name, a period, and the method name in parentheses with its matching parameters.

As we assign all of the other fields of the object firstStudent, notice how each statement matches this model.

```
firstStudent.setAddress (newAddress);
firstStudent.setAge (ageNow);
firstStudent.setGpa (trueGpa);
firstStudent.setYearOfGrad (year);
```

The term object-oriented programming becomes more meaningful once you understand that the object initiates all of the action on itself. Also note that there are as many parameters in the call made by the object as are in the method's parameter list. My examples here happen to have only one parameter, but that is just a coincidence.

Calling from Inside the Class

When you make calls to methods within a class, the syntax is simpler. There is an understanding that if you are already inside a class, you got there because some object came into existence. This object is understood to exist, but if one is pressed to give it a name, it's called "this." That's right—this.

Here is an example. Let's say I have an additional method called isHigherGPA, which will return a boolean value of true if the calling object has a higher gpa than the object in the parameter list. It will return false otherwise. Here is the code for the method:

```
boolean isHigherGpa (Student otherStudent)
{
if  (this.getGpa() > otherStudent.getGpa () )
return true;
else
return false;
}
```

So the important line is the first line of code following the brace:

```
if  (this.getGpa() > otherStudent.getGpa () )
```

We can see that the same syntax we used when we made a call outside of the class applies here. The object is calling the method by using a period followed by the method name and the necessary parameters, which are none in this case. As I mentioned previously, you do not have to use the word this to make a call. Look at the same example:

```
boolean isHigherGpa (Student otherStudent)
{
if (getGpa() > otherStudent.getGpa () )
return true;
else
return false;
}
```

Think of how efficient this call really is. When getGpa( ) is called, the compiler knows that the main object must have called it because there is no other object name given.

Summary

Object-oriented programming describes a kind of program design where the object initiates all calls and is the center of its behavior.

Class syntax was introduced, followed by constructors, accessors, and modifiers—the main methods that are present in a class. A method, which is public, can be accessed outside of its class. The fields of an object should be private to prevent any uncontrolled modification.

There are two kinds of constructors: default and normal. Accessors allow the programmer to get at the fields of an object. Modifiers allow the programmer to alter a field of an object after it has been constructed.

There are two places where objects call the methods of its class: inside or outside of the class. The syntax is almost the same: the object name, a period, the method name, and any parameters that the method requires. Within the class, the object name, which is always this, is optional.

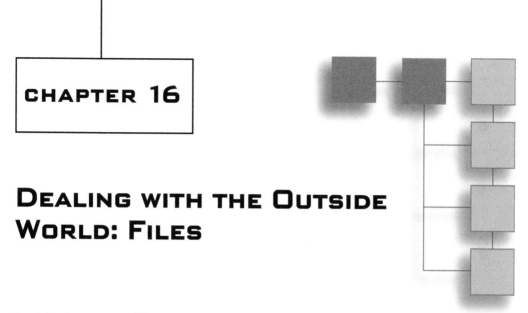

CHAPTER 16

DEALING WITH THE OUTSIDE WORLD: FILES

In this chapter, you'll examine how computer programs get data from an outside source: the text file. Text files are useful because they hold large quantities of data separate from a program that would manipulate that data. These files consist of streams of data and markers that separate one line of data from another. When you work with a text file, you learn to use those markers to help pull data from the text file to use in your program.

In This Chapter

- The text file

- How to create a text file

- The `eoln` marker

- The `eof` marker

- The user vs. the file

- Streams of info and data

The Outside World from a Program's Perspective

So far we have seen that programs manipulate values, which are stored in variables. These values have come either from the programmer or from the user who interacts with the program. Whenever a program deals with a great quantity of data, the data usually comes from an outside source. (No user wants to sit at the computer typing for hours.)

An example of a program that uses a large quantity of data is a program that prints all the batting averages of all the Major League Baseball players in order from highest average to lowest average. Another example is a program that prints all the names of people with the last name Smith who live in the Manhattan borough of New York City. These programs deal with large quantities of data.

A. Smith

Al Smith

Allan Smith

Allan C. Smith

Allen Smith

Large quantities of data (information) can be stored in special files that are called *text files*. Just a couple of examples are the names of all the people in the local phone directory or the names and statistics of all the National Hockey League players. These files are different from programming files because what they contain is treated only as text (keyboard letters and symbols) rather than commands. Programming files are different from text files because a compiler will examine the programming file, looking for commands to translate, and then attempt to execute those commands.

Programs could become very tedious if they contained both the data to be worked on as well as the commands to carry out a task. Separating data from instructions can be useful for programmers. Imagine a program that alphabetized and updated a list—any list—like a telephone directory. The directory is like the text file and needs to be changed every year, but the instructions for alphabetizing contained in the programming file probably don't need to be changed. That's one reason why it is useful to separate files that contain only data from files that contain instructions.

In this chapter, we will learn how to create a text file. The next step is to learn how to access the contents of the text file. We need to write another program file that does this. There are certain things that are true about text files and the way a programming file "reads" a text file. As I mentioned before, a programming file (a program) generally gets its data from the programmer or the user. This time we want the program to connect itself to a text file. We want the program to open the text file and read data from it, much as you would open a book and read words from it.

Creating a Text File

The real power of programming comes when you can connect your program to a text file where much data is stored. In our first example, let's create a short text file of our friends' names and phone numbers so we can learn the basics about text file structure. Consider this list of friends with phone numbers:

Carl Brady	555-1234
Marlo Jones	789-0123
Jason Argonaut	888-4567
Jim Collins	456-2345
Jane Austen	234-8765

The text file should be thought of as a large piece of lined paper on which we will write data on each line. Data (information) should be put into the text file with some organization. In this file, we have chosen to put a name and then a phone number on each line. But first, we need to create the text file and name it appropriately.

When you open a new file and save it for the first time, use some name like

```
MyFriends.dat
     ↓              ↓
file name   extension
```

We can use the extension .dat to indicate that we are writing a *text file*, not a programming file. (Recall that extensions are used to classify files—you have probably already seen .gif, .jpg, and .doc files, as examples.)

Organizing a File Through Markers

When you write a text file (also called a data file), it is important to give it some structure. As far as the compiler is concerned, a text file is just a sequence of letters and symbols. It looks like this:

```
Carl Brady555-1234 Marlo Jones789-0123Jason Argonaut888-4567Jim
Collins . . .
```

The compiler does not care what names you have typed at the keyboard, since it is not looking for programming commands or keywords, such as int, main, void, endl, for, while, do, and so on to translate. It will, however, look for *markers* on the file. Markers are used to separate data. Since data appears in a stream (just like our cin stream), the markers are used to provide some organization to what would otherwise be a continuous stream. For this reason, the compiler needs to have some organization imposed on the file. The organization in a file will come from the spacing (the blanks that surround a value) and two types of markers that are put onto the text file.

The End of Line Marker

The first marker is an *end of line* marker (written eoln). This is used to organize the data in the text file. When you write a file and decide what data will be inside of it (for example, names followed by phone numbers), you then need to use an eoln marker to separate each piece of unique information. In this case, we want to write a person's name followed by a phone number on each line. After every new person's name and phone number we hit the Return key, which causes an eoln marker to appear on the file. The file is organized with data followed by these line markers.

The End of File Marker

When you finish typing a text file, there is an additional marker automatically put onto the file. It is called an *end of file* marker (eof). I have used a bullet symbol (●) to represent the marker so you can see where it is placed. This mark is necessary for the compiler or translator that uses the file. See Figure 16.1.

Screen View

Carl Brady	555-1234 □
Marlo Jones	789-0123 □
Jason Argonaut	888-4567 □
Jim Collins	456-2345 □
Jane Austen	234-8765 □ ●

Stream View

Carl Brady   555-1234 □ Marlo Jones   789-0123□ Jason Argonaut   888-4567□
Jim Collins   456-2345 □ Jane Austen 234-8765 □●

Figure 16.1
The file is shown as it appears on the screen and as it appears as a stream where each name and phone number is followed by an eoln marker [here, a box symbol (□)] and then at the end of the file, an eof marker is used [here, a bullet symbol (●)].

Reading from a Text File

Once you have created the text file, it is necessary to think about the next step—reading from the text file. First, we need to examine how text files are read. A text file behaves like a CD. You can go back to the beginning of a CD, or all the way to the end, just by pressing a button on your CD player. You can also burn a CD or just listen to it. A text file behaves in almost the same way. When we first use a text file, we have to open it and indicate that we are going to read from it. Reading a text file is like listening to a CD. Reading means that we will move through the text file, extracting (pulling out) copies of values (like the names and phone numbers in MyFriends.dat) that are in the file so that we can use them in our program. When we read a text file, we are not altering it or "recording" over it—just "listening" to it.

The term *writing* a text file is used to describe creating or changing an existing text file by sending values out to the text file. We use the same terminology to describe "burning" a CD—we are writing new material onto the CD as opposed to just reading (listening to) the CD.

The steps involved in reading and writing text files (data files) are the same for most programming languages. The first step is to open the text file and then indicate whether you intend to read it or write onto it in the program. Before we do these steps, you need to be familiar with two streams that are used with text files. If you recall, streams are like channels through which values can travel or be stored temporarily.

Streams Used with Files

Text files are an outside source of information for the programmer. Just as the user (another outside source) can provide values for the programmer, a text file (often called a data file) provides values as well. Once a text file has been created, it is necessary to access the values from the file so that they can be used in a program.

It is important to familiarize yourself with the streams associated with a text file, since these streams provide us access to the file—whether we intend to read from or write to the file. In Chapter 2, we talked about the cin stream (in the C++ programming language) associated with the keyboard. When you work with files, you will probably have to define a stream that connects to the text file. Recall that the cin stream is already being used and is "connected" to the keyboard.

There are two types of streams used with text files: an *in* stream and an *out* stream. In the programming language C++, the in stream type, called `ifstream`, allows data (values) to travel from the text file into the program. The out stream type, called `ofstream`, allows values to go from the program out to the text file.

These streams are very similar to the `cin` and `cout` streams we studied previously. If you recall, the `cin` stream is like a channel through which values come into a program from data entered at the keyboard. The `cout` stream allows values to go from the stream out to the screen.

Some languages do not bother with letting the programmer access the stream directly. For example, in the programming language Pascal, the programmer just uses commands like `read` and `write` which simplify this process but also make it more difficult to understand how the computer does what it does.

How to Access the Values in a Text File

When you begin a program that will use values that come from a text file, you need to indicate to the compiler that your program will be communicating with an outside file by using an `open` command in the programming language.

We tell the compiler that we will open a file for the purpose of reading from the file. The command could look like this:

```
open ("MyFriends.dat");
```

The next step is to declare an "in" stream that will connect to the text file. The "in" stream type is called an `ifstream`. (This variable type is found in the header file called `fstream.h`.) Think of this type as short for an *in-from-file stream*. We will call the new stream `file_in`. We can call it anything, even x, but we want to give it a name that reminds us that it is a stream used for *reading from* a text file.

```
ifstream              file_in;
   ↓                     ↓
type of file stream   name of file stream
```

Notice that it follows the grammar of declaring a variable of some type.

```
int x;
char initial;
double m;
ifstream  file_in;
```

Once you have declared the stream type, you are ready to use it in the same way you use the `cin` stream, which allows you to get values from the user. We use the same extraction operator (>>) that we used with `cin`. We also need to use variable holders for the values that will be pulled out of the stream. In the text file we created previously, we have two strings on each line: a string for the name of our friend and a string to hold a phone number. All of these are variable holders.

```
string name, number; /* declaring two strings to hold values from the file */

file_in >> name >> number ;
   ↓                  ↓
stream name      string names
```

Accessing the Contents and Displaying Them on the Screen at the Same Time

The most useful thing to do with a large file is examine its contents by opening a text file for reading. Then we use the appropriate stream with a loop to get copies of all the values from the file.

We will use the previous example and expand it in two ways. The first statement we will add is a `cout` statement so that we can see the values that came from the text file (they were copied into our variables, `name` and `number`) and display them on the screen.

```
string name, number; /* declaring two strings to hold values from the file */
file_in >> name >> number ;
cout << name << "   "   << number << endl;
// this statement allows you to view name's and number's values.
```

The example only lets you see the *first two* values in the text file—`Carl Brady` and `555-1234`. Every time you use the extraction operator with the file stream, you are reading from the file, which is like playing a CD. If you want to read the entire file (like playing a CD all the way to the end), you will have to use the extraction operator repeatedly until everything has been copied out of the file.

Note

> Reading from a file does not change a file. It is similar to listening to a tape or playing a CD. The song is not changed.

If you want to see all the contents of the text file, you will need to use a loop so that you can get all eight lines of data from the file.

```
string name, number;
int y;

for ( y = 1 ; y <= 8; y = y + 1 )
{
file_in >> name >> number;
cout << name << "   "  << number << endl;
}
```

Each time this loop spins, a new name and number get copied into the two variable holders. Then the cout line allows the program to print the values on the screen. Think of the file_in stream with the >> operator as something that pulls copies of values out of the file and then puts them into the variable holders, in this case, name and number. The next line uses the cout stream to send those variables' values to the screen.

Note

When using a loop with the *same* two holders (as in the previous example) the values in the variables will constantly change as the loop spins.

Some Elementary Commands Used with Files

There is a small group of commands (or functions) associated with using files in any programming language. Let's look at these commands so that you will be familiar with the types of operations that you can perform on a file.

How to "Rewind" a File

When you open a file, there is an imaginary pointer that moves back to the beginning of the file. This pointer keeps track of where you are in the file as the file is being read. It's like moving to track 1 on a CD or pressing the restart button on a CD player. When you read from a file using the file stream we mentioned earlier, the pointer will move through the file as you read from the file. See Figure 16.2.

Writing Values to a File

If you want to add another number or name to a file, there are two ways to do this. The first way is to type more data directly into the file, just as we did when we first created the file MyFriends.dat. Just add more names and numbers onto the bottom of the list you already have.

⇓
Carl Brady   555-1234☐ Marlo Jones   789-0123☐ Jason Argonaut   888-4567☐
Jim Collins   456-2345 ☐ Jane Austen 234-8765 ☐•

⇓
Carl Brady   555-1234☐ Marlo Jones   789-0123☐ Jason Argonaut   888-4567☐
Jim Collins   456-2345 ☐ Jane Austen 234-8765 ☐•

⇓
Carl Brady   555-1234☐ Marlo Jones   789-0123☐ Jason Argonaut   888-4567☐
Jim Collins   456-2345 ☐ Jane Austen 234-8765 ☐•

Carl Brady   555-1234☐ Marlo Jones   789-0123☐ Jason Argonaut   888-4567☐

⇓
Jim Collins   456-2345 ☐ Jane Austen 234-8765 ☐•

Figure 16.2
A pointer ↓ is shown in different places in a file.

```
Carl Brady                  555-1234
Marlo Jones                 789-0123
Jason Argonaut              888-4567
Jim Collins                 456-2345
Jane Austen                 234-8765 //this was where the file used to end
William Shakespeare         789-1564 //now it ends here
```

The other option is to open the file and use the stream that allows data to go out to a file. This type of stream is called an `ofstream` stream. (I think of it as an *out-to-file stream*.) Let's declare a stream of the `ofstream` type.

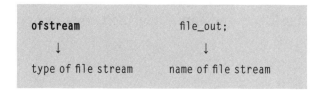

Now we can use the insertion operator (<<) that we used with the `cout` stream from Chapter 5. The insertion operator will allow the two variables' values to be sent out to the stream and then to the file.

```
string A = "hello!";
int B = 78;
file_out << A << B;
```

The text file will look like this:

```
hello!78
```

If we want to put *spaces* between values in a text file, we will have to put spaces into the stream that is the channel to the text file. Look at this next example where we insert spaces between the values that are going to the stream.

```
file_out<< A << "   " << B;
```

The text file will look like this:

```
hello!      78
```

To keep the file structured with values on separate "lines," we will put a line marker into the stream with the endl command so that a line marker goes onto the file itself.

```
file_out << A << "   " << B << endl;
```

Note

The Return key is used to put a line marker directly onto the text file; the endl command must be used to put a line marker into a stream that will send its values to a file.

Adding Values to the End of a File

If we want to get to the end of a text file we will have to read it all the way to the end—like playing a CD to the end. Some languages provide a command that allows you to go to the end of a file so that you can add more values there. This command is called append. When you append something, you are adding it onto the end of something (for example, an *append*ix appears *at the end* of a book.)

Let's start by opening the file MyFriends.dat and appending another name and number to it.

```
open ("MyFriends.dat");
append ("MyFriends.dat");
string A = "Mark Holden";
string B = "456-1234";
ofstream file_out;
file_out << A << "   " << B   << endl;
```

Now the file should look like this:

```
Carl Brady          555-1234
Marlo Jones         789-0123
Jason Argonaut      888-4567
```

```
Jim Collins                    456-2345
Jane Austen                    234-8765
William Shakespeare            789-1564
Mark Holden                    456-1234
```

Closing a File

The last thing to do when you are finished with a file is to close the file—just like closing a book when you are finished reading it.

```
close ("MyFriends.dat");
```

Every language has its own commands for using files. It is important to see how each new language handles files. You need to check to see how you can open the file, write to it, read from it, and then append, if possible. The last thing is to remember to close the file.

On the CD

A program in C++ that creates a text file. Also available is a program that reads data from this text file and displays it on the screen.

Summary

Text files (also called data files) are outside sources of data (files of data) that can be introduced into a program. Text files can be one or more lines of data or text and do not have any programming commands. The big advantage of a text file is not having to rely on the user or the programmer as sources of large quantities of data. Phone directories, lists of students at schools and universities, and statistics for members of professional sports are just a few examples of large quantities of data. When you name a file, you should use the .dat extension, which indicates that the file type is not a programming file.

Text files have two different kinds of markers used to organize information within them: the eoln marker and the eof marker. When you create a text file directly, you need to hit the return key to place an eoln marker onto the file. An eof marker is automatically placed onto a file when a file is closed after it has been created.

Reading from a text file allows copies of values to come out of a file for use in a program. Writing to a text file sends values out to a file through a program. In order to perform either of these tasks, you need to use the two streams associated with text files. In C++, these streams are called ofstreams and ifstreams (out-to-file streams and in-from-file streams). They work in the same way as the cout and cin streams we discussed earlier.

Basic commands associated with file use include commands for opening, closing, and appending to text files. There is an imaginary pointer (like a counter for a CD player) that sits above a file and keeps track of where you left off in the file. When you open a file, the pointer moves to the beginning of the text file. When you append to a file, the pointer automatically goes to the end of the file. Closing the file will cause the file to be closed, just like closing a book.

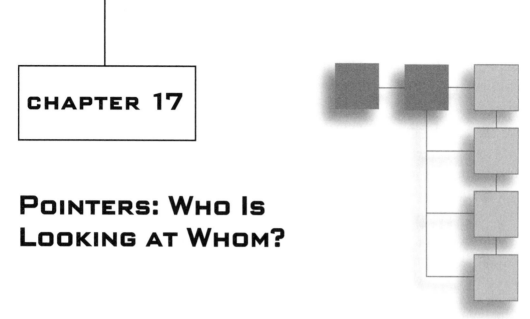

CHAPTER 17

POINTERS: WHO IS LOOKING AT WHOM?

In this chapter, I cover the two main kinds of variables: static and dynamic. These names refer to how memory is used for the storage of data. *Dynamic* variables are sometimes called *pointer* variables because they actually contain addresses that allow them to "point" to another location in memory. A pointer variable has two uses: it allows the programmer to save memory by referral instead of copying everything, and it allows him to release the variable when he is finished with it. Finally, I will discuss how to declare and use pointer variables.

In This Chapter

- Static variables

- Dynamic variables

- Introduction of pointer variables

- How pointer variables work

- Why use pointer variables?

Static vs. Dynamic Variables

There are two kinds of variables, and before you understand the basic difference between them, you need to consider an analogy. Imagine you are taking an around-the-world trip where you will visit different countries in different climates. The first part of the trip you expect to spend in northern countries where the climate is cold. The second part of the trip, you will be visiting southern countries where the weather is warmer. Strategically, you will pack half your luggage with clothing for the cold weather and the rest of your luggage with clothing for the warmer climate in southern countries.

After you spend the first part of the trip in the cold weather, you plan to send that luggage home so you don't have to continue to carry it around with you—as, literally, excess baggage. Now you can travel more easily, carrying only what you need for the remainder of the trip.

Variables can be likened to the baggage on a trip. Some variables you are stuck with for the entire program. You can't get rid of them, even if their purpose was long over after the first few minutes of running a long program. They are called *static* variables because they exist for the duration of a program. Other variables, called *dynamic* variables, are convenient in the way that they can be "unloaded" at any point through the execution of a program.

Static and Dynamic Variables—Their Role in Memory

There are two classifications of variables beyond the types we mentioned earlier in the book. These classifications describe how variables use memory. The first classification of variables is called *static*. Static variables exist for the duration of a program. Once you declare a static variable, it occupies a spot in the memory of the computer until the program ends. All the variables we have studied so far have been static variables.

Dynamic variables behave differently. They can be declared during the execution of a program. What that means is they can come into existence during the running of the program if they are needed. They can also be destroyed during the running of the program. When a dynamic variable is destroyed, the space it occupied in memory is released back to the computer. This is important if you are running a program that uses huge amounts of memory and you don't want to waste any of it on variables that no longer serve any purpose as the program continues to run.

The Pointer Variable: A Dynamic Variable

In this section we examine the *pointer* variable, which is a dynamic variable. A pointer variable (or *pointer*, for short) is a variable that holds an address rather than a value. Think of a variable as a container. Normally a variable holds a value. Regular variables look like holders with values inside. See Figure 17.1.

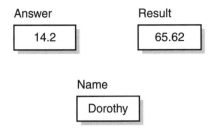

Figure 17.1
Three static variables are shown with their values inside.

Pointer variables, unlike static variables, do not contain values. They contain addresses that look like a combination of letters and numbers. See Figure 17.2.

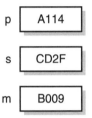

Figure 17.2
Three pointer variables are shown with addresses inside of them.

Since pointer variables contain addresses where data is stored, programmers can make use of them in functions. Functions, as you may recall, often have parameters that are sent into the function to be manipulated. Some of these parameters are called variable or *reference* parameters (see Chapter 8). Reference parameters are really pointer variables because they allow you to refer to another location where contents are stored.

Normally, when a variable is needed in a function, it needs to have all of its contents copied into a new memory spot for the function. A pointer variable just passes its address to the function so that the function can get at its contents without having to copy its contents. Programming with pointer variables allows programmers to conserve memory.

Imagine four separate functions that all alter the same variable, called check- amount. If static variables are used, each function must have copies of that variable and will use memory to make those copies. If pointer variables are used instead, each function can simply store the address of checkamount. This saves a lot of memory space.

How a Pointer (Variable) Works

Now that you know that pointers contain addresses, the question is, "How do they work?" The first step is to get the address that is contained in the pointer. The next step is to go to that address (where another variable is found). Then you can go inside of the other variable to get its value. Because the pointer contains an address, it really "points" to another place in memory. At that other place in memory, you will find a variable that contains a value. See Figure 17.3.

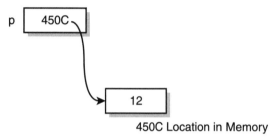

450C Location in Memory

Figure 17.3
A pointer is shown with its address. Another variable containing a value is shown at that address.

Operations Associated with Pointers

There are different tasks, or operations, associated with pointers regardless of the language you are using. Once you understand the concepts behind each of these tasks, you will be ready to learn the different syntax rules particular to each language. Let's examine each of these tasks.

Declaring a Pointer

When you *declare* a pointer, you are telling the compiler to treat the variable in a different way. The compiler will understand that it will be dealing with memory addresses rather than direct values. When you declare a pointer variable, you need to tell the compiler what type of value the pointer will ultimately be "looking at." It is understood that a pointer will contain an address, but we need to tell the compiler an address for what type of variable. Will it contain an address to an integer, to a character, to a string, or to a record/structure? These are important concerns for the compiler.

Just like the declaration of a static variable, we first state the type of variable followed by the pointer's name. The only difference between static variable declarations and pointer variable declarations is the use of an intermediate symbol to indicate it is a pointer. In the C++ language, we use an asterisk (*) between the pointer's name and the variable type it will point at.

```
int * p ; // p will "look at" an integer
// p will contain the address of an integer variable.
// p, itself, is not an integer!
```

The pointer variable has a name, but the variable it looks at does not always have one. The other variable is known as "the variable the pointer looks at." See Figure 17.4.

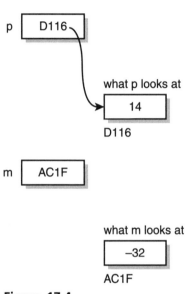

Figure 17.4
Two pointer variables are shown with their own variable names and the addresses they contain. At each address, another variable is shown containing a value and labeled "what p looks at" and "what m looks at."

Allocating Memory for a Pointer

The term *allocate* means to set aside for use. If you allocate funds for a project, such as building a bridge, you set aside funds to build the bridge. When you allocate memory, you are reserving memory for use by the pointer. The command to set aside the memory is the new command. This command is used with the type of variable the pointer will look at. The compiler will look for an available space, get the address of that space, and assign that address to the pointer. The pointer now contains that address. Consider the following example:

```
int * p; // p is declared as a pointer variable
p = new int; // memory is set aside (allocated)for p
```

We don't have any control over the address that the compiler finds in memory for the pointer. The compiler will look for a place in memory that is open or unoccupied. It will then assign the address of that spot to the pointer. The next step is to assign a value to that address according to the type used in the declaration. Once you have allocated memory for a pointer, then you want to assign it.

Assigning the Variable at Which the Pointer "Looks"

There are two kinds of assignments for pointer variables, depending on how you want the pointer to be used. The first type of assignment is when you assign the variable the pointer looks at. This assignment is just like the other assignment statements we have used previously. The only difference with this kind of assignment is that we need to clearly tell the compiler that we wish to assign the variable the pointer looks at—not the pointer itself. Let's call the variable the pointer looks at the *referred* variable.

Let's look at how we name this other variable. If we can use the correct syntax for naming the variable, then we use that name in the assignment statement to make the statement work. When calling this other variable, we use the asterisk symbol (*) again, but we put it *after* the pointer name. Consider these three statements used with the pointer called p.

```
int * p; // The compiler is informed that p is a pointer.
p = new int; // memory is allocated for p
p* = 6 ; // "what p looks at" is assigned the value, 6.
```

Here are some other examples of pointers being declared, then assigned, after memory has been allocated to them.

```
char * g; // g declared as a pointer to a character
g = new char; // memory is allocated to g
g* = 'm'; // "what g looks at" is given the value, 'm'.

double * num;
num = new double;
num* = 45.65;
```

Caution

It is very important to use the asterisk symbol (*) properly. In *declaration* statements, it is used on one side of the pointer name. In *assignment* statements, it is used on the other side of the pointer.

Distinguishing Between the Pointer and the Referred Variable

In the following examples, consider each of the values in the variable. Either the value is an *address*, contained in the pointer, or it is a *value* of the variable type referred to by the pointer. Also note the names of each variable, both the pointer names and the variables referred to by the pointer names. See Figure 17.5.

Pointer Variables

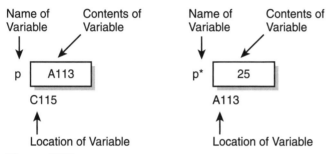

Figure 17.5
Each variable, whether a static variable or a dynamic (pointer) variable, is located at an address and contains something—either an address or a value.

In this section, we will examine statements that either use the pointer or use the referred variable. Because pointers contain addresses, sometimes it is necessary to consider the address contained in a pointer. In the first example, we want to check to see whether two different pointers are looking at the same variable. The easiest way to do this is to compare the addresses contained in the pointers. Let's start by declaring two pointers and assigning their referred variables.

```
int * p;// both p and m are declared as pointers
int * m;// The compiler now "knows" they will contain addresses.
p = new int; m = new int;//memory is set aside for both
p* = 15;// the "referred " vars are assigned
m* = 34;
```

Next we want to compare the pointers themselves using a relational operator. Let's assume that p's address is AB14 and m's address is C12A. The next statement will compare their addresses to see if they are the same.

```
//addresses contained in both p and m are compared
if ( p == m )
cout << "These pointers are looking at the same variable."
```

The compiler will check to see if the relational expression, AB14 == C12A is true, which it is not. If we use the following statement with the pointer variables, the relational expression will be true because AB14 does not equal C12A.

```
if ( p != m )
cout << "These pointers are not looking at the same variable."
```

Let's look at some other examples where we use either the pointer or its referred variable. The statements are shown at left and the values printed on the screen are shown at right. Notice that for the last two examples, we do not know what the user will type so the question mark (?) indicates this fact.

Examples

```
cout << p << endl;                        AB14
cout << p* << endl;                       15
cout << m << endl;                        C12A
cout << m* << endl;                       38
//Letting the user assign p*
cin >> p* ;                               ?
//Letting the user assign m*
cin >> m*;                                ?
```

How to Assign the Pointer Another Pointer

So far we have assigned only the variables "referred to" by the pointers. It is also possible to assign the pointer itself. You can assign the pointer an address contained in another pointer. This is equivalent to making two pointers look at the same variable. One pointer's address will be copied into another pointer variable after executing these statements:

```
int * p; // declaring a pointer to an int
int * snaker; // declaring a pointer to an int

snaker = new int; // allocating memory for the snaker
p = snaker; // p will look at the same variable as snaker
```

De-allocating Memory

When we speak of *de-allocating* memory, we really mean that we are releasing occupied space back to the compiler for its use. If you recall, it's like sending the luggage home during the long trip. How it works is best explained in this way. When we allocate (set aside) memory for a pointer through the new command, the compiler finds a block of memory both suitable for the variable type and unoccupied and assigns that address to the pointer. The pointer is the gateway to that other variable's contents. This variable, the one we call "the variable looked at by the pointer" is the *referred* variable. If we need this variable for the duration of the program, it behaves much like the static variables studied previously.

However, if you find that you need more memory and this referred variable is no longer useful, then you can release this memory back to the compiler. Releasing the memory is called *de-allocating* memory. We do this through the delete command.

```
//p is a pointer variable
delete p; // p's address is given back to the compiler
```

A variable containing some value occupies memory space. When the pointer is used with the delete command, the address of the referred variable is returned to the compiler for future use.

Note

De-allocating memory is the same as releasing the memory occupied by the referred variable. The address is given back to the compiler for future use.

Summary

This chapter introduced static variables and dynamic variables. Static variables exist for the duration of a program, while dynamic variables do not. The pointer variable is a dynamic variable, which contains an address to a location in memory. At that other address is a variable called a *referred* variable, or the variable the pointer looks at.

I gave different examples of the syntax for assigning the referred variable of a pointer. You have no control over the address the compiler chooses to set aside for a pointer. The pointer is given a spot in memory—this is called *allocating* memory for a pointer, and it is done through the `new` command. Likewise, releasing memory once referred to by a pointer is called *de-allocating* memory, and this is executed with the `delete` command.

The asterisk (*) symbol is used in pointer syntax. When you declare a pointer variable, the asterisk is used in the declaration to indicate that a pointer is being declared rather than a static variable. (All the variables we have worked with so far have been static variables.)

CHAPTER 18

SEARCHING: DID YOU FIND IT YET?

This chapter examines how to look for a data value stored in an array. There are two main algorithms for finding a value in an array: the linear search and the binary search. The linear search moves through the array looking at each slot to check whether the value has been found. The binary search relies on cutting the array in half and deciding which half should be examined for the value. Through a combination of a loop and the right relational expression, you can program the computer to find the value you are seeking.

In This Chapter

- Searching through a list

- Using the array in your search

- Examining one member at a time using a loop

- Inserting a relational expression to find something

- The linear search

- The binary search

- Defining indices—left, middle, and right

- Using indices in the binary search

Searching

This chapter covers the topic of *searching*—that is, looking for a value amid a large group of values. Generally you search though an array for a value. The array, you might recall, is a data structure that can hold a large number of values. Consider this array, called list, of values that were assigned by the user.

Array Member	Containing Value
list[0]	22
list[1]	–5
list[2]	6
list[3]	10
list[4]	0
list[5]	–37
list[6]	14
list[7]	2
list[8]	141
list[9]	59
list[10]	46

The programmer does not know which values are in the array, since the user thought of the values that went into each slot.

Searching for a Value in the Array

Let's say the programmer wants to know whether the value –37 was typed by the user. (He does not yet know it is in member list[5].) You can write a fragment of code to search through the array, looking at each member of the array to see whether it is the value –37.

Is it in list[0]? Is it in list[1]? The programmer writes code to check each slot of the array until he finds the slot that contains –37. He will eventually find that –37 is in the 6th slot of the array. We will look at the code that accomplishes this in the next section.

Tip

Remember that the 1st slot in the array is called slot[0], the second is called slot[1], and so on. So when I refer to slot[5], I am referring to the 6th slot because slot[3] is the 4th slot followed by slot[4], which is the 5th slot followed by slot[5], which is the 6th slot.

Searching for a Value Not in the Array

Now if the programmer wanted to know whether the value 100 were in the array, he would be disappointed because it is not there. The programmer would write code to look at each member of the array to see whether 100 was in one of the slots of the array. list[0] does not contain 100. Nor does list [1], list[2], or list[3].

The programmer must write code so that the computer looks at each member. Eventually he will get to the last few members of the array—list[8], list[9], and list[10]. He'll confirm that 100 is not in any of them.

Note

The only way to confirm that a value is not found in an array is to check *every* slot of the array first.

Developing the Linear Search Algorithm

The programmer needs to methodically move through the array, examining one member at a time. *Linear search* is the name for this method of searching—looking for a value by examining one member at a time in an array.

How to Examine a Member

The easiest way to examine array members is to use a *relational expression* with each member of the array and the value for which you are searching. Let's call the holder for this value Number. In the previous example, Number contained −37. We need to examine each array member. We will use a relational expression with the equality symbol, ==. This is the general form of the expression we will use.

```
Array Member == Number
```

Does the value in Array Member equal the value in Number?

The programmer must have the computer check to see whether this relational expression is true. He'll program the computer to check each slot of the array until he finds one (a slot or member) that contains −37.

	Value of Relational Expression
Does list[0] == Number?	
22 == −37	False
Does list[1] == Number?	
−5 == −37	False
Does list[2] == Number?	
6 == −37	False

```
Does list[3] == Number?
   10        == −37                        False
Does list[4] == Number?
    0        == −37                        False
Does list[5] == Number?
  −37        == −37                        True
```

Once the relational expression is true, then the computer can stop searching. It has found the value in member 5 of the list array.

Writing a Loop to Examine Each Member

A pattern has developed in the previous questions containing relational expressions. In each expression we are examining

list[*slot#*] == Number

Let's use a variable to represent the slot in the array. Let's declare it an integer called x.

```
int x;
x = 0;
              Does list[x] == Number?
                      ⇓
              Does list[0] == Number?
                 ⇓         ⇓
                22    ==  −37        False
```

If x changes in value and becomes 1 then we can check the next slot (member) of the array:

```
x = x + 1; // x is now 1
              Does list[x] == Number?
                      ⇓
              Does list[1]== Number?
                 ⇓         ⇓
                −5    ==  −37        False
```

If x changes again, we can check the next slot (member) of the array:

```
x = x + 1; // x is now 2
                    Does list[x] == Number?
                              ⇓
                    Does list[2] == Number?
                         ⇓          ⇓
                         6    ==   −37        False
```

We are ready to develop a loop that will move through each member of the array:

```
for (int x = 0; x <= 10; x = x + 1)
{
// does list[x] == Number?

}
```

Developing an If Statement with the Relational Expression

We want to write an if statement that contains the relational expression. First we need to decide what to do when we find the member that contains the same value that is in Number. Let's allow the user to know *where* we found the value by printing a message on the screen to him.

```
if ( list[x] == Number )
cout << Number << "is in the array at position" << x << endl;
```

The next step is to put this statement *inside* of the loop we just constructed. Now the entire fragment will look like the following block of code:

```
for ( int x = 0; x <= 10; x = x + 1)
{
if ( list[x] == Number )
cout << Number << "is in the array at position" << x << "." << endl;
// this is a very long output statement
}
```

The Binary Search

There is another kind of search that is very efficient at finding a number in an array. The *binary search* can be performed on an array that is already in some kind of order. Before we examine the binary search, we need to talk about an array that is "in order."

Ascending Order

The word "ascend" means to go up—like ascending a mountain. The phrase *ascending order* means that numbers increase as you move through a list. Let's look at a list that is in ascending order. Notice that you can skip a lot of numbers in a list and still be in ascending order.

3   4   6   17   21   24   32   43

These numbers increase as you move through the list from left to right. Let's construct an array that contains these numbers. We'll use an array of eight members called group.

```
int group[8];

group[0] = 3;
group[1] = 4;
group[2] = 6;
group[3] = 17;
group[4] = 21;
group[5] = 24;
group[6] = 32;
group[7] = 43;
```

Once an array is in order, we can begin to use a binary search on the array to look for a number. We will examine the case where the number we are searching for is in the list.

What Is a Binary Search?

You know that a search is a procedure by which you methodically look for a number. You have to remember that you can't always see what is inside an array—especially if the user loaded the numbers through an input statement like this:

```
for ( int x = 0; x <= 8; x = x + 1)
{
cout << "Please type a number." << endl;
cin >> group[x];
}
```

You need to keep in mind that you do not know the contents of an array, although for the binary search to work, you need to know that the numbers are *in order*.

The word *binary* is used to indicate that during the search execution, we will examine two halves of the array. The binary search is a method that involves cutting the array in half, figuratively. See Figure 18.1.

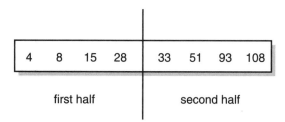

Figure 18.1
An array is shown cut into two halves. For this reason, we call the search a *binary* search.

Understanding the Binary Search

Now imagine that you were playing a game with a friend who was fond of numbers and had lots of free time on her hands. The game is for you to guess the number that your friend is thinking of. Rather than telling you whether you have guessed correctly or not, your friend will give you one hint for each guess. She will respond whether your guess is higher or lower than the correct answer. You and your friend, Eloise, have the following conversation:

Eloise:	"I am thinking of a number between 1 and 100. Guess what it is." (Eloise is thinking of 34.)
You:	"Is it 50?"
Eloise:	"No, it's lower than 50."
You:	"Is it 25?"
Eloise:	"No, it's higher than 25."
You:	"Is it 37?"
Eloise:	"No, it's lower than 37."
You:	"Is it 31?"
Eloise:	"No, it's higher than 31."
You:	"Is it 34?"
Eloise:	"That's it!"

It took you five guesses to figure out what number Eloise was thinking of. (If you had used the linear search it would have taken 34 guesses!) There is also a pattern to the guesses you made. Each time Eloise responded with a hint—saying that the answer was *higher* or *lower* than the guess—you, correctly, no longer considered the numbers that were out of range. Another interesting pattern occurring in the game is that your guess was always in the *middle* of the part of the list being examined.

Examining the Middle of a List

The guessing game is a good way to see how the binary search works. You always start by picking a number in the middle of your list as your first guess. Then if you find out that your guess was wrong, you need to know whether the correct answer is higher or lower than your guess. Once you know that, you can cross off the part of the list that is out of range.

Think of the first guess you made in the example. You guessed the number 50 and Eloise's response was that the answer is lower than 50. Now in your head, you can throw out the numbers 50, 51, 52, . . . , 99, 100, since the answer must be less than 50. This is the advantage of the binary search at work. You are able to cut out an entire half of the array so that your next guess will come from a smaller section of the array. See Figure 18.2.

Guessing the middle of the list is very efficient because it maximizes the numbers you can eliminate. If you were to make a guess that was not in the middle, it would be very inefficient. Consider what would happen if you played the same game with Eloise but this time you had the following conversation:

Eloise:	"I am thinking of a number between 1 and 100. Guess what it is." (Eloise is thinking of 34.)
You:	"Is it 1?"
Eloise:	"No, it's higher than 1."
You:	"Is it 2?"
Eloise:	"No, it's higher than 2."
You:	"Is it 3?"
Eloise:	"No, it's higher than 3."
You:	"Is it 4?"
Eloise (exasperated):	"No, it's higher than 4!"

1 2 3 ... 47 48 49 50 51 52 ... 98 99 100

Is it 50?
No, it's lower.

1 2 3 ... 47 48 49 ~~50 51 52 ... 98 99 100~~
⇓
1 2 3 ... 23 24 25 26 27 ... 47 48 49

Is it 25?
No, it's higher.

~~1 2 3 ... 23 25~~ 26 27 ... 47 48 49
⇓
26 27 ... 36 37 38 ... 48 49

Is it 37?
No, it's lower.

26 27 ... ~~36 37 38 ... 48 49~~
⇓
26 27 28 29 30 31 32 33 34 35 36

Is it 31?
No, it's higher.

~~25 26 27 28 29 30 31~~ 32 33 34 35 36
⇓
32 33 34 35 36

Is it 34?
YES!

Figure 18.2
A list with each guess is shown and a successive part of the array eliminated. Notice how the actual part of the list that you examine gradually becomes smaller and smaller.

By now Eloise has figured out that you will probably continue your pattern of guessing the next biggest number. (You are actually performing a linear search by going through the list of members, one at a time.) You might now begin to see the advantage of guessing a number in the middle of a list. It allows you to throw out a large section (half) of the list that you know does not contain the answer.

Most people who have not studied the binary search would randomly guess numbers, as that would seem like a better alternative than guessing the numbers one at a time from left to right. You might get lucky or you might not. For that reason, we guess a number in the middle of the list.

Caution

Remember that the binary search can only work on numbers that are arranged *in order.*

Moving to the Right or to the Left

When you make a guess that is incorrect, you need to know whether your guess was lower or higher than the answer. This is where the binary search saves you time—eliminating half of the list. When you make a comparison between your guess and the answer, you need a relational expression with the greater than (>) operator like the following:

```
if (my_guess > answer)
/* I'll throw out all the numbers greater than (to the right of) my_guess. */
```

This is what happened when you first guessed the number 50. Eloise responded that the answer was "lower than 50." That is, your guess was too high a number. Your guess (50) was *greater than* the answer (34). As a result, you start to consider only the numbers that are lower than 50, or to the *left* of 50, as if these numbers were arranged in a list, left to right.

In another guess you made, you guessed 25, and Eloise responded that the answer was "higher than 25." In this case, your guess was too low a number. So the answer must be higher than 25, or to the *right* of 25, if we lined up the numbers left to right in a list. Here a relational expression using the "less than" (<) operator would be appropriate:

```
if (my_guess < answer )
/* I'll throw out all the numbers less than (to the left of) my_guess. */
```

Every time you lose half the array, you have just saved some time in your searching process. In an ordered list of the numbers 1 through 1,000, your first guess using the binary search would be the number 500. If the guess were not correct, you would immediately be able to throw out 500 members of the list (either those numbers less than 500 or greater than 500). What a great time saver when you are searching for a number!

Note

Remember that with a list written in ascending order, numbers to the left of others are *less than* them. Numbers to the right of others are *greater than* them.

How the Binary Search Works with an Array

Now that we have studied the basics of the binary search, we need to consider how programmers use it. I mentioned earlier in the chapter that we generally search via an array, since the array is a data structure that can hold quite a few numbers. Let's start to look at the binary search as a way of finding a number in an array whose values are in order.

Finding the Middle of the Array

In order to find the middle of the array, we need to find the middle member of the array. If the array has eight members, then the 4th member is the middle member. If the array has 50 members, then the 25th member is the middle member.

As you continue to use the binary search, you need to make adjustments in how you find the middle member. For example, if you eliminate the first 500 members of an array that has 1,000 members, you will need to find the middle of the subsection of the array that begins with the 501st member (slot 500) and ends at the 1,000th member (slot 999).

The subsection you are examining:

500   501   502   503   ...   748   749   750   751   ...   997   998   999

(the middle of that subsection of the array)

A vertical representation of the array:

```
list[500]
list[501]
list[502]
list[503]
.
.
.
list[748]
list[749] // the middle of the array subsection
list[750]
list[751]
.
.
.
list[997]
list[998]
list[999]
```

When we found the middle of the arrays mentioned previously, we used the size of the array to find the middle. In the array with eight members, we know that half the number of members would be four, so slot 4 is the middle of the array. (It is actually in group[3] because we began the array at group[0].)

An *index* is a slot of an array. All arrays in C++ begin with the index 0. We call this a *left index* because it represents the leftmost slot of an array when it is viewed left to right. Likewise, the last slot is the *right index*. In the case of an array with eight members, the right index would be 7. In an array with 500 members, the right index would be 499.

Note

You always need to remember that (in C, C++, and Java) you begin arrays with the 0 index.

As you eliminate halves of the array through the binary search, a new middle is found by using the left index and right index of the subsection of the array. Let's take the previous example where we were examining the right half of the array (we'll call it list) with 1,000 members.

500 501 502 503 ... 748 749 750 751 ... 997 998 999

With this subsection, the left index is 500 and the right index is 999. We find the *middle index*, the index of the middle member, by taking the *average* of the left and right indices.

middle index = (left index + right index) / 2

Let's see how middle index is assigned by doing this average. The left index (500) + the right index (999) is 1,499. Dividing 1,499 by 2 gives us the number 749.5. Since slots of the array are always *integers*, we throw out the excess (0.5) part of the number. So the new middle of the array is slot 749.

Let's find the middle index of the array group. The left index is 0 and the right index is 7, so the middle index is found by taking the average of the two indices. (0 + 7 is 7 and 7/2 is 3—since we eliminate the 0.5.)

How to "Eliminate" Half of the Array

The binary search is efficient because we are able to "throw out" half of the array each time we get the answer that the number we are searching for is higher than or lower than our guess. Let's practice the search on the example of the array group.

Let's start by searching for a number that is in the list. Here is the list again to remind you of the values that are in it. Let's ask the user for a number to search for in the array. We will store it in a variable called answer.

```
int group[8];

group[0] = 3;
group[1] = 4;
group[2] = 6;
group[3] = 17;
group[4] = 21;
group[5] = 24;
group[6] = 32;
group[7] = 43;
cout << "Please type a number and I will tell you if it is in the list." << endl;
cin >> answer;
```

Using the guessing game we played earlier, let's assume the user types a number that is in the list—like 4—and it will represent the answer. We'll now play the guessing game with the computer instead of our friend Eloise. You (the programmer) play the game by the rules of the binary search, which means you always make a guess—a value found in the middle slot of the array. (Your guess is *always* the value found in the middle slot of the array.)

Programmer:	"I am looking for a number in my array group. (The user picked the value 4.) I'll first check the number found in the middle of the array—at group[3]—the value 17."
Computer:	"No. Your guess, 17, is higher than the answer (4). Examine the left half of the array—that is, all the slots of the array to the left of the middle slot ([3])."
Programmer:	"Okay, I'll focus on members with indices, 0, 1, and 2, since that is all that remains to be examined according to the binary search. Is the value in slot 1?"
Computer:	"Yes! How did you get that so fast?"
Programmer:	"I chose the middle index of the subsection of the array. The left index was 0 and the right index was 2, so the average—the middle index—is 1. The value in the middle slot (group[1]) matches the value in the variable answer."

When we adjust the indices for a subsection of the array, we are giving new values to both the left index and the right index. Consider what happened in the game played between the programmer and the computer. After the first guess was made, the subsection of the array was the left half of the array. We get this left half of the array by looking at the members from the left index (0) up to the right index, which is the last index before the middle index—here, it is 2. After we establish the values of the left index (0) and the right index (2), we can use their average—(0 + 2)/2—to find the value of the middle index, which is 1. The answer is always found in the middle slot of some section of the array. Every time you eliminate half the members, that subsection gets smaller and easier to work with.

On the CD

The complete binary search is shown in a program in C++.

Summary

I began the chapter by defining what it means to search through a list for some value. We usually search through an array because the array can hold so many values. A linear search is a searching method by which we examine a list (an array) one member at a time. Because we repeatedly examine members of a list, we can use a loop to do this work.

We also use a relational expression to find a value in an array. The relational expression is put inside of the loop so that all members can be examined for the value. It is possible that the value is not in the list.

The binary search represents a search method that is very different from the linear search. It is more efficient than the linear search, but it can only be used on an ordered array—one whose values are listed in increasing size from left to right. We call this order *ascending order* because the numbers ascend as we move through the list.

The binary search can best be explained through a guessing game played between two people. Later in the chapter, the game was played between the programmer and the computer as an illustration of the binary search at work.

The binary search uses the middle of the list as its first guess in the guessing game. If the guess is incorrect, the next guess will be found in a subsection of the array—found either to the left or to the right of that initial guess. By focusing on one half of the array before making the second guess, we have eliminated half of the original list. For this reason, the binary search is very efficient.

An *index* is a slot in the array. The left index is at the first slot numbered 0. The right index will be the slot of the last member of the array. In order to find the middle index, we take the average of the values of the left and right indices. (If there is any fractional leftover, we discard it, since an index must be an integer.)

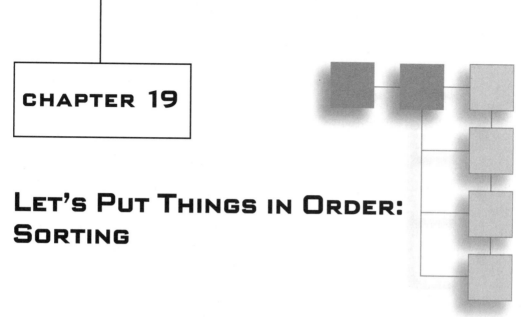

CHAPTER 19

LET'S PUT THINGS IN ORDER: SORTING

In this chapter, you'll examine the topic of sorting data—putting data in some order. Alphabetization is the process of putting words in order. When you order numbers, you decide whether you want those numbers to increase in value (ascending order) or decrease in value (descending order). Next you'll examine two specific examples of sorting algorithms: the selection sort, which relies on finding the minimum repeatedly, and the merge sort, which repeatedly halves the array.

In This Chapter

- Alphabetization defined
- Ascending vs. descending order
- The selection sort
- Finding the minimum
- The merge sort

How Data Is Arranged—Sorting

When we arrange data in order, we *sort* it. It is important to be able to arrange a list of words in alphabetical order or a list of numbers in increasing or decreasing order of value. If you had a list of lottery numbers, you would want to be able to arrange them so that you could easily look up a certain number in a list. There are many ways to sort data, and as you study the topic of programming, you will learn these different sorting methods. In this chapter, I will discuss the broad topic of sorting, and then study two particular sorts so that you can see how a sorting algorithm works. Think of each sort as a recipe for arranging data in order. Each sort has its own name, depending on the particular way data is arranged in order.

The ability to sort is an important task when you are dealing with large quantities of data. The most obvious kind of arrangement of data would be the alphabetization of strings—putting words in alphabetical order. Names (strings) are alphabetized all the time. Look at this list of names that are *not* in alphabetical order.

John
Nicola
Marie
Susan
Brian
Bridget
Margaret
Nick
Bernie
Al

If we alphabetize this list, we see that Al should be first, and then we will examine the names that begin with B. After handling those names, we can look to the next letter in sequence, the J. Then we find that the names beginning with M should be placed before those beginning with N, and last we follow with the name Susan.

Al
Bernie
Brian
Bridget
John
Margaret
Marie
Nick
Nicola
Susan

If you stop for a moment and analyze the work you did to alphabetize this list, you might not think it was much work at all. After all, you can see that Al is first because the name begins with an A. Next you might admit that it required a little work to arrange the three names that began with B in order. (You need to look at the second and third letters to see which name is first, second, and third among them.) Now stop to consider how a machine with no intelligence would go about organizing data in some kind of order.

Here we begin the topic of sorting—arranging data in order. First I will introduce two kinds of order—ascending and descending. In the last chapter, we examined ascending order. We will be sorting data in ascending order in this chapter.

Ascending vs. Descending Order

Ascending order is the order we introduced in Chapter 18 when we mentioned the requirement that a binary search can only be performed on an array that is in order. *Ascending* order means that numbers in the array increase in value as you move through the array. For example, as you move from member 3 to member 4, you expect the value found at member 4 to be greater than that found at member 3. Look at this example of a list of numbers in ascending order. (The numbers increase in value as you move from left to right.)

| −8 | −1 | 2 | 5 | 12 | 18 | 19 | 32 | 41 | 45 |

If an array were used to contain these values, the array's first holder slot would hold −8 and the second holder would contain −1, and so on.

−8	−1	2	5	12	18	19	32	41	45
list[0]	list[1]	list[2]	list[3]	list[4]	list[5]	list[6]	list[7]	list[8]	list[9]

Descending order is just the opposite—the values found at the front of the array (on the left) are bigger in value than those that follow (on the right). Look at the same list of values, which are in *descending* order.

| 45 | 41 | 32 | 19 | 18 | 12 | 5 | 2 | −1 | −8 |

This list is in descending order because every value (to the left) is bigger than every value to the right. Now let's take this list and put the values into an array.

```
int list[10];

list[0] = 45;
list[1] = 41;
```

```
list[2] = 32;
list[3] = 19;
list[4] = 18;
list[5] = 12;
list[6] = 5;
list[7] = 2;
list[8] = −1;
list[9] = −8;
```

As you move down through the list, the values become smaller. This array is in *descending* order. We will examine a few different sorts to see the basic method by which numbers are arranged in order.

The Selection Sort

For a computer to sort (organize) data, it must follow a very specific set of instructions. There are different kinds of sorts, depending on the method used. Each sort is named for the method it employs. The *selection sort* is a good sort to begin your study. As an analogy, let's start by looking at an example of a selection sort performed on a group of people at a party, and then we'll examine the sort applied to a list of numbers in an array.

An Analogy: The Partygoers

Imagine a group of people attending a party. Someone not in the party plans to make a list of the youngest to oldest people in attendance. We will call this person the organizer. The organizer enters the room where the party is and asks the first person he meets how old he or she is. The organizer continues to ask every other person how old each is. One by one, he tries to find someone younger than the first person he asked. If he finds someone younger, he considers that person *the youngest* now. He continues to ask each person his age. When he finishes querying everyone, he retains the name of the person who was the youngest.

The organizer asks that person to leave the room after he writes down the name first on his list. Returning to the room, he asks the remaining people, one at a time, their ages. He will find the youngest person in that group and ask that individual to leave the room. He writes down the name of the person leaving.

The organizer now holds a list of two people—the youngest person's name is at the top, and the next youngest person is listed second. The party is not as big as it was before, since *two people have left*. As the organizer polls the remaining group to find the next youngest person, he writes down that person's name and asks him or her to leave. Now the party is missing three people, and thus is a smaller group. He now has a list of three people—the youngest, second youngest, and third youngest of all the people that went to the party.

The algorithm we are developing is to select the youngest in a group and put that person's name at the top of a list. Then we select the youngest person (really the second youngest) from the slightly smaller group (the youngest is missing since we asked her or him to leave) and follow the same procedure: write down the name and ask the person to leave.

The organizer keeps a list of each "new" youngest person found at the party and also asks that individual to leave once he has written down the name. In this way, he can examine a smaller group each time to find the "new" youngest person.

The list he keeps is growing. It is a list of the youngest through oldest people who attended the party. By repeatedly selecting the youngest person from the group, he is organizing the names of all the people who attended the party in order from youngest to oldest.

Two Parts to the Selection Sort

The first part of the selection sort is to notice that we are selecting the youngest from a group and putting that person's name at the top. The second part of the sort is to recognize that we are examining a smaller and smaller group each time. See Figure 19.1.

Each sort you will study has some structure to its method. The selection sort selects the smallest number from a group and puts it at the top of a list. This number is removed from the group so that when you find the smallest in the remaining members of the group, you will be able to find the next smallest, and so on.

Finding the Minimum

Before we look at the selection sort performed on an array of numbers, we need to look at the part of the sort where we found the youngest person in the room. This requires some work.

Finding the youngest person in a room is an analogy for finding the *minimum* in a list of numbers. The minimum is the smallest value in a list. When you find the

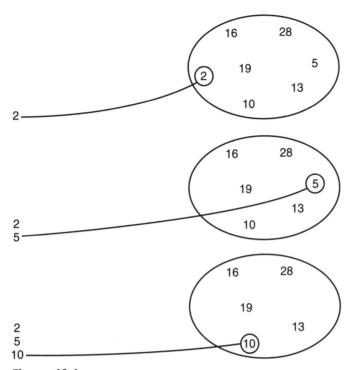

Figure 19.1
The smallest number (2) of a group is shown outside the group at the top of a list. Then the group is shown *without* that member. Next the smallest (5) is chosen from the group, and it is written second in the list. The third time, the smallest (10) is pulled from the group and written third in the list. This is how the selection sort works.

minimum of a list, you are really finding the smallest value in a list of numbers. Let's examine this list of six numbers:

 14   32   5   12   61   7

As you look at the list, you can immediately see that 5 is the smallest number in the list. The task is more difficult for a computer. It has to be programmed to find this minimum. Let's look at what the computer might think in order to better understand how finding the minimum works.

Computer.	Let's assume that 14 is the smallest number. Let's get the next number from the list—a 32.
	Is 32 less than 14? No. So 14 is still the smallest. Good. (Less work for me.)
Computer.	Let's assume that 14 is the smallest number. Let's get the next number from the list—a 5.
	Is 5 less than 14? Yes. I guess 5 is the smallest now.

Computer:	Let's assume that 5 is the smallest number. Let's get the next number from the list—a 12.
	Is 12 less than 5? No. So 5 is still the smallest.
Computer:	Let's assume that 5 is the smallest number. Let's get the next number from the list—a 61.
	Is 61 less than 5? No. 5 is still the smallest. (It has lasted longer than 14.)
Computer:	Let's assume that 5 is the smallest number. Let's get the next number from the list—a 7.
	Is 7 less than 5? No. So 5 is the smallest value in the entire list.

Let's do this exercise a second time showing at least two replacements of the minimum value as you move through the following list:

21   16   25   8   19   4   1

Looking at this list, you can see that 1 is the smallest. But consider the work the computer would do if confronted by such a list (an array)! Remember that the computer cannot "see" all the numbers in the list at once.

Computer:	Let's assume that 21 is the smallest number. We'll get the next number from the list—a 16.
	Is 16 smaller than 21? 16 is now the smallest in the list. (21 didn't last long!)
Computer:	Let's assume that 16 is the smallest number. We'll get the next number from the list—a 25.
	Is 25 less than 16? No. So 16 is still the minimum.
Computer:	Let's assume that 16 is the smallest number. We'll get the next number from the list—a 8.
	Is 8 less than 16? Yes. So 8 will replace 16 as the new minimum. (Fair enough.)
Computer:	Let's assume that 8 is the smallest number. We'll get the next number from the list—a 19.
	Is 19 less than 8? No. 8 is still the minimum.
Computer:	Let's assume that 8 is the smallest number. We'll get the next number from the list—a 4.
	Is 4 less than 8? Yes. So 4 is the new minimum. (The minimum has changed three times.)
Computer:	Let's assume that 4 is the smallest number. We'll get the next number from the list—a 1.
	Is 1 less than 4? Yes. So the minimum has changed again.

After the computer has exhausted the list by examining all the members, the minimum of the entire list is the value that *remains* in the minimum holder (variable) at the end of the algorithm.

When you program the computer to find the minimum, you first establish a value for a variable called minimum. Using the first value in the array is an efficient choice. Consider this fragment of code:

```
int collection[7];

collection[0] = 21;
collection[1] = 16;
collection[2] = 25;
collection[3] = 8;
collection[4] = 19;
collection[5] = 4;
collection[6] = 1;

int minimum = collection[0]; /* the first value in the array is
assumed to be the smallest since we have seen no other values. */
```

Now that the minimum has been assigned a value, the computer will need to look at all the other values in the array—one at a time—to make comparisons with the value in the minimum holder. If any "better" value is found (a lower value) then the minimum will need to be assigned that lower value. Look at this example of a statement that would cause the minimum to be replaced by a new lower value.

```
if ( collection[3] < minimum )
minimum = collection[3];
```

In the comparison between the values in collection[3] and minimum, the computer will evaluate whether it is true that collection[3] contains a value that is lower than the value contained in minimum. If the value of that relational expression is true, then minimum will be reassigned the value that is contained in collection[3]. The old value in minimum will be replaced.

Now look at all the work the computer does to find the minimum for this array of seven members. Here are six statements that will look for a better minimum (a lower value) than the minimum that is established initially with the value in the first slot of the array.

```
if ( collection[1]< minimum )
minimum = collection[1];
```

```
if ( collection[2] < minimum )
minimum = collection[2];
if ( collection[3] < minimum )
minimum = collection[3];
if ( collection[4] < minimum )
minimum = collection[4];
if ( collection[5] < minimum )
minimum = collection[5];
if ( collection[6] < minimum )
minimum = collection[6];
```

This is how the computer finds the lowest value in the entire list; it methodically looks for a lower value in *each* of the slots of the array. The most important thing to notice, however, is that whenever the computer finds a lower value, it replaces the value in minimum immediately.

You might have noticed that the preceding statements seem repetitive, and they are. We need to use a loop to save some time in our programming. Let's use a for loop to hit all the members of the array.

```
for (int x = 0; x < 7; x = x + 1)
{
if ( collection[x] < minimum )
minimum = collection[x];
}
```

Now we are ready to see the entire block of code that allows the computer to find the minimum from an array of numbers. This block of code will work on any array; you only need to adjust the for loop so that it will spin the appropriate number of times.

```
minimum = collection[0];//setting the initial (first) value
// for the minimum variable.
for (int x = 0; x < 7; x = x + 1)
{
if ( collection[x] < minimum )
minimum = collection[x];
}
cout << "The smallest value in the array is" << minimum
     << "." << endl;
// remember the cout line can wrap to the next line.
```

Note

Remember to assign the value of the `minimum` variable, slot 0, the first member of the array. In order to find the minimum, the computer needs to constantly compare a new array slot with the most recent value in the `minimum` variable. It is possible for the value in the `minimum` variable to change several times before the `for` loop ends

On the CD

A program that shows the complete selection sort.

Merge Sort: A Very Fast Sort

The next sort I will discuss is called a *merge sort,* which involves bringing together two halves of an array. The way it sorts numbers in order is quite different from the selection sort we just studied. For this reason, it is an interesting sort to study.

Let's take a list of numbers from an array in order to see how a merge sort works on the list to organize it into ascending order (numbers increasing as you move from left to right or from top to bottom). We will name each slot of the list underneath the number.

```
32    12    5    18    31    4    25    7
[0]   [1]  [2]   [3]   [4]  [5]  [6]  [7]
```

How the Merge Sort Works

Consider the array just presented. Initially, the array of eight elements is viewed as one array. After the first halving, the eight-member array is viewed as two separate four-member arrays. The next cut in each half produces four quarters. The next halving of each of those quarters produces the eight individual elements. Consider how the array has been broken into halves repeatedly. See Figure 19.2.

Now let's do this exercise again, but this time we will focus on the entire left half of the array—that is, the first four elements. We will ignore the right side of the array for now.

```
32    12    5    18                31    4    25    7
     one half                  ignore this half for now
```

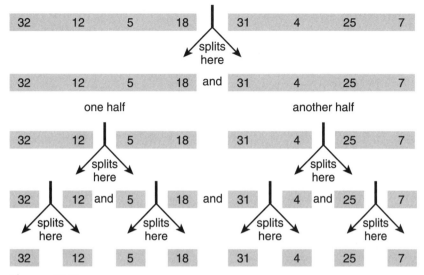

Figure 19.2
The array is shown broken in different places until each piece of the array is a single element.

If we cut the left half in half, we will have two quarters on the left side:

```
32        12     5         18              31    4     25    7
first quarter,  second quarter            ignore this half
```

Each of the left two quarters is then cut in half. Now there are *four* individual elements on the left side of the array while the right half is ignored.

```
32   12   5   18              31    4    25    7
four individual elements      ignore this half
```

The left half of the array is ready to be reassembled, or merged, into the proper order. It is important to notice that as we reassemble the left half of the array, the right half of the array remains out of order. Merge sort is programmed to work on one half of the array at a time.

Putting the Array into Order

Let's consider where we left off in the array. The first four elements need to be reassembled into the proper order. The first rule of merging is that you can only merge with the element that you most recently split from. What does that mean with our list? If you look back at the numbers, 32 and 12 can be merged, since they were split apart; but 12 and 5 cannot be merged because they did not come from the same quarter of the array. Likewise, 5 and 18 can be merged. Let's merge each of these pairs into the proper order.

32   12   will become

12   32

The two elements have been properly merged and are in order. Next the 5 and 18 can be merged:

5   18   will become

5   18

Now look at the left half of the array. It is still not in order but it has undergone some ordering. Each quarter is in order.

12   32   5   18

Now these two quarters of the array can be brought together (merged) into a left half of the array. The 5 will be first, followed by the 12, then the 18 will be next, followed by the 32.

5   12   18   32

Now the array (still undergoing the merge sort) looks like the following:

```
5   12   18   32              31    4    25       7
 left half in order              this half was ignored
```

Focusing on the Right Half

Let's do the same thing to the right half as was done to the left half of the array. (We will ignore the left half for now.) The right half, just like the left half, will be split into two quarters and then into four elements.

```
5   12   18   32              31    4    25    7
 ignore this half                the right half
```

If we cut the right half in half, we will have two quarters on the right side:

```
5   12   18   32              31        4    25          7
 ignore this half            third quarter, fourth quarter
```

```
5   12   18   32              31    4    25    7
 ignore this half            four individual elements
```

The last four elements should now be reassembled, or merged, into the proper order. We need to remember that we can only merge with the element that you most recently split from. The numbers 31 and 4 will be merged, since they were split apart in an earlier step. The numbers 25 and 7 can be merged. Let's merge each of these pairs into the proper order.

31   4   will become

4   31

The two elements have been properly merged and are in order. Next the 25 and 7 can be merged:

25   7   will become

7   25

Now look at the *right* half of the array. It is still not in order but it has undergone some ordering.

4   31   7   25

Now these two quarters of the array can be brought together (merged) into an ordered right half of the array. The 4 will be first, followed by the 7, then the 25 will be next, followed by the 31.

4   7   25   31

Now the array has two halves (a left half and a right half) that are ready for a final merge. Each half looks like the following:

```
5  12  18  32              4   7   25   31
left half in order         right half in order
```

The final step of merge sort is to merge these two "ordered" halves. The result of this merging is an array in ascending order. See Figure 19.3.

The merge sort works by a process that allows an array to be cut into halves *repeatedly* until individual elements are left. Then those members are brought together, each half with its other half into the correct order. Eventually the entire array is in order.

The programming code to execute the merge sort involves a process called *recursion*, which we will study in the next chapter.

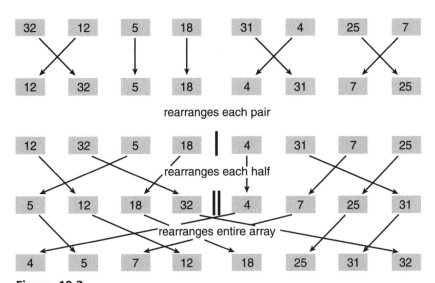

Figure 19.3
The array is shown as the merging of these two ordered halves. Each member from each half goes into its proper position.

Summary

Sorting means arranging data in order. Arranging a list of names in alphabetical order is an example of sorting. Sorting a list of numbers means arranging them in *ascending* or *descending* order. Ascending order arranges smaller numbers before larger numbers in an array. Descending order puts numbers that are greater in size first, followed by smaller numbers.

Next we covered the *selection sort,* which relies on the ability to find the minimum in a list. The selection sort was explained through an analogy of people attending a party. Then we looked at the selection sort applied to a list of numbers.

Next we defined the *minimum* of a list. It is the smallest number in a list. In order to find the smallest number, the first number from the array (slot [0]) is assigned to a variable called minimum. Then the algorithm works by looking at the rest of the numbers in the list—one at a time—through the use of a loop. As you look at each number, you test whether that number is smaller than the number that is presently assigned to the minimum variable. When the loop is done spinning, the value in the minimum variable is the smallest number in the list.

The *merge sort* was the second sort we examined. It works very differently from the selection sort. The merge sort repeatedly cuts an array into halves until there are only single elements of the array. Then those members of the array are assembled into their proper order, two pieces at a time. The sort gets its name from the merging that occurs as the pieces are put back together properly.

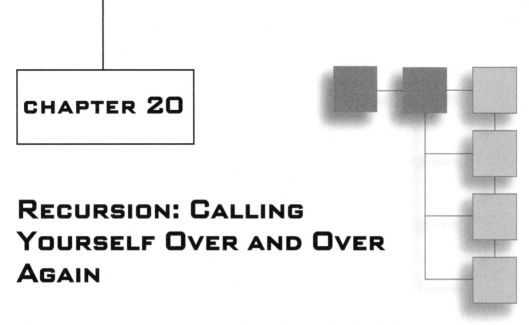

CHAPTER 20

Recursion: Calling Yourself Over and Over Again

This chapter examines recursion, which is a method of solving a problem by solving a smaller case of the same problem. I give examples of recursion and explain how the computer can carry out recursion through repeated calls to the same function, but each time using a different, smaller parameter.

In This Chapter

- Examples of recursion
- Definition of recursion
- Key features of recursion

Recursion—What Is It?

Recursion is a particular process involved in solving a problem. Webster's definition of recursion states that it is "a procedure that can repeat itself indefinitely." Essentially, the process involves solving a simpler problem of the same type as the original problem you were asked to solve. Let's first look at some examples outside of the context of programming to understand this process.

Example Using Words

Let's say we have a vocabulary word whose meaning we do not know. Your second impulse might be to look up the word in the dictionary. (Your first impulse might be to ask someone the meaning!)

Take the word *obstreperous*. If you look up obstreperous in the dictionary, it might say something like "recalcitrant or willful." When you read this meaning, at first you will be happy that there is a word you understand—willful—but then disappointed that you need to look up another word—recalcitrant. So you next look up the word recalcitrant to see what that means. This time the dictionary says something like "defiant." At this point, you might think you know what defiant means, but you need to check it to be sure. So once again you consult the dictionary, and you find that defiant means "unruly." You're almost sure of the meaning of the last word—unruly—but you look it up to be certain. Here the dictionary says "stubborn." See Figure 20.1.

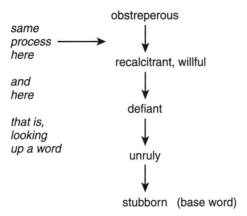

Figure 20.1
A word, obstreperous, is shown with other words used to explain its meaning. Each word below another word contributes to the understanding of the meaning of the original word.

So the word obstreperous at the base of all this work means something like stubborn, with some other shades of meaning picked up from the words along the way. Our process of discovering the meaning of this word has been a *recursive* process. We chose a method to solve our problem—finding the meaning of a word—by using the same process, looking up other words in a dictionary. Each time we looked up a new word, we came closer to understanding the meaning of the original word.

Recursion is this process of redoing a problem, but in a simpler context than the original problem we did. Consider the next example that uses recursion and involves numbers.

Example Using Numbers

It is often easier to see recursion in a numeric example than in an example that does not involve numbers. In order to understand this example, we first need to define the factorial of a number. The *factorial* of a number is a product of the number and all the numbers less than it—all the way down to 1.

The factorial of 6 is the answer you get from multiplying 6 by all the numbers less than it—5, 4, 3, 2, and 1. Recall that multiplication is represented by the asterisk (*).

```
6 * 5 * 4 * 3 * 2 * 1
 \ /
  30 * 4 * 3 * 2 * 1
   \ /
    120 * 3 * 2 * 1
     \ /
      360 * 2 * 1
       \ /
        720 * 1
       \    /
        720
```

So the answer to the factorial of 6 is 720.

Factorials quickly produce massive numbers because you are multiplying so many numbers, usually, to get an answer. The factorial of a number is represented by an exclamation point (!). The previous example looks like this symbolically: 6!

Before we get to the recursion involved in the problem, let's redo the problem with some creativity. Let's start with the symbol for a factorial and use it in writing the multiplication for the factorial.

```
6! = 6 * 5 * 4 * 3 * 2 * 1
     another factorial is here
```

The boldface part of the preceding statement is another factorial. It is called the factorial of 5, or 5!. Let's rewrite the previous statement using that information.

```
6! = 6 * 5!
```

The previous statement means that the factorial of 6 is found by multiplying the number 6 by the factorial of 5. If we only knew the factorial of 5, we could finish this problem right away. So the solution to finding the factorial of 6 rests on our ability to find the factorial of 5, and then to take that answer and just multiply it by the number 6. This way of solving the problem is a *recursive* method. We are solving the problem by solving a *smaller case* of the same type of problem.

Now consider the separate problem of finding the answer to the factorial of 5. Consider what the factorial of 5 looks like as a product of numbers.

```
5! = 5 * 4 * 3 * 2 * 1
     another factorial is here
```

Again, just as in the previous example, we can use another factorial to represent part of the work needed to get the answer to the factorial of 5. Let's rewrite the problem using that factorial.

```
5! = 5 * 4 !
```

And so the process continues like this. We find the factorial of 4 by finding the factorial of 3 and then multiplying that answer by 4.

```
4! = 4 * 3 !
```

The last two lines of work involve finding the factorial of 3 and the factorial of 2 (The factorial of 1 is the value 1.) Consider these last two lines of computation.

```
3! = 3 * 2!
2! = 2 * 1
```

Each line of computation involved finding the answer to a similar—but smaller—factorial problem. The important point to notice is that you are finding the answer to the problem using a smaller case of the same problem. The factorial of 6 used the answer from the smaller case, the factorial of 5. Another point to notice is that this process eventually stops. If it did not stop, then the recursive process would continue forever.

Two Features of Recursion

In order to understand the topic of recursion more comprehensively, we need to look at key aspects of a recursive solution, or what constitutes a recursive solution to a problem. We will also examine how the previous problems (the words in the dictionary and the factorial problem) modeled these aspects. Let's examine the key features of a recursive problem:

1. A smaller problem of the same type exists.

2. Eventually you reach a bottom case or *stopping state.*

Recursion would be useless if it continued indefinitely. We would never arrive at an answer if that were the case. In the examples we completed in the previous section, both of these features were present in the solution of the problem.

When we looked up the word obstreperous in the dictionary, we eventually found a simpler word whose meaning we did understand. The simpler word, stubborn, is a smaller case of the same type of problem (that is, the word is not as difficult as the original word). The stopping state for the word problem is finding a word whose meaning we do know, and then we can stop looking up words in the dictionary.

With the factorial example, the smaller case of the same type of problem is using a factorial of a number less than the number we started with. (The factorial of 5 is a smaller case than the factorial of 6.) The stopping state is reaching a factorial whose answer we do know—the factorial of 2, since it is the product of 2 * 1.

Infinite recursion is a problem that arises when one of these parts is not satisfied by the recursive design we make. For example, if we never arrived at a word we understood in the dictionary, we would always be looking up new words.

Using Functions in Recursion

In order to understand how recursion works, we need to look at how functions are the bedrock of recursion on a computer. Imagine if we defined a function called look_up. This function would look up any word that we did not understand. First we would call on it and send in the word obstreperous from the previous example. Then we would want to call the function again, but this time send in the word recalcitrant. We would want to call the function a third time, sending in the next word, defiant. The last time we call the function, we send in the word unruly, where the meaning we get (here, stubborn) is clear to us, so we can stop calling the function look_up.

The process of looking up one word and then another and another, until we get a word whose meaning we know, shows that we need to make several calls (four calls, in fact) to this function. See Figure 20.2

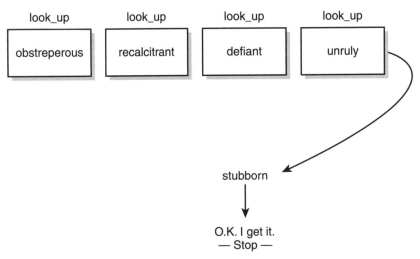

Figure 20.2
A chain of calls is shown with a new word sent to the function each time it is called.

One Function Calls Itself

The reality behind these repeated calls to one function is that the calling occurs within the function itself. Now what does that mean? I have always talked about the main program (the main function) making the calls to the function. In reality, any function can make a call to another function. In the case of recursion, *the function calls itself.* Let's see what this does.

In the look_up example, the main function calls the look_up function and sends in the word obstreperous. Once the look_up function starts its work—looking up a word in a dictionary—it finds another word it doesn't know. So it leaves in the middle of its own function and calls look_up again—this time with the new word it did not understand—recalcitrant. The idea behind the call to the function is that once it understands the new word, it can use that knowledge to understand the meaning of the first word, obstreperous.

How Recursion Is Executed

Recursion is dependent on the ability of a program to call a function over and over again. The first step in recursion is to define a function that will solve the first case of the problem.

Copies of Functions Are Generated

Each time a call is made to a function, the compiler will generate *a copy* of the instructions (the code) of the function in the memory of the computer. If you call a function repeatedly, then for each call there will be a copy of the function stored in memory. Let's say a function called Alpha (with an integer parameter) is called three times during a program's execution.

```
int x, y, z;
. // x , y, and z are assigned before the calls are made
.

.
Alpha (x);
.

.

.
Alpha (y);
.

.

.
Alpha (z);
```

Alpha's code will be copied three times in memory as each copy is made for each call. See Figure 20.3.

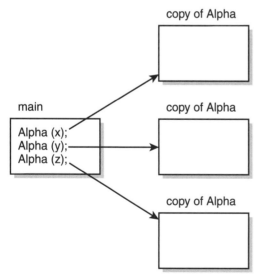

Figure 20.3
Three copies of the function Alpha are shown for each call made to the function.

Once the Call Is Made

Whenever a call to a function is made, the compiler immediately leaves the place where it is to go to the place that was called. (Recall that this call to a function just needs the function name with any necessary parameters inside.) In the `main` function of the program, there will be an initial call to the factorial function, perhaps followed by an output statement to show that answer on the screen. The initial call is the first call to start the recursive process. After recursion is completed, the next statement—here, a `cout` statement—is executed.

```
result = factorial (6); // a function is called here
cout << result << endl; // the answer will be on the screen
```

Once inside the function `factorial`, the recursive process begins, since the function includes a call to itself. However, this time the call is slightly different because `factorial` is called with a *smaller number* as a parameter. The statement that contains the call will look something like this statement:

```
answer = 6 * factorial (5);
         compiler leaves this statement to go to the factorial function
```

In this statement, the variable `answer` is assigned a *product* (the answer you get when you multiply two numbers). But the product, `6 * factorial (5)`, cannot be calculated because the computer does not know the answer to the factorial of 5! Before the product can be found, the compiler will leave the function it is in and go to another copy of the function to compute the value of the factorial of 5. We are doing the problem for a second time, but this time we are computing the factorial for a smaller number, 5. See Figure 20.4.

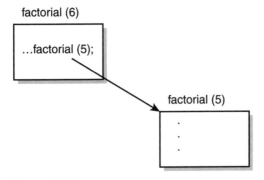

Figure 20.4
The function is shown with the value that was sent into it (6), and a copy of the same function is shown with a new (smaller) value (5) that was sent into it.

When the second function finishes its work in computing the factorial of 5, it will return a value to the exact place where it was called. The returned value is used to compute the product in the assignment statement.

```
answer = 6 * factorial (5); // inside factorial "6"
        // 6 * some value will be assigned to answer
```

What happens in the factorial function that had 5 sent into it? That function (we'll call it factorial "5") had its own assignment statement with a *call* to another function. Consider this statement:

```
answer = 5 * factorial (4); // inside factorial "5"
```

It looks like the exact same statement we saw in the first copy of the function (the factorial function with the parameter 6). Now we are in another copy of the function factorial "5". This statement includes another call to the factorial function—this time with the parameter 4. Let's call it factorial "4".

So factorial "4" is called, and we can expect to see the same kind of statement inside the function as we have already seen. Likewise, factorial "4" has the same assignment statement. Here it is:

```
answer = 4 * factorial (3); // inside factorial "4"
        the second last call in recursion
```

We are almost done with these calls. There are two calls left before we reach the *stopping state*—the end of recursion. The second last call is the call to the factorial function with the parameter 3 sent into it (let's call this function copy factorial "3").

Once you enter the factorial "3" function, you will see *the last call* in recursion. This is the statement:

```
answer = 3 * factorial (2);// inside factorial "3"
        the last call in recursion
```

Now the last call has been made, and we enter the factorial with parameter 2. Here is the stopping state of recursion. We have encountered a factorial problem whose answer we do know; we do not have to call anything else to get an answer. We have a partial answer to the problem.

```
answer = 2 * 1;// inside factorial "2"
        no more calls
```

Coming Back Up Through a Recursive Web

I just mentioned that we have a partial answer to the original problem. We need to examine the next stage of recursion to see how we arrive at the final (definitive) answer to the original problem: computing the factorial of 6 (6!).

So far we have just been calling other functions and not getting any results. With the call to `factorial "2"`, we have an intermediate answer—the value, 2, from the product of 2 * 1. The way to get the final answer is to check what happens next in each function. Consider this fragment of code from `factorial "2"`.

```
answer = 2 * 1;// inside factorial "2"
return answer;
```

What happens with the `return` statement? If you recall, it will cause the value in the variable `answer` to be sent back to the place that called it. Unlike all of the previous examples where we used the `return` statement, we were always sending values back to the `main` function (where the call was begun) of the program. In this example, we are sending the value back to the previous factorial function, `factorial "3"`. Watch what happens when we look at the statements in `factorial "3"`.

```
answer = 3 * factorial (2);// inside factorial "3"
                     ⇓
                     2
return answer; // from 3 * 2
          ⇓
          6
```

The value 2 is multiplied by the number 3, since 2 was returned from `factorial "2"`. But wait! After this statement, there is another `return` statement, which will cause another value to be returned to the place that called it. This time the value 6 (3 * 2) will be returned to the place that called `factorial "3"`. But which function called `factorial "3"`? It was `factorial "4"` that called `factorial "3"`, and here are two statements from `factorial "4"`.

```
answer = 4 * factorial (3);// inside factorial "3"
                     ⇓
                     6
return answer; // from 4 * 6
          ⇓
          24
```

The value 6, which was computed and returned from `factorial "3"`, is multiplied by the value 4. Next the value 24 will be returned to the function that called `factorial` "4"—`factorial` "5". The same process is repeated inside of `factorial` "5".

```
answer = 5 * factorial (4);// inside factorial "5"
                    ⇓
                    24
return answer; // from 5 * 24
         ⇓
        120
```

We have almost finished following the compiler back to all the places where calls were initiated to other functions. Now the value 120 will be returned to the function that called `factorial` "5", which was `factorial` "6".

```
answer = 6 * factorial (5);// inside factorial "6"
                    ⇓
                   120
return answer; // 6 * 120
         ⇓
        720
```

The final statement in `factorial` "6" will return the value 720 to the `main` function, where the first function call was made. Once inside the `main` function, that value is printed on the screen through the `cout` statement.

```
result = factorial (6);
              ⇓
             720
cout << result << endl; // 720 is printed on the screen
```

This is just one example of how recursion, the process of a function calling itself, is used to solve a problem. Recursive solutions tend to be very quickly computed, but they have the disadvantage of using up a lot of memory. Remember that every time a function is called, another copy of that same function (this time with a different parameter) is generated.

Note

Recursion always involves calls to the same function with different parameters each time. Another important part of recursion is understanding how the compiler moves from one function to another through the `return` statement that is used in each function.

On the CD

A program (written in the C++ programming language) that computes the factorial of a number.

Summary

This chapter covers the topic of *recursion*—a method of solving a problem by using a smaller case of the same problem. Functions are used in recursive solutions. As the same function is called over and over again, it is called with a different parameter each time. The value of the parameter is smaller for each successive call, and this is what is meant by a *smaller case* of the same type of problem. Eventually a smallest case is reached, called a *stopping state*, and the recursive process ends.

After all the calls have been made, the `return` statement of each function sends the compiler from one function back to the function that originally called it. This chain of recursion is what makes the process sometimes difficult to follow.

We covered two examples in this chapter. The first example was a situation where the meaning of an unknown word was found by repeatedly looking up simpler synonyms for the original word. In the second example, a factorial operation on a number was done by finding the answers to factorial operations of smaller numbers. A *factorial* of a number is defined as the product of the number and all numbers less than it, down to the number 1.

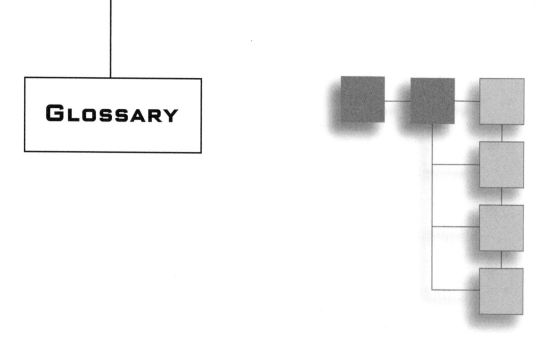

GLOSSARY

Accessor. A method in a class that returns the value of a field of the object.

Algorithm. A finite set of steps to solve a problem.

Alignment. The positioning of text or an image within a document.

Allocate Memory. Set aside memory for a variable. The amount of memory set aside depends on the variable type.

ALU. The arithmetic logic unit of a computer (found in the CPU).

Append. Add on to the end (of a file).

Applet. A small application launched through another file. It does not run independently.

Application. Programs that are designed to accomplish some task, like word processing, balancing a checkbook, or playing a game.

Arithmetic Operator. Any of the operators that represent addition, subtraction, multiplication, or division: +, −, *, /, %.

Array. A data structure that holds different values of the same type (an array of integers). Each slot of the array is a unique variable.

Ascending Order. Refers to numbers that are listed in increasing value (for example, 5, 7, 12, 16, 20).

Assignment. Giving a variable a value in a program.

Attribute. An additional quality given to a tag's function to expand the features of the tag (for example, the width attribute for an image tag).

Attribute Value. A value assigned to an attribute within a tag (for example, width = 100).

Background. The window area that is not the foreground.

Binary Operator. An operator that takes two operands.

Binary Search. Searching an ordered data structure (like an array) by eliminating one half of the data structure at a time.

Bit. A binary digit (0 or1) used to form a byte.

Boolean Expression. An expression that produces the value true or false.

Boolean Type. A variable type that holds the value true or false.

Browser. An application program (like Mozilla's Firefox or Microsoft's Internet Explorer) that accesses the Internet to find, display, or retrieve files.

Byte. A sequence of 8 bits.

Byte Codes. Semi-translated code generated from compiling a Java source program.

Case Statement. *See* Switch/Case Statement.

Character. One letter, symbol, or digit. Several characters together form a string.

cin Stream. The name of the input stream in C++.

Class. An object together with all its functions that create, access, and modify it.

Client File. A file that uses a class.

Comment. A descriptive remark in a program that is not executed by the translator. Comments help readers of the program to understand the programmer's intentions.

Compiler. Translator that translates an entire program at once.

Compiler Directive. A direction given to the compiler. In the C++ programming language, include is a compiler directive.

Component. A term in the Java programming language to describe an object that rests within a container (for example, a radio button).

Concatenation. Adding two or more strings together to create a new string.

Conditional Loop. A loop that executes upon some condition being true (for example, a while loop).

Constructor. A function that brings an object into existence (instantiates it) and assigns it attributes.

Container. A term to describe an object that contains other objects (for example, a frame).

Control Statement. A programming statement designed to manipulate the normal sequential execution of programming statements.

Control Unit. Found in the CPU. The control unit regulates program flow (that is, the order of statement execution).

Control Variable. A variable that controls the repetition of the `for` loop.

Copy Parameter. A parameter that generates a copy of the value of the original variable that was used in the call.

Counter Statement. A statement that increases (usually by 1) the value in a variable.

cout Stream. The name of the output stream.

CPU. The central processing unit of a computer. It contains the ALU and the control unit.

Data. Information that will be used in a program. Data can be numbers, words, or a combination of these.

Data File. A file that contains data.

Data Structure. A holder for data. Generally more elaborate than the simple data types like integers, reals, doubles, chars, and so on.

De-allocate Memory. To release memory that was being used (for a variable).

Debugging. The process of finding and correcting errors in a program.

Declaration of a Variable. Introducing a variable in a program by stating its type and name (identifier).

delete. The `delete` command releases memory set aside for a dynamic variable. Used with pointer variables.

Depreciated Tag. A tag that is no longer part of the most updated version of HTML. It is gradually phased out of general usage.

Descending Order. Refers to numbers that are listed in order of decreasing value (for example, 14, 11, 9, 6, 3, 1).

Digitization. The process of converting non-numeric information into numbers so that a computer can understand it.

do...while Loop. A post-test loop—that is, a loop that executes until some condition becomes false.

Dynamic Variable. A variable that can be "created" and "destroyed" during program execution.

End-of-File Marker. A marker that signals the end of a file.

End-of-Line Marker. A marker that separates one line of text from another (on a text file).

Event. An action taken on an object (for example, clicking a check box). An event is recognized by a special method called a *listener.*

External Drive. A drive outside of the computer used to expand the storage capacity of the computer.

Extraction Operator. Operator that extracts or pulls values from a stream.

Field. A variable type in a record definition.

Fixed Iterative Loop. A loop that spins a fixed (known) number of times (for example, a for loop).

for Loop. A loop that executes a fixed number of times.

Foreground. The front part of a window. Images drawn by the programmer are part of the foreground.

Function. A separate block of code that accomplishes some task.

Function Heading. A line of code that includes a function's name, parameter list, and whether it returns a value.

Global Variable. A variable that is recognized everywhere (globally) in a program.

Graphics. The topic of design and manipulation of images on a computer.

GUI. Graphical User Interface. A design that allows users to interact with the computer through visual components rather than text alone.

Hard Drive. Internal memory of a computer.

Hardware. The physical components of a computer.

Header File. In the C++ programming language, a file that defines a class, contains all the headings of all functions in that class, and the definition of the object itself.

High-Level Language. A programming language (for example, C, C++, Java, Pascal, Fortran, and so on) that requires more translation than a low-level language.

HTML. Hypertext Markup Language. A high-level computer language used to format documents (add images, sound clips, and so forth) and link them over the Internet.

Identifier. The proper name of a variable. The name refers to how the variable is identified in the program.

if Statement. A control statement that uses a boolean expression (after the word if) followed by a conclusion.

ifstream. A stream type in the C++ programming language. Data coming in from an external file will travel through this stream.

Implementation File. A file that implements (contains the code for) the functions defined in the class header file.

Index. Slot or member of an array. Most arrays start with the index 0 rather than 1.

Inheritance. The concept that one class can inherit all the characteristics of a base class.

Initialization of a Variable. Giving a variable its first (initial) value.

Input. What the user types at the keyboard.

Input Stream. A small channel that feeds from the keyboard.

Insertion Operator. Operator that inserts values into a stream.

Instantiate. To bring an object into existence by constructing it.

Integers. Positive or negative numbers that have no fractional part.

Internet. The immense interconnected network of other networks.

Interpreter. Translator that translates an entire program line by line.

Linear Search. Searching a data structure (like an array) one member at a time.

Link Tag. A tag that allows you to jump to another Web page by clicking the appropriate label.

Listener. A method that responds to an event.

Local Variable. A variable that is defined within a function.

Logic Error. An error that results from an unintended consequence rather than a syntax error.

Logic Operator. Any of the words *and, or,* or *not* or the symbols used to represent them (&&, | |, !).

Loop. A block of statements that executes a certain number of times or until some condition changes.

Low-Level Language. A programming language (for example, assembly language) that requires little translation to execute it at machine language level.

Machine Language. The native language of an individual computer. Programs must be translated into machine language.

Main Section. The main part of the program, where the compiler first goes to execute program code.

Matrix. A two-dimensional array.

Merge Sort. A sort that cuts an array into halves repeatedly until there are only single elements. Then those elements are merged into order.

Method. The name in the Java programming language for a class function.

Minimum. The smallest value in a list (an array).

Mod Operator. An arithmetic operator that produces the remainder from a division problem.

Modifier. A method in a class that changes the value for the field of an object.

New. This command causes memory to be set aside for a dynamic variable. Used with pointer variables.

Object. A data structure designed with certain functions in mind that are useful for that data structure.

Object Code. The translated program that is ready to run on the machine.

Object-Oriented Programming. Programming a problem while keeping the object as the center of focus and design, rather than keeping an action or task in mind.

ofstream. A stream type in the C++ programming language. Data going out to an external file will travel through this stream.

Operand. A number on which an action or operation is performed.

Operating System. The system programs that allow the computer to operate and perform its elementary functions, like creating, saving, and deleting files.

Operators. Symbols that cause actions to be performed on numbers and boolean or logic values. There are different kinds of operators—arithmetic, relational, and logic.

Output. Any data or messages generated and displayed on the screen.

Output Stream. A small channel that goes out to the screen.

Parameter List. The list of variables and their types required by a function.

Platform Independent. Hardware independent. Generally refers to programs (usually Java) that can execute on any machine regardless of architecture.

Pointer Variable. A variable that contains a memory address of another variable.

Post-Test Loop. A loop whose condition is checked after executing the body of the loop.

Pre-Test Loop. A loop whose condition is checked prior to entering the body of the loop.

Precedence. The ranking of an operator.

Private. A section of a class definition. Anything defined within this section cannot be accessed by a client file.

Program Flow. The sequential execution of programming commands in a language.

Program Fragment. A portion or section of a program.

Programmer. The person who writes the program.

Programming. Solving a program by designing an algorithm and expressing that algorithm in a programming language.

Protocol. How a computer communicates with another computer (for example, hypertext transfer protocol [http], file transfer protocol [ftp], and so on).

Public. A section of a class definition. Anything defined within this section is accessible in a client file.

RAM. Random Access Memory. Also known as volatile memory. It will be lost once the computer is turned off.

ROM. Read-Only Memory. Memory that is hard wired into the computer when the computer is made (that is, permanent memory).

Reals. Numbers that are represented by decimals. In computer languages, these are numbers that are not integers.

Record. Also known as a struct in C++. A data structure that is designed to hold different types of data (for example, an integer and a string).

Recursion. A method of solving a problem by using a smaller case of the same problem.

Reference Parameter. A parameter that refers back to the original variable used in the call. This variable will be altered if the parameter is altered through the function's code.

Relational Operator. Any of the operators that allow comparison between two operands (for example, <, >, <=, >=, ==, !=).

Reserved Words. Words that are reserved because they have a special use in a programming language. They may not be used as variable identifiers.

Resource. The file you wish to access from the host computer.

Return Statement. A statement in the C++ programming language (and Java). It allows a value to be returned to the place where the call to the function was made.

Return Type. The type of the return value sent back to the place that called the function. The return type is listed in the function heading.

Return Value. A value returned after a function has been executed.

Run-Time Error. An error that develops during the running of the program.

Scope. The extent of recognition of a variable. A variable's scope is limited to the function in which it is defined unless it is a global variable.

Searching. The process of looking for a value in a data structure (usually searching through an array).

Selection Sort. A sort that repeatedly selects the minimum value from a subsection of a list and then puts that value into a specific position in the list (the array).

Software. Programs that run on computers.

Sorting. The arrangement of data into either ascending or descending order.

Source Code. The original program before it has been translated.

Statements. The building blocks of a program. The "sentences" in a programming language.

Static Variable. A variable that exists for the duration of a program.

String. A sequence of characters usually used to represent words.

`switch/case` **Statement.** A statement that allows one of several options to be chosen, depending on the value of the variable controlling the statement.

Syntax. The grammar of a language (that is, the rules necessary for the language to make sense).

Syntax Error. An error that results from an error in syntax.

System Software/Programs. Includes the operating system, and so on. The programs that allow the computer to perform elementary operations and use applications.

Tag. In HTML, a tag is used to mark text in some manner (for example, a paragraph tag is used to begin a new paragraph of text).

Text File. A file that stores only text or characters.

Top-Down Design. Designing a program with the big tasks in mind before the smaller tasks.

Translators. Programs that translate high-level languages into machine language.

Type. The classification of data. Some common types are integers, real numbers, booleans, characters, and strings.

Unary Operator. An operator that takes one operand.

URL. Universal Resource Locator. An address of a resource (a file). A URL has three parts: protocol, host, and file name.

User. The person who interacts with a program.

Value Parameter. A parameter that generates a copy of the value of the original variable that was used in the call.

Variable Parameter. A parameter that refers back to the original variable used in the call. This variable will be altered if the parameter is altered through the function's code.

Variable. A holder for data. Variables are given names to identify them in a program.

Vector Graphics. The creation of images through lines that have length and direction.

Void. Term used to indicate that a function will not return a value after it has been executed.

`while` **Loop.** A pre-test loop (that is, a loop that executes while some condition is true).

INDEX

3D games, 152

A

accessors, 242
addition (+) operator,
   40–41, 45, 191
Add_New_Title function, 134
address1 record, 229–230
address_1 variable, 229–230
address2 record, 230
Adobe Acrobat, 3
algebra and variables, 19
algorithms, 76
   counting number of steps
      and ringing bell, 23
   decision making and, 14
   delaying computer to see
      images, 160–161
   finite steps, 14
   programming, 15
   real-world examples, 14–15
   repeatable steps, 14
   solving problems, 13–14
   verifying user's password, 125
   without variable, 20–21
allocating memory, 203
Alpha function, 305
alphabetizeList function, 79
Alphabetize_list function, 134
alphabetizing, 284–285
ALU (arithmetic/logic unit), 5
American Standard Code for
   Information Interchange.
   See ASCII (American

Standard Code for
   Information Interchange)
ampersand (&) symbol, 146
and conjunction, 49
and operator (&&), 49–51, 51
and reserved word, 225
answer variable, 28, 280,
   306, 308
append command, 256
application programs, 3.
   See also programs
applications, 2. *See also*
   programs
arithmetic expressions, 50
arithmetic operators, 45–46, 60
   precedence, 111
arithmetic/logic unit. *See* ALU
   (arithmetic/logic unit)
array of records, 231–234
arrays, 173
   assigning members value, 176
   assigning values to, 178–180
   binary search, 273–281
   C++ programming
      language, 280
   common name, 201
   control variable, 180
   copying array to, 186
   counting number of negative
      values in, 185
   data type, 203
   declaring, 176
   descending order, 285–286
   eliminating half of, 280–281
   examples, 183–186

finding middle of, 279–280
finding minimum, 287–292
finding value in, 269
holding collection of data,
   173–175
index, 280
initializing, 184
left index, 280–281
for loop, 291
loops, 180–183
members, 174
methodically looking for
   number, 274–275
middle index, 280
multi-dimensional, 199
name, 203
number of members, 203
printing, 184–185
putting in order, 293–294
real numbers, 178
repeatedly cut into halves, 295
right index, 280–281
searching for value in, 270
searching for value not
   in, 271
something unusual happened
   to, 197
storing data, 183
strings, 178–179, 190–192
syntax, 176–177
types, 176, 178
uninitialized variables, 179
user assigning members, 182
variables differing in values,
   175–176

License Agreement/Notice of Limited Warranty

By opening the sealed disc container in this book, you agree to the following terms and conditions. If, upon reading the following license agreement and notice of limited warranty, you cannot agree to the terms and conditions set forth, return the unused book with unopened disc to the place where you purchased it for a refund.

License

The enclosed software is copyrighted by the copyright holder(s) indicated on the software disc. You are licensed to copy the software onto a single computer for use by a single user and to a backup disc. You may not reproduce, make copies, or distribute copies or rent or lease the software in whole or in part, except with written permission of the copyright holder(s). You may transfer the enclosed disc only together with this license, and only if you destroy all other copies of the software and the transferee agrees to the terms of the license. You may not decompile, reverse assemble, or reverse engineer the software.

Notice of Limited Warranty

The enclosed disc is warranted by Thomson Course Technology PTR to be free of physical defects in materials and workmanship for a period of sixty (60) days from end user's purchase of the book/disc combination. During the sixty-day term of the limited warranty, Thomson Course Technology PTR will provide a replacement disc upon the return of a defective disc.

Limited Liability

THE SOLE REMEDY FOR BREACH OF THIS LIMITED WARRANTY SHALL CONSIST ENTIRELY OF REPLACEMENT OF THE DEFECTIVE DISC. IN NO EVENT SHALL THOMSON COURSE TECHNOLOGY PTR OR THE AUTHOR BE LIABLE FOR ANY OTHER DAMAGES, INCLUDING LOSS OR CORRUPTION OF DATA, CHANGES IN THE FUNCTIONAL CHARACTERISTICS OF THE HARDWARE OR OPERATING SYSTEM, DELETERIOUS INTERACTION WITH OTHER SOFTWARE, OR ANY OTHER SPECIAL, INCIDENTAL, OR CONSEQUENTIAL DAMAGES THAT MAY ARISE, EVEN IF THOMSON COURSE TECHNOLOGY PTR AND/OR THE AUTHOR HAS PREVIOUSLY BEEN NOTIFIED THAT THE POSSIBILITY OF SUCH DAMAGES EXISTS.

Disclaimer of Warranties

THOMSON COURSE TECHNOLOGY PTR AND THE AUTHOR SPECIFICALLY DISCLAIM ANY AND ALL OTHER WARRANTIES, EITHER EXPRESS OR IMPLIED, INCLUDING WARRANTIES OF MERCHANTABILITY, SUITABILITY TO A PARTICULAR TASK OR PURPOSE, OR FREEDOM FROM ERRORS. SOME STATES DO NOT ALLOW FOR EXCLUSION OF IMPLIED WARRANTIES OR LIMITATION OF INCIDENTAL OR CONSEQUENTIAL DAMAGES, SO THESE LIMITATIONS MIGHT NOT APPLY TO YOU.

Other

This Agreement is governed by the laws of the State of Massachusetts without regard to choice of law principles. The United Convention of Contracts for the International Sale of Goods is specifically disclaimed. This Agreement constitutes the entire agreement between you and Thomson Course Technology PTR regarding use of the software.